MISMANAGED DECLINE

What politicians won't tell you about the economy

Vicky Pryce & Andy Ross

\B^b\
Biteback Publishing

First published in Great Britain in 2025 by
Biteback Publishing Ltd, London
Copyright © Vicky Pryce and Andy Ross 2025

ISBN 978-1-83736-031-4

10 9 8 7 6 5 4 3 2 1

A CIP catalogue record for this book is available from the British Library.

Set in Minion Pro

Printed and bound in Great Britain by
CPI Group (UK) Ltd, Croydon CR0 4YY

FSC
www.fsc.org
MIX
Paper | Supporting
responsible forestry
FSC® C013604

CONTENTS

PREFACE

Mismanaged Decline offers an overview of the UK's economy from the Industrial Revolution to the present. We distil the lessons to be learned from the myriad forces that have shaped the UK economy, offering a comprehensive assessment of what UK governments can and can't achieve through policy. Drawing on extensive policy experience, we study both inexorable global forces and our many home-grown errors. The book does not always make for reassuring reading, as our message is often grave: unlike so many of our politicians, we explain why there are no magic solutions, why there will be no sudden economic 'reset' and why that only makes what we must do now all the more urgent.

The book tackles the reaction to globalisation and the trend to deindustrialisation, both of which have left a significant legacy, including on public finances. We consider the UK's place in today's much changed world order, while examining our ability to shape the structure of the economy and achieve sustainable growth in a post-Brexit, post-Covid, tariff-ridden environment, now also substantially altered by the wider impact of the war in Ukraine, AI and climate change. All this makes attempts at containing welfare spending, tackling inequality, managing immigration, strengthening skills and ensuring the regulatory environment serves us well much more difficult to achieve. And in such an environment, policy mistakes have a larger and longer negative impact. In this context, we question whether the lack of investment and the low growth and productivity of recent decades were all inevitable or if different courses of action could have helped. Evidence and analysis, based on solid scrutiny of the data, have become crucial for the road ahead.

In Part I, we look at the implications for policy arising from the UK's emergence as the first industrial nation, through deindustrialisation and globalisation to our largely service-based economy today. We consider the global events that have shaped our current economic standing, before running through a sequence of shocks that have troubled recent governments. Understanding the past, we argue, makes it easier to understand what needs to be done now.

In Part II, we look at the major economic issues facing the current government, informed by economic theory and real-world examples. We consider GDP, environmental imperatives, productivity, immigration and inequality, among other things.

In the third and final part, we look to the future, detailing our recommendations on what must be done to improve the UK's economic performance. We argue that painful trade-offs will have to be made in the pursuit of economic growth, despite what some (at times deliberately) disingenuous politicians may tell us.

PART I

HOW WE GOT HERE

CHAPTER 1

FROM TOP DOG TO LAP DOG

The performance of the UK's economy, and how we manage it, is vital to so much more than our material standard of living: it affects our wellbeing, drives much of our politics and shapes our society. It also largely determines our international status. The UK is still a relatively rich country, but our economy will not self-correct excessive inequality or automatically raise living standards, nor will it support public services on a sustainable basis based on current projections, even with record levels of tax.

Left to itself, a laissez-faire capitalist system does not automatically achieve these things. In truth, much of the private sector is dependent on government actions. The government can act in a number of important ways, including through the procurement of goods and services, such as from the pharmaceutical sector for the NHS or from specialist defence companies to meet military and security needs. They can use legislation, including regulations on banks to limit excessive risk-taking. They can control profits using windfalls and other sector-specific taxes, or use labour market rules and safety legislation, including setting the minimum wage and imposing non-discrimination rules or controlling salaries in the public sector. They can control prices, such as those for household energy since the war in Ukraine, or make trade and investment agreements with other countries/regions which can have a profound impact on sectors by altering the terms of trade and thereby affecting competitiveness. Immigration policy can alter labour and skills availability while also putting extra pressures on demand for social services. Competition rules can have an impact on market dynamics, while planning regulations can affect much of the housing and infrastructure sectors.

All these things, and many more, give governments considerable leverage to do 'good' if such controls are properly exercised. The list can go on and on, giving the government a lot of power – and with it, much responsibility. No country, of course, is either completely state-controlled or entirely capitalistic. But the first trick is knowing *when* to interfere or tweak what is already there and then, *how*. Of course, potential market failures have to be considered, as well as the value for money of each decision made. Where regulation and deregulation are concerned, proper impact assessments will be needed and unintended consequences and indirect and secondary longer-term effects will need to be considered.

Such things are, of course, bread and butter for economists. But, in the real world, there's a need to properly assess how to balance the public and private to achieve the best results, which is by no means easy in itself. No desk-based analyst can tell you what the trick is. Trial and error, learning from (and admitting) mistakes and listening to advice are all key. Even if all this is done to perfection, the question remains: how can one possibly build enough resilience to withstand the international winds of change in an environment now increasingly dominated by two superpowers, the US and China? Add to this the emergence of new, harder-to-control digital currencies, the growth of financial technology ('fintech') and non-banking financial institutions, the abandonment of the old world trade order and capital flows that can be reversed at the touch of a button, and it becomes clear that the UK's room for manoeuvre has become increasingly constrained.

In the meantime, of course, the underlying issues that plague most countries must be tackled while balancing the population's expectations of improving living standards. But politicians are reluctant to admit that painful economic trade-offs will have to be made. This is especially true as populations age and the effects of climate change and AI on jobs come up against attempts to contain fiscal imbalances and ballooning debt. Instead, our leaders procrastinate in the hope that the economy picks up and stays up of its own volition. It won't – not within this parliament or, most likely, the next.

Further deregulation, particularly of financial services, won't work, as the list of unintended consequences is a mile long and the fallout from the financial crisis of 2008/09 lingers in the form of lower growth and productivity. There is a case to be made for easier planning laws to allow for more houses and infrastructure – both of which this country sorely needs – but laxer rules won't do it, certainly not by themselves, as the UK's record for implementation of any major project remains particularly poor. Brexit, despite promises by politicians, has not done it either.

Sadly, no party has magic solutions, as we discovered post-Brexit, and 'magic money trees' don't exist. On the other hand, governments can certainly make things worse, even unintentionally. But the bullet will have to be bitten soon if our economic decline is to be halted and, if possible, reversed. This requires a good comprehension of what has and hasn't worked before, of what has changed and why. To understand the UK economy in our rapidly changing world, we need to properly understand its past. Economies are shaped by their histories, their evolving political structures and, crucially, their interactions with other economies and cultures. In the jargon it's called being 'path dependent': past choices and decisions dictate the path of the present.

*   *   *

We shall start this story with the Industrial Revolution, which we can safely say began in Britain and gave rise to the modern world. There is no precise date for when it started, other than that this revolution in both production and consumption is generally said to have found its momentum during the eighteenth century. Economic growth then was not considerably greater than the UK has since experienced, though it is still rightly called a 'revolution' as that increase in growth was sufficient to transform billions of human lives, helped by greater connectivity and expansion of trade and movement of people between countries and regions. After millennia of subsistence living for all but the wealthiest elites, the average citizen in the developed world today is materially rich beyond the wildest imaginings of those living in previous millennia. With our modern medicine, energy and clean water, plus a cornucopia of foods and myriad forms of entertainment, most of us in richer countries have a better and healthier standard of living than even those exulted emperors and monarchs of history and certainly better than the three-quarters of a billion people in the world still scraping a living or dying in absolute poverty.

From about the beginning of the eighteenth century, the transformation of production, as it spread out from the UK and then across the world, broke free from Malthusian constraints on living standards, producing a veritable 'hockey stick' upward kink in the historical graph of living standards when measured in centuries.

This revolution gave Britain a head-start in becoming the world's richest country. Adam Smith, who wrote the first 'textbook' of economics, *The Wealth of Nations* (1776), saw that a new epoch was arising but also reasoned that there would be new epochs in the future (an observation that is roundly ignored by contemporary free marketeers). For reasons we'll explain throughout this book, we are, perhaps, seeing the beginnings of a new epoch now. As economic power tends to beget military power, for over a hundred years Britain was the world's undoubted superpower, peaking in pre-eminence in the nineteenth century when Britannia truly ruled the waves and Victoria was not only the Queen but the 'Empress of India', sitting at the head of the largest empire the world has ever seen.

Britain's military dominance rested on an economy that was hailed as the 'workshop of the world' because of an early lead in manufacturing. Despite a shock defeat in the American War of Independence in 1783, Britain's relative military might enabled it to conquer poorer nations and capture colonies. It was an empire that at its peak included almost a quarter of both the world's population and land area; commanding such a vast portion of the globe gave Britain a sense of its own towering superiority that remained until the mid-twentieth century. Many concerns about that period are surfacing now, but at the time the British came to regard the existence of the empire as God's will, a belief summed up by Cecil Rhodes's maxim, 'I contend that we are the finest race in the world and that the more of the world we inhabit the better it is for the human race' – a maxim enforced towards the end of empire by the Maxim gun.

AFTER EMPIRE

During its long age of empire, Britain's economy came to rely heavily on its captive resources and markets, despite the claims of free trade. By the second half of the twentieth century, that order had well and truly crumbled and debts soared as the remains of empire became a liability rather than an asset; these debts were dramatically increased by two costly and bloody world wars. As late as the late nineteenth century, the UK was arguably still the number-one superpower, but other countries had been rapidly industrialising. Perhaps earlier, but certainly after two punishing world wars, it was clear that Britain had been comprehensively overtaken by the world's new superpower, the United States of America. It was a painful reality for a nation so long used to being the top dog. Despite clinging to the trappings of empire and repeating jingoistic themes, leaders were forced to adjust to Britian's relative decline as a superpower. Any uncertainty regarding such a decline was removed by the humiliating reality check of the Suez crisis, when the US under President Dwight D. Eisenhower effectively told Britain to 'mind its place' in the new world order.

Despite this, many ordinary citizens clung to patriotic delusions of grandeur and of British superiority. This romantic memory mixed with bigotry was so brilliantly parodied in the '60s and '70s by Johnny Speight with his comical creation Alf Garnett in the TV series *Till Death Us Do Part*. Even if the irony of Alf was lost on many of his fans, who relished him as a working-class hero of 'patriotic white supremacy', by the 1950s it had become clear to UK governments and informed observers that Britain's past as a superpower was just that: the past.

Fortunately, perhaps, the British Empire and economy had needed to develop sophisticated financial and commercial services to support its global trade and industry, and so during the second half of the twentieth century, as its manufacturing was replaced by imported manufactured products, Britain's role as a financier and provider of services became increasingly important as its primary source of wealth. Despite Winston Churchill's expressed wish to 'see finance less proud and industry more content', the percentage of the workforce in manufacturing dropped from around 40 per cent at the turn of the twentieth century to less than 10 per cent by 2020. By contrast, services employed less than 40 per cent of workers in 1900 but now account for over 80 per cent.

Such deep structural shifts in the economy are often driven by global changes in the competitiveness of nations, and they are not easily reversed by government policies even though they have profound social and economic impacts. They drive changes in employment patterns, entrench regional disparities, deepen feelings of prosperity and create resentment. The north of England, for example, had relied on textiles and heavy industry such as shipbuilding; the Midlands had engineering, particularly automotive production; Scotland had heavy industry and shipbuilding; and Wales had coal mining and steel. These activities had sustained their regional economies and infrastructure for many decades and inculcated strong local identities and attitudes.

THATCHER AND THE END OF 'BUTSKELLISM'

John Maynard Keynes is still a giant in 'macroeconomics': the study of how the economy as a whole works – and, sometimes, doesn't. Keynes (it rhymes with 'brains') ignited an intellectual revolution in the way economists thought about the properties of capitalism and hence the role and responsibilities of governments. His most celebrated work was *The General Theory of Employment, Interest and Money*, usually abbreviated to just the *General Theory*. The *General Theory*'s message that governments had a direct responsibility for protecting the populace from the vagaries of capitalism fitted well with the sociopolitical solidarity that had arisen as a result of the Great Depression of the interwar years and the horrors of two world wars.

This post-war consensus, born from much misery, came to be called 'Butskellism', combining the surnames of two Chancellors of the Exchequer: Hugh Gaitskell (Labour, 1950–51) and Rab Butler (Conservative, 1951–55). The name arose during the 1950s to describe the prevailing consensus between the two main parties, who largely agreed on using Keynesian economics to manage the macro economy, keeping unemployment low and providing a 'cradle to grave' welfare state to relieve poverty and mitigate inequality. They also agreed that there should be a mixed economy of private enterprise and nationalised industries. It was a one nation inclusive approach to economic policy and social issues. For a long time this 'Golden Age of Keynesianism' – mixed in with a dose of socialism – seemed to work: from the 1950s to 1965 the populace enjoyed an increase of around 40 per cent in their living standards, although growth was a rather stop-and-go affair. Harold Macmillan, the Conservative Prime Minister from 1957 to 1963, captured the mood of many with his boast, 'You've never had it so good.'

Rising living standards made falling behind other comparable economies more palatable for proud Brits. The UK's growth was considerably outpaced by competitors: France by 50 per cent, Germany 250 per cent and Japan 400 per cent over the same decade. This was compounded by the rapid deindustrialisation of much of the UK during the '70s and '80s, which saw the loss of millions of manufacturing and extractive jobs and brought unemployment, poverty and long-term decline to whole regions. The bitter resentment and loss of self-esteem this engendered was captured by the popular '80s TV series *Boys from the Blackstuff*, written by Alan Bleasdale. Set in Liverpool, the series depicted the deep resentments, desperation and strain on mental health brought about by unemployment, poverty and regional decline, summarised in the central character's constant plea for work: 'Gizza job – I can do that!'

This loss of 'traditional' industrial jobs was a result of numerous factors: global competition, technological change, poor industrial relations and, as the unemployment rate tripled, the deliberate economic policies of the Thatcher government from 1979. The experience of 'stagflation', the decline of traditional regional industries and poor industrial relations – particularly during the 'Winter of Discontent' of disruptive strikes under the Labour Prime Minister, James Callaghan – had given the political momentum to the Conservative Party for the general election of 1979. The first woman to be Prime Minister won a decisive victory that began some eighteen years of Conservative government. Under Margaret Thatcher's premiership, the Conservative Party, though not all Conservative MPs, broke with one nation Conservatives (whom Thatcher described as 'wets').

Mrs Thatcher viewed a mixed economy with its large state as simply 'backdoor socialism', an attitude epitomised by perhaps her most famous remark that 'there is no such thing as society' – though many of her admirers insist the quote has been widely misunderstood. To counter the greatly increased inflation of the 1970s – but against the advice of the strongly Keynesian stance of almost all economists of the day – her government embarked on a decidedly non-Keynesian 'monetarist experiment' (discussed further in Chapter 3), combined with high interest rates and financial deregulation, which clearly favoured finance over industry (despite Thatcher's proclaimed adoration for Churchill). Financial deregulation allowed increased competition, innovation and hence growth in the banking and financial sectors, but with an increase in risky loans and, in effect, bets. 'Reaganomics', named after Thatcher's contemporary and friend, US President Ronald Reagan, also pursued a policy shift to the right.

Many economists believe that such deregulation also allows for long 'Minsky cycles' of credit expansion that inevitably end in painful 'corrections' when the extent of the expansion is revealed, perhaps decades later, as discussed in Chapter 3. The fear is that this build-up of apparent wealth is merely 'funny money' and not grounded in real income-producing assets. The growth of finance, and the discovery of North Sea oil, likely prevented the value of the pound sterling decreasing as much as it would have done otherwise, but that didn't help UK manufacturing to remain competitive. To be fair to Thatcher, as we have seen, the process of deindustrialisation had started before she had become Prime Minister and would accelerate under the administrations of both Tony Blair and Gordon Brown. During her premiership, the high interest rates – implemented to restrain monetary expansion and combat inflation – also depressed the economy; this, combined with North Sea oil, kept the exchange rate up. The tragic result of reduced spending and high interest rates was a sharp increase in job losses, leaving a legacy of greatly increased unemployment. Sadly, instead of North Sea oil revenues being used to set up a sovereign wealth fund, it was largely squandered on welfare payments for the unfortunate victims of widespread economic decline – a decline accelerated by the Margaret Thatcher/Keith Joseph ideological 'monetarist experiment'.

Not surprisingly, the break with the post-war mixed economy consensus – which in effect abandoned whole regions to industrial decline and eschewed the Keynesian principle that it is a prime responsibility of government to keep unemployment at low levels – was bitterly resented by many. Thatcher's supporters, on the other hand, saw her as an 'Iron Lady', a radical political giant taking on left-wing vested interests who were challenging the democratic will with their industrial unrest. She was hailed as a modern-day Boudica, resolute in making tough decisions to steer the UK away from post-war decline, and on towards a bright new future. Most notably, in a bitter and protracted dispute, she defeated the powerful miners' union that had all but destroyed the previous Conservative government led by Edward Heath.

Under Thatcher, London and the south-east benefitted from global trade, heavy deregulation and investment in infrastructure, while leaving the deindustrialised regions stuck in vicious circles of high unemployment, poverty, poor health, de-skilling and social discontent, with underperforming schools and shorter life expectancies. Inequality soared, though that was largely the result of the top incomes pulling away from the pack. Meanwhile, as Oliver Bullough has described in his book *Butler to the World*, too few questions were asked about the propriety and origins of the money flowing into the UK finance sector. The hedonistic excess of financial deregulation was perfectly captured by Gordon Gekko's 'Greed is good' speech in the 1987 film *Wall Street*. By contrast, the desperation of the 'left behind' UK workless was portrayed in the popular bittersweet 1997 comedy *The Full Monty*, where unemployed men feel compelled by their desperation and humiliation to organise and perform a local strip show for money, in an attempt to restore some self-respect.

This regional disparity remains very much alive. Today, London is home to only an eighth of the UK's population, but it alone accounts for almost a quarter of the UK's GDP (or gross domestic product, the nation's aggregate level of output, discussed at length in Chapter 6) and together with the south-east, for well over a third of total UK GDP. For better or worse, the whole of Britain is now deeply reliant on the economic success of London and the south-east, although large cities such as Edinburgh and Manchester have their significant part to play. The forces behind these regional differences also persist today: in terms of job creation, London has experienced a relative boom since 1997, with 54 per cent more jobs, while the north-east and west Midlands created fewer than 10 per cent more jobs, despite a population growth in some regions of almost 20 per cent. Deindustrialisation, of course, continues to be a powerful factor behind these entrenched regional disparities.

This pattern of contrasting regional fortunes, together with tax cuts for higher earners, deregulation and reductions in social welfare spending, all led to a very sharp increase in inequality during the Thatcher government, and that substantial increase remains to this day, with the top 1 per cent having pulled even further away from the mass of the population. The much-vaunted 'levelling up' initiative was never going to seriously dent this historically embedded and globally charged inequality. It's hard enough to turn a tanker, let alone the direction of a country, a fact that Donald Trump will be finding out to his country's, and the rest of the world's, cost.

THE GREAT MODERATION

Increased income and regional inequality became structurally embedded and were not reversed to a significant extent under the subsequent Labour governments of Tony Blair and Gordon Brown (1997–2010). Nevertheless, from 1993 to 2007, consecutive Conservative and Labour governments enjoyed a more stable period for the economy that came to be known as the 'Great Moderation'. This period saw low inflation, high employment and steady growth, earning it the nickname 'NICE' as an acronym for 'no-inflation continuous expansion' (discussed further in Chapter 3). With further deregulation and increased innovation, financial services grew substantially and the City of London remained a global financial hub; retail businesses enjoyed growth fuelled by rising disposable incomes and consumer confidence, as well as from their own impressive increases in productivity; the construction sector boomed because of low interest rates, financial deregulation and rising incomes; the technical sector grew rapidly with heady advances in IT and telecommunications. These concurrent booms fostered the attendant growth of professional services such as consulting, legal work and accounting. Although the Great Moderation had set in under Conservative Ken Clarke's chancellorship, it was Gordon Brown who presided over most of it as Chancellor, from 1997 to 2007, leading him to proudly, if recklessly, proclaim that New Labour had 'ended economic cycles of boom and bust'. Cue much rejoicing and hubris among economists who felt that their profession was, for once, riding high in public opinion.

Financial deregulation, both in the UK and the US, allowed for great innovation in 'exotic' financial services and instruments, often complex and little understood even within finance. This fostered a massive increase in private debts, often arising due to fancy things like 'derivatives' – which are really just bets. Although Gordon Brown did add more to government debt than he should have done, it was the private sector debt overhang caused by 'debts and bets' that caused the Great Financial Crisis of 2007/08, and hence the Great Recession from 2008; it certainly wasn't the level of UK government debt as was so widely and gleefully blamed in the media. Put simply, the crisis wasn't caused by too much government spending, or, as the comedian Alexei Sayle pithily put it, because of 'too many libraries in Wolverhampton'.

THE GREAT FINANCIAL CRISIS

The impact of the Great Financial Crisis and the resulting deep recession on government dept was huge, due mainly to the consequent decrease in tax revenue as GDP contracted (see Chapter 3 for more detail). This sharp increase in the 'national debt' was used by the Conservative Chancellor George Osborne to justify dramatic public spending cuts, with rather daft memes such as Labour having 'maxed out the government's credit card'. Osborne made 'getting the debt down' his top priority, though it can be cogently argued that his policies in fact made it harder to reduce government debt. They certainly slowed subsequent growth – as the then newly created fiscal watchdog, the Office for Budget Responsibility (OBR), felt bound to report at the time – and weakened the UK's capacity for longer-term growth. Given the impact of the Great Recession on tax revenues, some longer-term fiscal realignment was always going to be necessary, but to cut spending while the economy was still so weak went against the advice of most economists.

The authors of this book, having both worked at the centre of government at the time, acknowledge that there was indeed 'no money left' in the Treasury's coffers once the emergency was over. It's also true that everything that could possibly be done was thrown into the economy to support it during the crisis at huge cost; this included nationalising the Royal Bank of Scotland. And it exposed the perils of too much dependence on the contribution of the financial sector to the UK's productivity, much of which proved to be an illusion. But it also revealed the dangers of lax regulation at a time of rising financial interconnectivity, meaning controlling events in other jurisdictions could have serious indirect, and sometimes direct, consequences back home. The global financial system was in peril with another recession looming. Without decent public infrastructure, business investment is discouraged, which contributes to low growth. The Eurozone went into an even more severe existential crisis due to mistaken over-tightening and the UK itself is still keenly feeling the impact a decade or more later.

Even the fiscally conservative then Permanent Secretary to the Treasury, Lord Macpherson, seems to have conceded that, with hindsight, the Treasury should have borrowed more when interest rates were low, in order to foster higher investment in public infrastructure and education. Not that it didn't borrow – in fact, as a result of the need to sustain the economy and prop up the financial system, the size of public sector debt trebled between 2010 and 2019. But while the cost of servicing the debt fell significantly as bond yields were slashed and the Bank of England cut the central bank rate to nearly zero, the benefit of extra spending was not seen across the population as a whole. Little went into supporting or rebuilding infrastructure, which has held the economy back ever since.

Low growth and austerity heightened the social resentment of those who felt left behind, particularly in the regions that had already experienced relative weakness as traditional industries went into long-term decline. This discontent has shaped populist political developments ever since and can be blamed for the 'slow economic puncture' of Brexit (of which, more in Chapter 5). Largely against their own interests, the regions hit hardest by deindustrialisation voted overwhelmingly to leave the EU.

In 2019, incoming Prime Minister Boris Johnson attempted to counter this resentment and to boost overall growth with his 'levelling up' policy. Despite gallant efforts by some outstanding officials and the former chief economist of the Bank of England, Andy Haldane, such policies lacked the resources to significantly reverse the UK's regional disparities. Funding for regions across England had suffered since the abolition of the regional development agencies in 2011 by the Conservative/Liberal Democrat coalition (bodies like the non-partisan think tank Centre for Cities argue that the cost of reducing disparities has increased since). More recent developments such as Covid, the war in Ukraine and US tariffs haven't helped. Regions outside London and the south-east are, in general, more dependent on manufacturing exports, which have been hit by persistently higher business electricity costs than competitors elsewhere. The disturbances during Covid and the supply chain issues that ensued also affected shipping costs and general access to essential inputs. With world trade and 'globalisation' slowing down, this poses a big and costly problem for the regions, and for the whole economy, to overcome.

All of this risks the perpetuation of a 'doom loop' for poorer regions, as young people choose to leave for better opportunities in richer cities (although we saw some movement out of London during Covid, this seems to have been reversed in recent years). As the local workforce dwindles, so the local authority's funds are reduced, placing further strain on the local authority's already stretched debts and making regional disparity worse, so more people leave. This kind of loop is already prominent in some other countries including Italy, Japan and South Korea.

It is not even clear that attempts to focus on regions are necessarily good for overall economic performance as, in a global world, it is perhaps cities rather than countries that now compete with one other. Indeed, studies show that it is the fact that government, regulators and the entire ecosystem of lawyers, asset management, stock exchanges and commodity exchanges, as well as accountants, actuaries and hedge funds, are all centred in London that supports the city's standing as the globe's number two financial centre after New York. Despite this, Labour's latest spending review, industrial strategy and defence industrial strategy – all produced within a few weeks of each other in mid-2025 – have a strong 'place' dimension in relation to public funding and encouragement of the private investment behind it. But the cost may prove too high.

The problem was that, overall, wealth appeared to be increasing rapidly during the Great Moderation, meaning a buoyant financial sector and so more tax revenues for the Treasury. Perhaps because of this, few people in government paid the issue of burgeoning private debt much heed. Unfortunately, the UK's academic macroeconomists had largely taken their eye off the financial ball, preferring to immerse themselves in highly abstract models which overlooked the importance of the finance sector and, too often, bore scant relation to the real world. Some practice-oriented economists did call out warnings of impending financial crisis, but perhaps there were just too many stakeholders in important places who were enjoying the political success of a buoyant economy (not to mention significant bonuses). Or perhaps it was simple complacency as things seemed to be going so well. To be fair, identifying an asset bubble isn't overly straightforward, as asset values depend on a future that cannot be known with any certainty. That said, it's widely known that unless private debt is in the longer term 'justified' by being anchored to real returns from assets, then eventually the bubble will burst. And burst it did, dramatically and globally, in 2007.

During the financial crisis, a substantial proportion of the UK's apparent wealth was exposed as a complex network of 'debts and bets', rather than being based on real income-generating assets. And so, inevitably, this financial house of cards came tumbling down. It works a lot like this: Peter owes Paul who owes Mary who owes Osama who owes Simon who owes Khaleda. If Peter defaults, then Paul can't pay Mary who can't pay Osama who can't pay Simon who can't pay Khaleda. Now, replace these names with financial institutions and the scale of the problem rapidly becomes huge due to such extensive financial 'contagion'. The problem for anyone trying to predict when the bubble will burst is that, until the defaults begin, the balance sheets can look healthy, as the liability of debt on one balance sheet appears as an asset on someone else's balance sheet. This makes so-called 'macro-prudence' difficult – as the billionaire investor Warren Buffett put it, 'It's only when the tide goes out that you learn who has been swimming naked.'

The financial system could withstand some more minor financial institutions going bust, but when the major investment bank Lehman Brothers became the biggest ever bankruptcy in 2008, it sent shockwaves throughout the global financial system. Modern financial systems are sustained by confidence, and so the failure of such a large and well-respected finance house as Lehman Brothers led to a severe loss of confidence in financial markets. This caused widespread panic and a desperate selling off of assets as they tumbled in price, followed by a subsequent credit freeze that affected economies worldwide. The 'NICE' party had ended suddenly in a crash.

It was all rather like holding a party in a visibly dangerous building. If you're not in the building then you're not at the party, and so you enter, while keeping one eye fixed on the exit. The problem is that everybody else at the party is doing the same. When the fire breaks out, everybody rushes for the door, quickly causing a block, and all but a lucky few get burned. That is – to stretch the analogy – unless the government steps in, but to save those at the party they'd have to singe everyone else. All the bonuses enjoyed in the finance sector had already been pocketed, so to prevent an even more disastrous crash the public were forced to suffer, as the banks were bailed out while public services were severely cut. As a tented village of protestors appeared outside St Pauls, Andy Haldane, yet to become chief economist at the Bank of England, bravely said, 'Occupy has been successful in its efforts to popularise the problems of the global financial system for one very simple reason: they are right.' Many of the financial organisations that had in many ways contributed to the crash were rescued as 'too big to fail' because of the implications for the system as a whole.

The financial crisis caused the Great Recession, from which growth has yet to properly recover. Productivity – the output an economy receives from its inputs, which is what ultimately matters for rising living standards – suffered across the developed world and has been almost flat in the UK since 2007. It's worth remembering that growth in the economy is achieved by getting more people in employment to produce more goods and/or improving the output per worker or, an even better measure, output per hour. With a given labour force, output per hour worked must keep rising if growth is to be sustained. By simply increasing population through immigration, growth could improve, but often at the expense of GDP per capita, unless the people arriving have higher skills and less need for public services. Higher productivity growth therefore boosts growth and improves tax take while feeding into improved public services and infrastructure and reducing the need to resort to more borrowing.

Taking in the severe negative shocks of Brexit, Covid lockdowns and the invasion of Ukraine brings our outline of the UK's recent economic history almost up to date. It's worth noting at this stage a few damning facts: the UK has one of the highest levels of inequality in the developed world – it would be the third highest, after Bulgaria and Lithuania, if measured against EU countries. Our public services are in a poor state. Business investment is chronically lower than in comparable countries, especially important as productivity remains flat. GDP per head is about 20 per cent down on where it would have been had the 'NICE' period continued, with stark impacts on tax revenues and the fiscal balance. Indeed, the estimates suggest that if growth had continued along its pre-crisis trend, GDP in the UK would now have been some 36 per cent higher, a larger impact than that experienced by the UK's major competitors. GDP per head is instead some £11,000 lower than it would have been according to Institute for Fiscal Studies (IFS) analysis in mid-2024, and an ageing population will likely add further strain to public finances.[1] But sadly, there is no longer a centrist consensus across the main parties; indeed, there has been divisive fragmentation, especially in the era of Brexit, and a disturbing rise of far-right populism, stemming from regional decline, austerity and the scapegoating of immigration as the cause of all our ills.

The links between economic stagnation, inequality, globalisation and the rise of neoliberal oligarchs and the far-right are complex but very real, with profound political consequences. The US is the most unequal country in the G7, though even in Europe the richest 10 per cent of the population receive 30 per cent of the Continent's entire income and own 50 per cent of all its wealth. The UK is similar, languishing thirty-fourth in the Organisation for Economic Co-operation and Development (OECD) inequality list of thirty-eight countries. When factors relating to education, such as length of schooling, are added, the UK's ranking in the UN's Human Development Index (HDI) index is a slightly more respectable thirteenth – still far from good enough.

The opening up of markets as a result of globalisation, usually encouraged by economists, has its downsides as well as its benefits. The upside is a dramatic reduction in global poverty; the downside is that the free movement of capital and goods and the financialisation of economies has exacerbated the inequalities in many countries, creating structural changes and resentments that have fuelled right-wing populism, leading to Trump's two administrations.

In short, although our troubles pale into insignificance when compared to the world's most desperate people, the UK economy is not an encouraging sight to see. Before looking in more detail at some of the major economic events outlined in this chapter, we'll bring our economic history up to the present.

CHAPTER 2

WHERE ARE WE NOW?

Following Liz Truss's infamous 2022 mini-budget, there were many claims that the economy was broken. 'Broken' is journalistic hyperbole, not a term used in economics, and it isn't strictly true that Truss, the UK's shortest-serving Prime Minister, crashed the economy. In September 2022, the interest rate on UK gilts (government IOUs are called 'gilts', as they once had gold edges and today are metaphorically 'as good as gold', in that the government is extremely unlikely ever to default on them) rose by over 100 basis points in four days, which clearly came with the risk of increasing the interest the UK has to pay to service its national debt. But GDP did not 'crash', though the turbulence in the bond market was most unhelpful. Of course, as with Conservatives MPs and the Great Financial Crisis, Labour MPs felt duty-bound to insist Truss did crash the economy (to such an extent that the beleaguered former PM sent a 'cease and desist' letter to Keir Starmer, warning him against repeating the claim).

We will never know exactly what the long-term consequences of the 2022 mini-budget might have been, as Truss quickly ditched her Chancellor, Kwasi Kwarteng, and appointed Jeremy Hunt. Hunt reversed most of her policies, except the sorely needed electricity price cap which Rishi Sunak had failed to introduce as Chancellor.

The delay in introducing this cap can be blamed for much of the UK's subsequent rise in inflation, which was above the G7 average in the period following Russia's invasion of Ukraine. As energy prices were perceived to be rising out of control, inflationary expectations shot through the roof; the government offered little support and were soon met with higher wage demands.

The day was also saved by the Bank of England reversing its intention to embark on further quantitative tightening at the time of the 2022 budget; that is, it started selling the bonds it had bought during the long period of quantitative easing. Quantitative easing had started with the financial crisis and risen substantially after the Brexit vote, only to rise further during the pandemic when the government's fiscal stimulus was sorely needed to sustain the economy. Instead of its intended tightening in 2022, the Bank of England started buying bonds again, albeit in a limited way and for a limited period, to calm the markets and prevent part of the financial sector entering serious difficulty. This reduced pressure on capital markets and brought bond yields down. At the time of writing, however, we are very much back to those high borrowing costs again, with the current Labour government engaging in extra borrowing, ostensibly to finance investment. Bond rates are also back where they were during the short-lived Truss era, and so the UK government must spend some £100 billion-plus a year just servicing the national debt.

To be fair to Liz Truss, it wasn't all her fault. Her action on the energy price cap probably saved money by avoiding a fall in GDP, and she has a point when she says the Bank of England played a large part in the mini-budget debacle. Indeed, following the shock to bond markets, which had a 'contagion' effect on other countries, Kwarteng was in Washington DC for a key International Monetary Fund (IMF) meeting. He was privately trying to reassure US bankers, politicians and diplomats at the British Embassy that the UK 'was committed to fiscal responsibility' and even that the Bank of England was one of the UK's 'finest institutions'. Apparently, his claim about the Bank of England prompted applause from just one person in the room, who turned out to be a board member of a British bank.

The unprecedented market movements were down to two key factors: the September mini-budget announcement of expansionary fiscal policy and the forced sales by liability-driven investment funds (LDIs). LDI funds are an investment strategy mostly used by pension funds and insurance companies to match assets with their long-term liabilities. The aim is to ensure that assets grow and are available in a way that matches the timing of the amounts that they need to pay out. The mini-budget hit a pensions industry that had over-leveraged with LDIs and a Bank of England reversing quantitative easing. As the value of the LDI investments held by pension funds fell in value, they were forced to sell off bonds to maintain their balances. That only made the value of bonds fall even further, forcing the Bank of England to start purchasing bonds to drive the price back up. The unofficial blog written by Bank of England staff, 'Bank Underground', estimated blame was split equally, with LDI-selling accounting for half of the decline in gilt prices during this period and fiscal policy accounting for roughly the other half.[1]

LEARNING FROM LIZ

It is always important to keep an eye on the market for the IOUs that the government issues. Of course, an excess of gilts, or a loss of confidence in them, will lower their price and hence make government borrowing from the markets by selling gilts more expensive. Equally, an expected fall in their price – say, because a future rise in interest rates is expected – can lower their price in the present. Around the time of Liz Truss's mini-budget, neither her Chancellor, Kwasi Kwarteng, nor the Bank of England was being particularly prudent. Although the Bank of England subsequently took decisive action to restore market confidence, and Truss subsequently sacked her Chancellor and then stepped down herself, there was a worrying period when it seemed that the UK might be lumbered for some time with a 'moron premium' on its debt. In the event, the damage is probably largely confined to those unfortunates who were seeking mortgages or renewals of loans at the time.

Liz Truss has since admitted that her plan to cut the 45p top rate of tax may have gone too far, but she insists it was not fair to blame subsequent interest rate rises on her mini-budget. She was never exonerated, and despite her cherished vision of ending a 'low growth high tax spiral', the unfunded tax cuts were seen as inflationary and hence likely to lead to higher interest rates and thus a fall in the price of gilts – in short, an increased cost of government debt. Truss is correct that it was all exacerbated by the preceding attempt at unwinding quantitative easing by the Bank of England, though this was known shortly before the infamous budget. In addition, her telling the OBR to 'keep out of it', in effect, was not likely to inspire confidence that she hadn't precipitated an ever-increasing deficit and higher interest rate. If all this wasn't bad enough, her sacking the well-respected Permanent Secretary to the Treasury, Sir Tom Scholar, added to the impression among many that she was reckless. What the Truss debacle does demonstrate, however, is that nowadays the market for government debt can't be taken for granted.

As explained earlier, so long as the UK government can call on the Bank of England to buy up its debt, it can never actually default. That does not mean, however, that there is no problem in running an ever-increasing structural deficit. It will eventually lead to a loss of market confidence in the value of gilts and could even engender accelerating inflation. If the government has to offer a higher interest rate to borrow, then more of the revenue it collects must go towards servicing its debt. Again, borrowing, and even sometimes the 'printing' of new money to finance investment, can lead to self-sustaining long-term fiscal health. And eventually, the bill for social support and public services must be paid for through taxation to avoid long-term damage to the economy (notwithstanding shorter periods of recession when the debt should be all but ignored to get the economy going again). No amount of clever playing around with accounting identities removes the long-term real resource constraints.

When Liz Truss was forced to step down in humiliation, her failed co-contender for the leadership of the Conservative Party, Rishi Sunak, took over, becoming the UK's first British Asian Prime Minister. His Chancellor, Jeremy Hunt, quickly reversed almost all the Truss/Kwarteng mini-budget fiscal proposals, but he didn't reverse the direction of government debt. In fact, Sunak was rebuked by the statistics watchdog, the UK Statistics Authority, for claiming that his government *had* reduced the debt.

*   *   *

For all that we have said above, Britain remains a rich country, with considerably lower taxation than in many other western European countries. However, as we have seen, there certainly wasn't an encouraging backdrop for the incoming Labour government in July 2024.

Perhaps scarred by the persistent and oft-repeated myth that

Labour caused the Great Financial Crisis through overspending, Keir Starmer and Chancellor Rachel Reeves made much of their 'fully costed' manifesto proposals. Predictably, after they won the general election, Labour 'discovered' a £22 billion 'black hole' in the nation's finances, left by the previous government. It's certainly true that some imminent costs to the Exchequer went shamefully undeclared to the OBR by the Conservatives. This amounted to perhaps £6 billion, including the asylum hotel costs which hadn't had funds allocated and the recommended wage rises for public sector workers (such as doctors and train drivers) which weren't allocated in the departmental budgets for the years ahead. And there's no doubt Jeremy Hunt did leave Labour with a £20 billion hole in terms of the two cuts of 2 per cent each in the National Insurance contribution (NIC) for employees, amounting to some £10 billion in January and then again in April 2024, just before the elections in July 2024.

Labour's position wasn't helped by their promise not to raise income tax, NIC or VAT in their manifesto. Rachel Reeves felt she could 'excuse' harsh fiscal measures by citing this 'black hole'; the problem she faces is that this doesn't placate those losing out, nor their supporters and lobbyists, including many of Labour's own backbenchers. And constantly banging on about how grim things are is hardly a boost to the confidence that encourages consumer and investment spending.

In truth, it was apparent to any informed observer well before the election that, unless public services were destined to become even poorer after an already lean decade of funding, or government debt be raised even higher, taxes would have to be increased. The IFS had been plain about the matter for a considerable time, claiming to anyone who would listen that both parties were maintaining a 'conspiracy of silence', and mocking any notion of 'fully costed' manifestos. Of course, the IFS also pointed out that the Liberal Democrats had even higher spending plans, while the Greens and Reform offered substantially larger numbers that were deemed 'wholly unattainable'.

DOES LABOUR HAVE 'FISCAL SPACE'?

The *Telegraph* journalist Tim Stanley, in his review of our 2015 book *It's the Economy, Stupid,* claimed the authors ignored the fact that Gordon Brown had severely diminished the 'fiscal space' left to tackle subsequent crises. Indeed? The Conservative Party's continued accumulation of debt during the Great Recession, the extra support after the Brexit vote, additional expenditure on furlough during Covid and the subsidisation of fuel bills after Putin invaded Ukraine all prove that Stanley is wrong. Now, it's true that some economists get dangerously close to the belief that government debt doesn't matter at all; when the economy is in a recession such an approach has merit, as recovery takes priority at such times and a recession is particularly bad for government debt anyway. Other economists, typically to the right, say reducing debt must always be paramount, and so they advocate large cuts in spending and in the size of the state, often while hoping somewhat contradictorily for tax cuts.

As usual, the truth lies somewhere in between. The oft-made claim that government debt must be a burden on future generations is more tenuous than many believe; if it was this straightforward then debt could be passed on by future generations to their future generations and so on. Also, if fiscal multipliers are sufficient, and in a recession that is more likely, then increased government spending may in fact reduce the ratio of debt to GDP over the short to medium term. Importantly, as with any sound business investment plan, if borrowing is used wisely to increase future growth, then longer-term debt may be permanently reduced, and markets can appreciate that. The OBR seems to accept this, including the positive productivity impact. That said, there is no doubt that the direction of the economy is disconcerting for any government that wishes to preserve, let alone improve, public services without further tax increases.

WHAT ABOUT THE FISCAL RULES?

Low economic growth and depleted public services facing ever-rising demands make it hard for any Chancellor to meet their own 'fiscal rules' – those rules set by individual Chancellors as a constraint upon themselves – and breaking these is not a new phenomenon by any means. In June 2010, then Chancellor George Osborne declared that the 'deficit will be eliminated to plus 0.3 per cent in 2014/15 and plus 0.8 per cent in 2015/16. In other words, it will be in surplus'. Having missed that target by some £75 billion, Osborne then committed himself to a surplus by 2020. When David Cameron felt obliged to resign as Prime Minister following his gamble with the Brexit referendum, incoming Prime Minister Theresa May and her Chancellor Phillip Hammond could see that even Osborne's new target was unrealistic. Inevitably, May moved the goalposts in 2016 and kicked the surplus target down the road, stating, 'We have not abandoned the intention to move to a surplus. What I have said is, we will not be targeting that at the end of this parliament.' This was followed by Hammond announcing in 2018 that the deficit should be 'falling to just 0.8 per cent by 2023–24'. *Quelle surprise*, this was also unrealistic. Covid, of course, allowed Rishi Sunak to prioritise dealing with a pandemic and so not to worry about the fiscal rules, with a declared promise to do 'whatever it takes'. This was echoed by Boris Johnson, with his reassurance, 'We are absolutely not going back to the austerity of ten years ago.'

When Johnson was forced to resign in 2022, he was replaced by Liz Truss. As her premiership notoriously lasted barely longer than the shelf life of a lettuce (forty-nine days, to be precise) it is hard to say what she and her Chancellor thought of fiscal rules, though it certainly doesn't seem she held them in particularly high regard. She wasn't keen on the OBR – unsurprising considering the IFS judged that the tax cuts in her Chancellor's budget would lead to 'unsustainable debt'. When Truss was replaced by Sunak in October 2022, Sunak's Chancellor, Jeremy Hunt, reinstated a fiscal rule: 'Public debt should be falling as a share of gross domestic product five years from now.' Of course, rolling targets can by their very nature be rolled forward at any time, meaning it was scarcely a constraint at all.

Given that government spending under Labour is now set to rise at 2.3 per cent a year over inflation for this parliament, after 3.6 per cent a year over the previous parliament – while the economy grew by just 0.8 per cent – the OBR's GDP forecast in March 2025 of 1.5 per cent a year looks optimistic. It's not surprising that Chancellor Rachel Reeves likes the rolling target idea. To give more scope for her plans for much-needed investment for growth, she reworked the fiscal rules to distinguish between day-to-day spending and investment.

Sensibly, the fiscal rules now require that only the current budget must be brought into balance, so that day-to-day spending is met by revenues by 2030 but the government is still able to borrow for investment. This means, provided the government invests wisely in assets, there should be a return in terms of GDP growth. So, to allow some more space for investment, Reeves has introduced an investment fiscal rule that incorporates the tax revenues from such investment-induced growth. Her investment rule is to reduce 'net financial debt' – i.e. public sector net financial liabilities (or PSNFL, often whimsically dubbed 'persnuffle') – as a proportion of GDP. Persnuffle is meant to capture not just the debt that government owes but also to consider assets that are expected to generate future returns. Examples include student loans, as these are expected to be repaid over time, providing a return to the government; equity investments in private companies that yield dividends or capital gains; funded pension schemes, as these assets generate returns that can offset future liabilities; and council housing that returns rents. The rolling target 'rule' and persnuffle obviously leave scope for some creative accounting to maintain a Chancellor's claim that their fiscal rules are being met. Moreover, as the OBR is powerless to question the government's spending plans, and some of its plans on tax, this gives room for the Chancellor to 'game the system', for example by forecasting unrealistic spending plans or tax rises that then fail to materialise, such as the much-delayed increase in fuel duties. Obviously, all this means that the role of OBR scrutiny becomes more, not less, important, as is argued by some opponents of evidence-based economic policy.

But why have any fiscal rules at all if they are so routinely ignored? Proponents of these rules typically claim that they reassure the markets and that Chancellors will always claim, 'This time we really mean it.' Perhaps the main practical reason, though, is that fiscal rules allow the Chancellor to say a resounding 'no' to fellow ministers who naturally want a bigger budget for their department. Any fiscal rule regarding the overall deficit, however, is only a rule about the balance of public sector spending and revenues, and so when cutting spending becomes too painful, a government can always raise tax. As we will see, we can, and should, get more tax revenue from the better-off to meet the ever-increasing need for government spending, though that won't be enough by itself.

Labour ruled out raising income taxes and other taxes on working people when going into the election, as they feared it could cost them votes. Since then, there have surely been enough well-publicised reasons to claim that the world has changed to such an unexpected degree that a rise in the basic rate of income tax, and perhaps some reversal of Jeremy Hunt's employee National Insurance cuts, is regrettably essential.

HEMMED IN BY PROMISES

It has often been said that in a democracy voters get the politicians they deserve. The problem, however, is that voters often underestimate the complexities of running a country and expect too much from politicians, perhaps hoping for European levels of public services with only US levels of taxation. As we'll argue throughout this book, such a hope just isn't feasible. Hence, politicians often feel they must be elusive or disingenuous – or even lie outright – to get elected. They may even feel they have a moral imperative to do this to keep their political foes from wrecking the country and doing all manner of evil things. Meanwhile, parties new to the political fray, or whose past failures have faded from voters' memories, offer magic solutions with little to no chance of success.

Though both national finances and public services are in a poor condition, Starmer felt hemmed in by the press and the electorate when he made the reckless pledge not to raise income tax. Labour should certainly follow some other countries and consider imposing a levy on commercial banks to address the unintended boost to their profits from quantitative easing, but beyond this, raising income tax would have been the fairest way to close any 'fiscal gap'. Instead, Rachel Reeves was forced to look elsewhere. She played semantics with the manifesto pledge of a 'tax lock for working people' and instead placed the weight of tax increases on employer National Insurance contributions, while leaving employee National Insurance rates unchanged. The truth is that just about all taxes end up hitting most pockets to some extent, and the most elementary economics of tax incidence reveals that raising employers' National Insurance contributions will certainly hit workers' pay packets and that the biggest distortions can come from over-reliance on particular taxes.

Despite Labour claiming to have placed economic growth at the centre of their economic strategy – like so many governments before them – their leaning so heavily on employers hit the business confidence that is needed if we are to see the investment that creates economic growth. An unintended side effect is likely to be a reduction in employment, too; not only workers in businesses, but also care homes, schools and the NHS. It is worth noting that in May 2025, the National Institute of Economic and Social Research, a respected think tank, concluded that reversing the previous Conservative government's cuts to employees' National Insurance contributions would have been less damaging to economic growth than raising those paid by employers.

Of course, most of the flak from the populist press centred on the cutting of the winter fuel payments to all but the poorest pensioners. Starmer's attackers largely ignored the fact that, since the payment was introduced in 2000, its real value had nearly halved and pensioners' incomes had grown at twice the rate of those of working age. They also made light of Labour extending the 'triple lock ratchet' that will continue to increase state pensions; the policy increased state pensions in 2024 by over 4 per cent, with a rise of £363 a year for those on the basic pension, or £472 for those on the new pension. This will most likely mean pensioners as a group will again have faster average income growth than those in work.

Of course, Labour has already come to regret passing the winter fuel payment cuts off as a demonstration of fiscal necessity forced by the parlous state of the economy they inherited. Cutting the payments proved particularly painful politically, a reminder that fiscal freebies once given can't easily be reversed without protest, and, of course, the argument that it was fiscally necessary was quite ridiculous given the rather modest savings, if any. Given the Labour U-turn on these payments, no doubt Starmer rues the day he posed the reasonable argument that giving money to better-off pensioners wastes public money. Simply freezing and taxing the allowance would have saved a similar amount, and Starmer would have avoided revealing to the bond markets his inability to drive through even a fairly modest cut despite a large Commons majority.

The triple lock on pensions, which Labour has reaffirmed, is more fiscally costly than the already frozen winter fuel payments. The triple lock is the rule that the state pension will rise every year by whichever is highest out of price inflation, earnings growth or 2.5 per cent. It has been very expensive because growth has been so poor; pre-2008, it would, in effect, have cost next to nothing. Earnings really should grow more than prices and certainly more than 2.5 per cent; if they don't, the burden of supporting an ageing population's pensions on those still working becomes greater. This means, as our population ages over the next forty years or so, poor growth could well mean lower living standards for non-pensioners. That said, living longer is clearly a good thing, and with a decrease in the percentage of manual workers the traditional 16–64 age measure of the working population becomes more redundant as people increasingly work past traditional pension ages.

Another likely Labour U-turn could come from ending the two-child universal benefit cap. The government is under increasing pressure to scrap the cap, as studies have shown that there is a strong correlation between this and child poverty. For example, the annual analysis from Loughborough University for the End Child Poverty Coalition reports that at least one in four children is in poverty in two-thirds of the UK's constituencies. Despite this, the Conservatives have said they will keep the cap, while the Liberal Democrats and the Green Party have both committed to abolishing the limit in their manifestos and Reform have said they would abolish it and reintroduce the winter fuel payments (no doubt to appeal to the age demographic of their voters). Labour have said they would abolish the cap only 'when fiscal conditions allow'. However, it is often overlooked that scrapping the two-child universal benefit cap would make the overall cap more significant. The two-child cap limits the amount of universal credit families can receive for more than two children, so if this cap were removed then some families in poverty could claim additional benefits for subsequent children, but the overall benefit cap on the total amount of benefits a household can receive – £22,020 per year for households outside London and £25,323 for those within London – would then become a more important constraint.

The ever-vigilant IFS has not overlooked the increased impact of the overall benefits cap. In 2024, they reported that 110,000 households are not directly affected by the two-child limit, as the benefit cap already limits their entitlements. Almost all of these are in the poorest fifth of households. Nevertheless, the IFS estimates that removing the two-child limit would reduce relative child poverty by approximately 500,000 – about 4 per cent of all children – at a cost of about £3.4 billion a year. For a sense of scale, the IFS points out that this would be equal to roughly 3 per cent of the total working-age benefit budget, or approximately the same cost as freezing fuel duties for the next parliament or cutting the basic rate of income tax by half a penny. The IFS also points to evidence suggesting investments in young children can reduce later fiscal costs; in their words, these investments might 'entirely pay for themselves by causing better outcomes for those children in later life'.

It has often been noted that once a fiscal benefit has been given it is politically costly to withdraw it. And so it has inevitably proved for Labour, particularly with the winter fuel payments and the squeeze on incapacity and disability payments. The government sought to address legitimate issues but were far too rushed and clumsy, despite having so much time to prepare while in opposition. It may still be relatively early in their administration, but the public perception of the party's cruelty and incompetence could well end in tears for Labour at the next election. This, combined with a stagnant economy, the failed promises to reduce immigration and the constant stream of grossly misreported accounts of the impacts of such immigration, both legal and illegal, means it is easy to see why Labour has lost so many of its working-class voters.

History shows that the more neglected and discontented voters feel, the more susceptible they become to radical demagogues offering apparently simple solutions, even when their sums just do not add up. As Andy Haldane has warned, it is perhaps no wonder that for many, Nigel Farage is now seen as the closest to a 'tribune' for the working class:

> I don't think there's any politician that comes even remotely close to speaking to, and for, blue-collar, working-class Britain. I think that is just a statement of fact and in some ways, that underscores the importance of the other parties doing somewhat better to find a story, to find a language, and to find some policies that speak to the needs of those most in need.

Labour, and their supporters, also need to do more to expose the sheer incompetence of Reform's policies and its ludicrous sums, the farce of many Reform councillors and exactly whom Reform are set up to serve.

DID THE FIRST BUDGET FROM THE UK'S FIRST FEMALE CHANCELLOR TURN THE TIDE?

Rachel Reeves's first budget was certainly not all bad: £22 billion for the NHS should do a lot to reverse the dramatic decline in recorded public satisfaction since it peaked in 2010. Although, with such a large financial increase all at once, it may not all be spent wisely, it could certainly help get people back in to work and raise overall productivity. The change in fiscal accounting that now allows Labour to borrow more for investment was also long overdue.

Reeves has claimed that her first budget 'drew a line' under her dismal economic inheritance from the Conservatives, but the truth is that her first budget didn't do much at all to change the direction of the economy. That may seem a strange thing to say about a budget that increased spending by an extra £70 billion a year, borrowing by £30 billion a year and taxes by £40 billion a year more through the parliament to 2029/30, by comparison with the March 2024 budget (the last Conservative fiscal event before the July 2024 election). The result was that the first post-election budget raised taxes to their highest ever overall level, although it was just a continuation of the sharp increase in tax and spending we saw under the previous Conservative government. The big decisions on public service spending were simply delayed, and despite the fury over farm inheritance, there was barely any tax reform. In short, it was more of a stop-gap budget than a portent of things to come. But by not reversing the £20 billion or so giveaway in terms of a 4 per cent cut in employee National Insurance contributions before the election by former Chancellor Jeremy Hunt, Reeves, who had talked herself into a corner by promising not to raise income tax, VAT or NIC on 'working people', has left herself taxing companies, which discourages hirings and investment and negatively affects growth. Further tax and spending changes are certain to be made, particularly as the OBR forecast in October 2024 that Rachel Reeves would meet her key fiscal rule, requiring her to balance the current budget – which excludes investment spending – by only a very narrow margin of £9.9 billion. In July 2025, Richard Hughes, chair of the OBR, noted that just a 0.1 percentage point reduction in the OBR's productivity growth forecast over five years would wipe out Reeves's £9.9 billion of headroom against her key fiscal rule, an already low margin that has since been completely erased by flatlining growth, higher-than-expected borrowing figures and higher interest rates charged for government debt than when the OBR reported its forecasts in March 2025, accompanying the Spring Statement.

Given the increased burden on employers and the nature of the investment spend, together with severely reduced forecasts for global growth, it is most unlikely that recent and future budgets will lead to sustainable growth by themselves. At least under Reeves we have seen an end to the cuts. Even if all this does indeed spur some turnaround in growth, most of it will be longer term rather than providing revenues in the short term. This means, unless Labour is lucky and the economy spontaneously accelerates, higher costs for employers, an ageing population, refusal to accept EU conditions for closer trade, raised tariffs by the US, commitments to net zero and a cross-party agreement to increase defence spending will worsen public services and likely prompt the sourcing of more tax revenues. Although spending cuts would perhaps be more likely under the Conservatives, the same underlying economic dynamics would apply to them as well.

Unfortunately, improving the performance of the economy requires a long-term, consistent and persistent direction, something that a democracy often can't guarantee. That is not the same thing as saying the situation needs a particular ideology, as adherence to ideology may be doggedly consistent but it can also be simply wrong and inflexible, as we discuss in the final chapter. To better understand why UK growth has, overall, been so flat since 2008, we should note that the root of all four of the biggest economic failures – the financial crisis, austerity, Brexit and Trump's tariffs – have all been the result of ideology. Sadly, it is economic folly to stick to ideology or reckless manifesto promises when circumstances alter. In words attributed at various times to both Keynes and Churchill: 'When the facts change, I change my mind. What do you do, sir?'

WHICH WAY TO TURN?

From global dominance to a nation diminished by the own goal of Brexit, the UK now often feels like a cork on a stormy global sea. Our finances and public services are under increasing strain, earnings have barely advanced for almost two decades and structural inequality feels embedded and hard to reverse. In some ways, the deep discontent of the electorate is understandable, as average earnings have barely risen for some twenty years. They are at least £10,000 a year below where they would have been had they continued to increase at the rate prevailing for the previous sixty years. In the face of this discontent, extremist parties offer their seemingly simple solutions – or, rather, fantasies – that seem attractive to people full of resentments.

One theme, echoed by Liz Truss and others in the Conservative

Party and Reform, is that an establishment 'blob' has been responsible for many of our woes (an idea we return to in Chapter 12). At various times this blob has included judges, 'lefty' lawyers, universities, the BBC, media figures and the civil service. It is, of course, almost complete nonsense, but the growing support for previously fringe ideas and parties makes the mainstream parties even more reluctant to admit that public services and support for the vulnerable require sacrifices if they are to be funded. And that includes all of us, not just the rich.

Externally, we desperately need good trade deals to boost GDP and job opportunities. Even though the electorate is considerably more pro-EU than in 2016, the rise of Reform and the continuing political influence of other anti-EU politicians does not bode well for any application to rejoin. We will never have the same advantageous deal as the one we had. The US is not proving to be the trustworthy partner that the long-expired myth of a 'special relationship' promised. Indeed, Trump seems to be inadvertently hastening the US's relative decline in its global economic footprint with little apparent care for whom it takes down with it. Any new deals we may broker with the US will come with heavy conditions and, once agreed, experience already shows they can be followed by subsequent threats of withdrawal and/or more demands. Of course, unlike our former voting and influence in the EU, the UK has no vote in the US. Overall, it is no exaggeration to say that Brexit has probably cost us net sovereignty. Any new deals should be seen as attempts to lessen the impact, rather than as net gain, as the theoretical advantages of gravity models of trade – that is, the comparatively greater benefits of trading with close neighbours rather than with trading partners far away – prove to be also correct in practice post-Brexit.

*   *   *

The legacy of the Industrial Revolution, followed by deindustrial-isation and our increased reliance on finance and other services – policies which bolstered a globalising agenda – have left a pattern of inequality that will take progressive policies and spending to overturn. The UK has no empire to retreat into and our economy is wide open to trade and financial movements across the globe. That means the decisions of the EU and the US, as well as China and India, will continue to be a vital part of our success or failure. Great skill and guile – and a good dose of luck – will be needed to get a balanced position with these countries, and we must avoid over-reliance on the US. We must explore moving closer to the EU, our closest giant market, consider new deals with India and other nations and do more to woo China for investment and easier access to its massive population and the huge trading blocs where China dominates.

That ends our whistlestop tour of the UK's economic history since the Industrial Revolution. It's now worth looking in more detail at the particular events that have shaped the UK's economic fortunes.

CHAPTER 3

EVENTS, DEAR BOY

Since 1900 there has been a succession of macroeconomic policy regimes that have come and gone, almost always in response to major events in the economy rather than advances in economic theory. This chapter gives a bird's-eye view of how economic policy has intertwined with events since the Great Depression.

KEYNES AND THE GREAT DEPRESSION

As we saw in the first chapter, the period up to and including the First World War had greatly damaged Britain's highly integrated global economic system, a system that was largely centred around the British Empire and London's financial supremacy. As Britain celebrated victory with her allies, it pursued policies intended to restore its pre-eminent status quo. But the world, and Britain's position in it, had changed. Regardless, Britain's policy was being dominated by the unrealistic and forlorn hope of restoring the nation's former economic strength. Winston Churchill, as Chancellor of the Exchequer in 1925, had taken the ill-judged decision to fix sterling to its pre-war parity by returning to the gold standard, whereby a pound could be exchanged for a specified amount of gold, which fixed the value of the pound and didn't allow it to depreciate, allowing the UK to become more internationally competitive. Pride in the pound sterling led to a seriously over-optimistic exchange rate for the pound, which restricted policy options and made UK exports – vital for such an open economy – uncompetitive. It was a major contributor to poor growth and hence to a distressingly high level of unemployment.

The stock market crash and US economic crisis from 1929 onwards further pulled down the UK which was caught in its wake; it showed that even politically independent countries are often strongly linked economically by their trade and financial flows (an idea we'll return to at length when discussing Brexit in Chapter 5). The Great Depression of the early 1930s saw widespread banking collapses, painfully high unemployment, price deflation, plummeting equity prices and political instability. Historians have extensively noted how these economic conditions contributed in no small degree to the origins of the Second World War. Unemployment climbed to reach some 25 per cent, with the accompanying misery unmitigated by a comprehensive welfare state. Financial meltdown in central Europe in 1931 then placed the overvalued pound sterling under massive speculative pressure, and the UK was forced off the gold standard, but not before the incumbent minority Labour government had collapsed amid demands for fiscal 'austerity'. But sterling's humiliation proved a blessing in disguise, similar, as we shall see, to the UK's forced exit from the European Exchange Rate Mechanism (ERM) some sixty years later in 1992. It was the countries which had abandoned the gold standard that had the earliest economic recovery. The Great Depression was ended by dramatic demand stimulus, as part of a deliberate reflation of the economy in the US under Roosevelt's 'New Deal', copied to a much lesser extent in the UK, and then later by the preparation for the Second World War.

Leaving the gold standard in 1931 allowed the National Government – the coalition which replaced a Labour government badly divided over how to tackle the financial crisis – to conduct a new policy regime, including a more competitive exchange rate. That is, a weaker pound made UK exports cheaper for foreign buyers and allowed cheaper money through lower interest rates (as we shall see, lower interest rates are associated with a weaker pound sterling). This also worked to dislodge deflationary expectations and led to an upturn in the economy even before the massive re-armament of the Second World War boosted output and virtually eliminated unemployment.

Calls for more state intervention post-war had been made even before the end of the war, with the demand arising for a number of reasons: the misery for so many unemployed in the great slump of the interwar years; the horrors of the war itself; the strong performance of the largely planned economy during the war; and the perceived threat of a Russian revolution and growing socialist movements. Despite Churchill's great success as a wartime leader, there was a landslide election victory in 1945 for the radical socialist-orientated Labour government of Clement Attlee. By then, all the main political parties had come to accept the Keynesian objective of full employment, together with some aspects of a planned economy, such as the nationalisation of some major industries. Fiscal intervention to 'correct' macroeconomic performance, the need for a welfare state and a belief in the virtues of a mixed economy became part of a broad cross-party consensus. As we saw in Chapter 1, this consensus on a mixed economy with macro-intervention came to be referred to as 'Butskellism'.

The economic and political trauma of the Great Depression had cast a long shadow over economic policy. Ever since, whenever the global economy has suffered a serious recession – in 1975, 1982, 1991, 2008 and 2020 – there has been speculation that a repeat of the Great Depression might be around the corner. In the post-war years, admiration for Keynes's 'General Theory' and the change in the political climate had led to a general acceptance across the political spectrum of the state's responsibility for economic performance, particularly for controlling unemployment through the adjustment of aggregate demand in the economy, which was so closely associated with Keynes. As we saw, the macroeconomy seemed to grow relatively smoothly during the 1950s and 1960s, decades with no recessions, growing prosperity and low unemployment, even though the UK's GDP grew slowly compared to comparable economies. This slower relative growth, along with the relative industrial decline and deteriorating industrial relations (with frequent strikes and other industrial action), was also more pronounced than in comparable countries. Characterisation of the UK as the 'sick man of Europe' in the media helped plant the seeds for a later counter-revolution against Keynes's macroeconomic prescriptions as a response to the economic woes of the '70s.

Despite many misgivings, in the post-war period up to the late 1960s demand management had almost wholly displaced the previous orthodoxy of neoclassical economics, which had asserted that the economy was self-righting without government intervention. This shift in prevailing thought was often called the 'Keynesian revolution', the central tenet being that the intrinsic instability of capitalism could be cured by governments using their own budgets and their influence over monetary conditions to affect the level of demand in their economies and thereby offset economic slumps.

THE BRETTON WOODS SYSTEM:
DO WE LEARN FROM HISTORY?

Keynes was also influential in advocating an international frame-work for richer post-war nations, in which countries would coop-erate in their macro policies to avoid mutually damaging 'beggar thy neighbour' races to the bottom. In short, Keynes sought to pre-vent countries trying to undercut each other through, for example, currency depreciation reducing the relative prices of a country's exports, or reducing competition through 'protectionism' (erecting barriers to imports). This new cooperative framework was known as the Bretton Woods Agreement. In 1944, the world's major indus-trial nations of the time (excluding Russia), agreed to sign up to an obligation for each to hold to a monetary policy that maintained their currency's exchange rate by tying their currencies to gold. In practice, this was in fact tied to the US dollar, as the dollar was directly convertible to gold at the time. Unlike the classical gold standard, capital controls were permitted to enable governments to stimulate their economies – by lowering interest rates, for exam-ple – without suffering financial market penalties from an outflow of their currency as financiers moved their cash around the globe seeking the highest return.

The International Monetary Fund (IMF) was also set up under Bretton Woods to bridge temporary imbalances of payments for struggling member countries by pooling loans from other member countries. This was provided as an alternative to aggressive deflation and devaluations, which, if copied, would also hurt other countries as global demand fell. The Bretton Woods agreement was driven by the shared experience of countries in the international order of the interwar years, which had failed to deal with the economic problems after the First World War, problems which would also play a large part in fomenting the Second World War (as Keynes himself had warned). Germany had been saddled with huge debts it could not – and didn't want to – repay, knowing such repayments would bring tremendous hardship and political unrest. The Treaty of Versailles following the First World War blamed Germany for the conflict and demanded large reparations, with a view to humiliating and punishing Germany.

The weakened economy and reparation payments meant that the German economy could not recover to the extent that it could meet these debts, at least without also risking political turmoil. Germany regularly defaulted on reparations payments; Wall Street resisted plans to allow the issue of German debt on favourable terms, fearing the competition and with its own serious problems. All this meant that the German government of the time, the Weimar Republic, was in effect bankrupt. It tried to keep the German economy going and to placate anger among the German population over payments to former enemies by simply printing new money. This printing started intermittently from 1921, but accelerated sharply in 1923 when German workers embarked on a general strike in protest against the occupation of the Ruhr Valley by French troops, who were themselves stationed there to force the payment of reparations. The Weimar Republic decided to support the strikers by paying their wages with newly printed money. Eventually, this led to hyper-inflation caused by too much money chasing too few goods, and this added greatly to a meltdown of the German economy.

By 1929, the Weimar economy was beginning to stabilise, but the Wall Street crash led to capital being recalled to the US, a huge blow for the German economy that caused renewed economic misery and fuelled extreme politics. As we are seeing today, poor economic growth is strongly associated with discontent and the rise of extreme views. Keynes had foreseen the folly of the Treaty of Versailles and so warned of the dangers of saddling countries with debts that kept them in permanent recession; he understood that economic recessions not only inflict misery on millions of people but, if prolonged, could lead to the rise of dangerous political extremes. The rest, as they say, is history, as the Third Reich came to power even in what was a democracy.

* * *

The chief obligations of the Bretton Woods system were for member countries to cooperate rather than compete in terms of macro policy by:

a) Adopting a monetary policy that maintained their exchange rates against gold;

b) Using capital controls to avoid speculation destabilising a country's currency and to allow expansion of a country's aggregate demand without impacts on its exchange rate;

c) Contributing to the ability of the IMF to bridge temporary imbalances of payments for countries that fell into trouble and then support them, preventing them from turning to actions that would be adverse to other countries in the agreement;

d) Avoiding the mutually destructive policies of 'protectionism' that had exacerbated the Great Depression, whereby a lack of cooperation among countries had led to competitive devaluations of currencies and attempts to engineer export-led recoveries through suppressing home demand and setting barriers to imports such as tariffs and regulatory measures.

National policies that had sought to eliminate trade deficits by reducing demand and devaluing currencies are an example of a 'fallacy of composition': what might work for an individual nation can have mutually adverse effects when all nations try it at once. Bretton Woods was a means of avoiding the damaging trade policies that had led to mutually negating devaluations and trade protectionism (a lesson that was resoundingly ignored by the Trump administration in 2025). As we have seen, Bretton Woods was part of a 'Golden Age' for Keynesian policy which contributed to the steady – albeit mostly modest – growth and relative stability that continued up to the late 1960s.

Some critics of the Bretton Woods system argued that although the fixed exchange rates favoured trade by removing exchange rate instability and hence uncertainty, the capital controls also hampered profits, particularly in the UK finance sector. Despite its notable successes, the system had been under increasing strain, and in August 1971 the US unilaterally terminated convertibility of the US dollar to gold, effectively bringing Bretton Woods to an end. As a result, many previously fixed currencies (such as the pound sterling) lost their benchmark and became free-floating. That is, they were determined freely by day-to-day market forces, rather than being maintained at specific levels by loans, market interventions and capital controls to prevent movement in exchange rates. Indeed, by the time US President Richard Nixon had declared, 'I am now a Keynesian in economics', the whole Keynesian consensus was being displaced by events and politics.

THE GOLDEN KEYNESIAN ERA

Today, Keynes is mostly known for his thoughts on how to 'rescue' capitalism from severe recessions and depressions by using fiscal policy – that is, using government fiscal deficits to smooth out fluctuations in aggregate demand, and hence output and employment. If unemployment rises, so Keynes suggested, the government should spend more and tax less; if the economy appeared to be overheating, threatening inflation, then do the reverse. This naive Keynesian view that such fine-tuning of the economy was appropriate was summed up by Sir Edward, later Lord Bridges, then Permanent Secretary to the Treasury, in the 1950s:

> The budget is second-to-none in importance, since by its influence on the flow of income it can be used both to sustain a high level of employment and keep total demand within the limits of total supply.

However, as Geoff Tily documents in his book *Keynes Betrayed*, Keynes was primarily a monetary theorist and not the 'high tax and big spender' he is often claimed to be. He regarded fiscal policy as an emergency backstop only, to be used in cases of crisis, rather like an economic defibrillator. He argued it was the responsibility of the public authorities to avoid and prevent such crises in the first place, especially financial crises, and that interest rates should generally be set to stimulate the level of private investment required to prevent deficiencies in aggregate demand and to encourage growth. Although, in practice, during most of the 'Golden Age of Keynesianism' low interest rates were chiefly seen as a means of keeping government debt repayments down.

Of course, correlation doesn't equal causation, particularly as economies are complex and there are usually other competing explanations, but for a long period up to the early 1970s naive Keynesianism appeared to be working. Stability was accompanied by steadily improving living standards, as governments of all political stripes embraced Keynesian policies. That was, until the 'stagflation' of the 1970s.

THE GREAT INFLATION AND THE NEOCLASSICAL COUNTER-REVOLUTION

The 1970s saw economic instability and crises, with the industrial and financial situation worsening through the decade. The 'Great Inflation', which took root in the late 1960s and peaked during the 1970s, saw inflation rise to double-digit annual rates, partly accounted for by the quadrupling of world oil prices in 1973, a big negative supply-side shock for the economy. 'In the 1974/75 recession, the first since the early 1930s, unemployment reached levels not seen since the Great Depression. The sum of inflation and unemployment rates, the so-called 'misery index', also reached record levels. In 1976, the Labour Prime Minister James Callaghan felt obliged to ask the IMF for a massive loan, which was seen as a national humiliation for a still-proud former superpower (especially as IMF bailouts were typically reserved only for profligate emerging markets). Not surprisingly, the financial markets were also performing badly.

The combination of high inflation and rising unemployment, or 'stagflation', seemed to pose an insuperable policy dilemma for Keynesian demand management policy: injecting more demand to reduce unemployment could raise already high inflation, while reducing aggregate demand might reduce inflation but also increase unemployment. At the Labour conference in 1976, the first since Callaghan became leader, he said:

We used to think that you could spend your way out of a recession and increase employment by cutting taxes and boosting government spending. I tell you in all candour that that option no longer exists, and that insofar as it ever did exist, it only worked on each occasion since the war by injecting a bigger dose of inflation into the economy, followed by a higher level of un-employment as the next step. Higher inflation followed by higher unemployment. We have just escaped from the highest rate of inflation this country has known; we have not yet escaped from the consequences: high unemployment.

Most Keynesian economists of the time continued to argue that unemployment could be reduced through government spending. 'Monetarists' blamed high inflation on an excess of money in the economy, driven by government in effect printing money to pay for their public sector deficits. Keynesian economists blamed inflation on myriad other things: sharply increased oil prices following the 1973 oil crisis, when members of the Organization of Arab Petro-leum Exporting Countries proclaimed an oil embargo targeted at those nations perceived as supporting Israel during the Yom Kippur War; the international financial deregulation following the break-up of Bretton Woods; in the UK, the 1971 'Competition and Credit Control' scheme whereby banks were granted permission by the Edward Heath government to lend more freely; the dramatic falls in the value of the pound due to this rapid expansion of credit; the lack of an effective incomes policy that prevented unions 'leap-frogging' each other's wage increases to push all wages up; and, as inflation tends to be international, the fact that there was a rise in inflation across all OECD countries.

Modern Keynesians do often concede that the 1960s had been a period of over-optimism during which aggregate demand had been allowed to expand too much in the pursuit of economic growth.

British economist Ann Pettifor puts a large part of the blame for the subsequent inflation on unrealistic growth targets:

> The setting of ridiculously high, unsustainable growth targets for the British economy by the OECD in the 1960s naturally led to the expansion of economic activity, beyond the capacity of the economy. This, in turn, led to inflation – which was promptly blamed on the trade unions.

In spite of Keynes's own more restrained recommendations for the use of demand management, post-war governments may well have seen aggregate demand as a 'magic' tool for growth and hence electoral popularity. And even after the collapse of the Bretton Woods system, when capital controls were lifted and domestic financial markets were deregulated, the rapid expansion of the private sector was not seen by policymakers as a potential threat to macroeconomic stability, despite history showing that credit booms are often the best predictors of financial crisis. As Pettifor says:

> The Latin American debt crisis launched another series of sovereign debt crises in 1982. Thanks to financial deregulation of the American 'thrift' industry, the Savings and Loans crisis of the 1980s was followed by the 1987 stock market crash; the 1989 Junk Bond crash; the Tequila crisis of 1994; the Asia crisis of 1997–8; the Dotcom bubble of 1999–2000 and then the global financial crisis of 2007–9.
>
> But while markets, banks, firms and millions of individuals 'crashed and burned', the supply-side economic theory and policies of financial deregulation and capital mobility that

underpinned the concept of 'limitless growth' were untouched. They remain intact to this day.

THE CHICAGO SCHOOL

By the 1970s, politicians were increasingly listening to US 'Chicago school' economists such as Milton Friedman of the University of Chicago. Their 'restatement' of pre-Keynesian economics led to a reconsideration of macroeconomic theory and policies that lasts to this day. Friedman argued that there is only a short-lived trade-off between inflation and unemployment, and that increasing government spending in an effort to keep unemployment below its 'natural rate' merely increases the money supply and the dangers of ever-accelerating inflation. Essentially, the doctrine of monetarism held that a government's primary macroeconomic duty was to restrain its own budget and thereby reduce excessive growth and fluctuations in the amount of money in the economy. The claim was that this would control inflation, leaving unemployment and growth to settle down at their 'natural' rates as driven by the market forces of supply and demand. We should note that there is no direct way of measuring these 'natural' values in a real economy; they arise from pure theory and in practice are estimated from merely statistical extrapolations. Even if they are valid concepts, they would frequently change as the underlying conditions of the economy change.

Trade unions were at that time an integral part of the Labour Party and had grown accustomed to their own inclusion in 'beer and sandwiches' policy discussions, often held in rooms thick with tobacco smoke. James Callaghan's shift to the right in the 1970s – and his government's efforts to control inflation by capping wage increases, even in the face of high inflation with the potential for sharp falls in real wages – therefore led to widespread union disputes. To some, it seemed that economist Jacob Viner's 1936 prediction, which he made when reviewing Keynes's General Theory, was finally coming to fruition:

> Keynes's reasoning points obviously to the superiority of inflationary remedies for unemployment over money wage reductions. In a world organized in accordance with Keynes's specifications there would be a constant race between the printing press [to print new money] and the business agents of the trade unions.

The level of industrial action peaked in the 1978/79 Winter of Discontent, which saw the largest withdrawal of labour since the 1926 general strike. A widely publicised series of strikes and much industrial unrest led to alarm and severe inconvenience for the public: car and railway workers, many public sector workers, lorry and ambulance drivers and even grave diggers took industrial action. Rubbish went uncollected and formed towering piles in the streets, attracting rats and providing photographs which the right-wing press used to denounce a Labour government they felt was responsible for a thorough breakdown in the social order. The direct action by workers, often followed rather than led by unions and their leaders (despite the press claiming it was the other way round), did help stem the tide of effective pay cuts caused by inflation that threatened the real value of wages. However, the disruption to ordinary life in the Winter of Discontent was a major factor in voters' decisions, contributing to the Conservative election victory of 1979, a considerable turning point in UK politics. Campaigning on the election slogan of 'Labour Isn't Working', the Conservative Party leader Margaret Thatcher lent a close ear to her long-term intellectual adviser, political colleague and monetarist convert, Sir Keith Joseph.

THE RISE AND FALL OF MONETARISM

In the mid-1970s, Sir Keith Joseph made major speeches about the economic principles which should guide the Conservative Party. The principles he espoused were in effect a vigorous restatement of classical economic liberalism, a rough synthesis of the contemporary academic teachings of both Friedrich von Hayek and Milton Friedman. Hayek was arguably the most prominent free-market anti-socialist philosopher of the twentieth century, while Friedman was the prophet of monetarism, itself part of a resurgent neoclassical type of economic thought. The central message of monetarism, and hence its name, was that all the government had to do for macroeconomic policy was to control the growth of the money supply, mostly by eschewing the creation of new money used to pay for government deficits. It was essentially a more modern version of the earlier neoclassical 'quantity of money' theory. As we have seen, the prediction was that controlling the money supply would curtail inflation and then unemployment would simply sort itself out through natural market forces – a return, of sorts, to the pre-Keynesian neoclassical notion of the self-righting economy. Joseph's shift away from Keynesian orthodoxy was criticised by the more sympathetically Keynesian former Prime Minister Edward Heath, who had led the Conservative Party until he was supplanted by Thatcher. Heath mocked Sir Keith as 'a good man fallen among monetarists'.

Rejecting Keynesianism, Margaret Thatcher famously likened good management of the nation's public finances to 'prudent housewives' who kept household expenditure within their budgets. The notion that a government's budget is just like a household budget, or a credit card that can be 'maxed out', has been a recurring and powerful rhetorical device among right-wingers, even though economists do not think the analogy is particularly accurate. Indeed, a great deal of confusion about the constraints on government spending could be cleared up if people understood that *government spending minus taxes must equal new borrowing from the private sector plus new money created by the state.* This is akin to an identity rather than an equation – just as 'men who have never married are bachelors', it is simply true by definition. We can't just make blanket assertions – for example, that the government can't borrow its way out of debt – as there are no assertions of causation in the identity at all. It is certainly not true that a government can only spend more if it taxes more, although longer term there are likely to be good reasons why increased government spending does need more taxation.

Clearly, the political pendulum in the lead-up to Thatcher's government had been swinging to the right, caused by the apparent failure of Keynesian approaches and fading memories of the Great Depression as well as by soaring inflation that destroyed people's savings and by the decline of socialist influence. This rise of the political right, in both the US and the UK, rehabilitated neoclassical free market approaches to macroeconomics. By contrast, formerly prominent macro theories that emphasised the exercise of power and conflict, as well as the determinants and consequences of relative shares between labour and capital, faded away. These were replaced by neoclassical and 'new classical' approaches that emphasised the role of individual choice rather than structural interdependency and systemic malfunctions. Free market economists such as Friedman and Hayek, who had previously been overshadowed, even ridiculed, by the 'Keynesian revolution', were being taken seriously again.

Academic macroeconomists began to reassert 'neoclassical micro-foundations', built on the assumption that economic agents – that is consumers, firms and even governments – optimise their own self-interest and that their optimisation drives macroeconomics towards a natural rate of employment and growth and hence also a natural rate of unemployment. At this natural rate of unemployment, anyone who wishes to work at prevailing wages can, at least after a bit of searching, find employment. If they can't, then wages will fall until there are enough jobs for all those who still wish to work. In short, no *involuntary* unemployment remains at this 'natural equilibrium'. New sophisticated iterations of older neoclassical models were designed, to provide theoretical explanations that Keynesian effects of policy were weak, temporary and, in the long run, self-defeating. Increasingly, these temporary effects were portrayed as deviations from the naturally efficient equilibrium states of the economy, but then later 'new classical' theory began to eschew even temporary Keynesian aggregate demand influences. In these abstract models, government macroeconomic interventions simply muddied the waters, making it harder to see true values and thus also making it difficult for economic agents to optimise.

In the real world, away from these highly abstract economic models, Mrs Thatcher's 'monetarist experiment' in the 1980s was associated with unemployment levels not seen since the Great Depression. She fought a bitter battle 'for Britain's economic future' against the power of unions, especially against the coal miners, whose industrial actions had earlier led to the downfall of Edward Heath. Following Thatcher's victory over the National Union of Mineworkers, poorly led by Arthur Scargill, in a bitter, protracted and sometimes violent dispute, the union movement has not been nearly as powerful, although the movement's long-term decline was largely due to other factors such as technological change, as union-isation declined around the world.

The intentions of Thatcher and Joseph had been signalled in advance by 'The Right Approach to the Economy' policy document of 1977, but the speed with which the Thatcher government sought to implement its new agenda still took most observers, including most economists, by surprise. Income tax rates (a progressive tax) were slashed in the budget of June 1979 and VAT (a regressive tax) almost doubled from 8 per cent to 15 per cent. Public spending was cut back in an effort to avoid the government budget deficits that Friedman had blamed as the root of uncontrolled expansion of the money supply and hence inflation. The overriding policy objective was to bring inflation down by achieving tight targets announced for the growth supply of money and, later, high interest rates to stave off the demand for credit. The problem for the monetary targets was that this demand for credit was from private sector banks, not government spending, which actually created most of the money supply in the form of commercial bank deposits.

In believing that the money supply could be controlled simply by limiting the creation of money by the Bank of England, Thatcher's deregulation of private sector finance institutions built on earlier financial deregulations, such as the 'Competition and Credit Control' relaxations at the beginning of the 1970s, which had also seen a surge in the creation of credit. The UK's capital controls on the flows of currency out of the country were abolished and restrictions on consumer lending were relaxed; high street stores freely offered credit, as the use of credit cards boomed. As such, consumer borrowing tripled during the 1980s. Building societies were also allowed to lend more and foreign banks were allowed to set up in the UK. In short, 'liberated' finance began to take more risks. The

Bank of England did not control this expansion of credit, and some economists see the roots of the subsequent financial crisis of 2007 in the deregulation of credit from the Thatcher years.

The policy trajectory had been set and Keynes was firmly out of favour, with the intellectual argument being led by right-wing economists in the US. These are often called 'freshwater' economists after the Great Lakes, in contrast with the more Keynesian 'saltwater' economists (also called 'fiscalists' in the US) from universities on the east and west coast such as Berkeley, Harvard, Princeton and Yale. In academia, although many older economists were still Keynesians, the younger academic macroeconomists were being increasingly trained in such complex-sounding ideas as 'neo-classical constrained maximisation micro-foundations' as 'complete' explanations for macroeconomic phenomena. The 'fallacy of composition' and 'animal spirits' (Keynes's term for the level of confidence) of Keynes were discarded in the new models, which were prized for their internal logical consistency, increasingly expressed in impressive-looking mathematics. Indeed, logical consistency of a model seemed to be more highly prized than correspondence with actual economic events, empirical data or an informed historical narrative. Unemployment came to be portrayed again in terms of individual choices rather than as the unemployed being hapless victims of a dysfunctional macroeconomy, as in Keynesian theory. As such, the lived experience of so many unfortunate people was grossly overlooked.

In short, demand stimulus policies, as associated with Keynes, were portrayed as unnecessary; at best, they were impotent and at worst, harmful and dangerously inflationary. Despite its strong backing by interested parties, the monetarist experiment was not wholly successful even on its own terms. As said, monetarism promised that all macro policy required governments to do was to prevent the supply of money in the economy expanding too fast and this would prevent excessive inflation; the rest of the economy could be left to sort itself out. Hence, Milton Friedman famously said, 'Inflation is always and everywhere a monetary phenomenon in the sense that it is and can be produced only by a more rapid increase in the quantity of money than in output.'

The first years of the monetarist policy regime saw recession, rising unemployment and continued high inflation. It spurred bitter political opposition to such a tough fiscal and monetary stance. Throughout, Thatcher was adamant that her 'monetarist treatment' would be maintained. Her determination, or her callous stubbornness and inflexibility, depending on one's views, was immortalised by her speech at the 1980 Conservative Party conference in which she infamously claimed, 'The lady's not for turning.' Monetarism had up to then showed little sign of delivering the relatively painless eradication of inflation that it had promised. Many saw it as a crude and brutal regime motivated by ideology, one that was deliberately seeking to discipline workers by imposing unnecessary recession and unemployment upon them.

As we have noted, the Conservative Party had previously marketed itself as a one nation party and had publicly supported the postwar consensus on the need for a mixed economy, while accepting that it was the government's responsibility to keep unemployment low. In contrast, Thatcher made no pretence about holding collective values. She was determined to destroy what she saw as creeping socialism and Keynesianism (which was, in her words, simply 'socialism through the back door'). She later summed up her views on society, or the lack thereof, in a notorious interview with *Woman's Own* magazine in 1987:

I think we've been through a period where too many people have been given to understand that if they have a problem, it's the government's job to cope with it. 'I have a problem, I'll get a grant. I'm homeless, the government must house me.' They're casting their problem on society. And, you know, there is no such thing as society. There are individual men and women, and there are families.

To this day, Thatcher remains a hero for many and for others a callous and divisive leader who destroyed the collective values of the post-war period. Some supporters, determined to claim she turned Britain around, point to the small increase in the long-run average rate of growth after the monetarist experiment, though this is alternatively explained by many economists as the effect of joining the European Economic Community in 1973 (this would later become the European Community before it was absorbed into the EU).

DID THE 'MONETARIST EXPERIMENT' WORK?

Although inflation did eventually fall under the Thatcher government, this was driven more by a suppressed economy and high unemployment than by any control of the money supply, especially as attempts to control the money supply had so very clearly failed. The targets for monetary growth were repeatedly breached and so were eventually forgotten without ceremony, even though they had previously been held up as the lynchpin of economic policy. Meanwhile, the high interest rates aimed at controlling the money supply through stemming demand for credit had reduced aggregate demand and increased the sterling exchange, hence making exports uncompetitive. Again, monetarism offered a simple macroeconomic panacea: government just needed to control the money supply, which would then control inflation and allow the economy to self-adjust to its natural levels. To control the money supply, it was necessary to prevent government deficits creating debt that could be used as reserve assets by commercial banks to create credit or, worse, could lead to the government directly printing money. To reduce the government's deficit, strongly deflationary policies were implemented: taxes were raised, government spending cut and interest rates increased. These deflationary fiscal and monetary policies did have the effect of reducing inflation, at a cost of falling aggregate demand and lower economic growth. By the middle of 1980, the economy had been plunged into recession, yet the government still pursued its deflationary policies.

Increasing taxes and cutting government expenditure in the middle of a recession was the opposite of Keynes's prescription for dealing with severe recessions and was hence in stark contrast to preceding governments' policies since the war. In March 1981, an open letter to *The Times* from 364 leading economists – including five retired senior government advisers – expressed the view of the vast majority of UK economists of the time: attempts to reduce the budget deficit, combined with the contractionary monetary stance of high interest rates, was too brutal a method of attacking inflation. Their letter stated:

> There is no basis in economic theory or supporting evidence for the government's belief that by deflating demand they will bring inflation permanently under control and thereby induce an automatic recovery in output and employment … Present politics will deepen the depression, erode the industrial base of our economy and threaten its social and political stability.

It was a very similar letter to those that would later be written by economists criticising the austerity policies of George Osborne from 2010, the majority of whom still turn to Keynes in the face of a deep recession. In fact, Thatcher was asked in a heated debate in Parliament if she could name even two economists who supported her programme. In reply, she named Alan Walters and Patrick Minford, both advisers to her government. On returning to Downing Street, a civil servant remarked to her, 'It is a good job he didn't ask you to name three!'

However, soon after the famous letter in 1981, Britain and the US did see a recovery. Ironically, by cutting taxes and increasing military spending in the US, President Ronald Regan was in effect engaging in a traditional Keynesian reflation. In the UK, on the other hand, the recovery may well have been due to decreased interest rates, seen by some as facilitated by the tight fiscal stance and by others by the abandoning of monetary targets. Also, most economists believe that economies, unless systematically destroyed by extreme policies, will always tend to recover in the long run. The question is: how long is the long run and what can be done to shorten it?

'With a delightful irony, the recovery in the economy began almost immediately after the letter from the 364 appeared in *The Times*,' wrote economist Tim Congdon, who remains sympathetic to monetarist economics. On the twenty-fifth anniversary of the letter, Congdon added, 'The academics at the time were in thrall to "naive Keynesianism", without regard for the potentially more powerful changes in the money supply.' He was pointing out that although fiscal policy was tight, and therefore deflationary, this was offset by credit control relaxation and subsequent falling interest rates. Indeed, some economists argue that Thatcher's fiscal restraint may have quickened a fall in inflation as it then allowed more expansionary credit conditions. We should note, however, that higher unemployment persisted for some twenty years after the monetarist experiment.

As is so often the case in macroeconomics, things are seldom settled beyond debate; in the absence of a macroeconomic laboratory for controlled economic experiments, there is always a shortage of counterfactuals and a surplus of alternative explanations, known as 'confounders'. In 2013, *The Economist* concluded, 'While Britain's 1981 budget almost certainly subtracted from aggregate demand, this was more than offset by monetary easing as interest rates fell. Indeed, the fiscal restraint probably hastened the fall in inflation, making more aggressive monetary relief possible.' But it also added, 'Evidence that this programme turned Britain's long-term economic performance around is more elusive than fans of Thatcherism would like. British real growth averaged 2.5 per cent from 1969 to 1979; it averaged 2.7 per cent in the subsequent decade, an improvement but no renaissance.'

As GDP had fallen by over 2 per cent in 1980 and remained flat in 1981, and manufacturing output fell by 15 per cent in two years, it is perhaps not surprising that inflation fell. As outraged Keynesian economists of the time observed, 'There is no inflation in a graveyard.' All that said, it's also the case that inflation rates and GDP often move in similar directions in economies that are linked internationally, and so the impacts of domestic policy are easily exaggerated. Overall, this was far from the relatively painless adjustment promised by monetarism. The high unemployment led to prolonged unemployment due to what economists call 'hysteresis' effects, whereby chronic unemployment leads to deteriorating morale and skills, as well as a mismatch of skills with jobs and worsened mental health. With hysteresis, the natural 'equilibrium level' of employment gravitates towards the actual level, rather than vice versa, as is usually assumed in economic theory. Therefore, if unemployment rises to high levels it will tend to lock-in a higher unemployment rate for subsequent periods compared to the period before the rise. Following the monetarist experiment, many young people had their life chances blighted by chronically poor employment prospects and many older unemployed people never worked again. This was exacerbated by the regional nature of the unemployment, which led to widespread discontent throughout entire communities.

Inflation had seemingly been cured, but perhaps only as it had also reduced across the world. After such severe recessions in the early 1980s, economists searched again for gentler ways of coping with economic cycles. The Bank of England, which oversees interest rates today, would not raise these rates as quickly as we saw during the monetarist experiment to control inflation. One reason for this is that, although the bank's primary remit is inflation, it is also charged with considering impacts on growth and unemployment (this is discussed further in Chapter 6).

Even with the chosen money supply targets growing well above forecast, the disinflation costs were higher than monetarists themselves had predicted; for monetarism to work, the relationship between inflation and the targeted monetary aggregate had to be reliable, which it wasn't. Indeed, the central tenet of monetarism – monetary targeting – became a high-profile embarrassment for the Thatcher government because it was so frequently exceeded and so was eventually, quietly, abandoned. But why did it prove so difficult to control the money supply? Charles Goodhart, an eminent monetary economist at the Bank of England, gave an explanation at the time that became known as 'Goodhart's Law': 'As soon as the government attempts to regulate a particular set of financial assets, these become unreliable as indicators of economic trends.'

This could be because once banks know a particular part of the money supply is being targeted, they simply move to increase other parts of the money supply. Today, it is widely accepted that in a modern banking system, within which bank deposits created through the provision of loans for profit are the biggest element of the money supply, money is largely 'endogenous'. This means that money is generated from *within* the banking sector itself in the form of commercial deposits and loans, so that its volume is determined by the demand for credit rather than a fixed 'supply' being set by the country's monetary authorities (an outdated view that can still be found in too many textbooks).

Monetary authorities can usually, but not always, play a large part in determining market rates of interest, but often have little influence over the volume of credit demanded – that is, the volume of bank deposits created by banks, which are a form of money. To avoid a common confusion, we should add that the fact that the money supply is often largely endogenous is not the same as saying that the monetary authorities – such as the US's central bank, the Federal Reserve, and the Bank of England – cannot 'soften or tighten' credit and monetary conditions. The rate they charge to commercial banks will usually feed through to market-determined interest rates through such things as expectations, competition, arbitrage or commercial banks changing the rates they charge to customers to reflect the opportunity cost of the interest rate they could get on their deposits with the central bank. So, a lower policy rate set by the central bank for commercial banks will usually feed through to lower rates charged by commercial banks to their customers. Quantitative easing, formerly called 'open market operations' – such as the central bank buying government bonds from private sector holders of bonds – can also inject liquidity into the economy, and in effect inject new money into the economy through interaction with the Treasury selling bonds and spending the revenue.

These 'monetary transmission mechanisms' can seem very confusing, even to professionals. To summarise, the Bank of England acts to adjust the price of credit money rather than acting directly on the volume of credit. Hence, in modern endogenous monetary frameworks, monetary policy is better described as 'interest rate policy'.

THE LAWSON BOOM

The Lawson Boom is the name given to the contrasting period of rapid economic expansion in the UK during the later years of the 1980s. The boom was named after Nigel Lawson, who was Chancellor under Margaret Thatcher from 1983 to 1989. The name entered popular economic parlance when Lawson resigned in protest at Thatcher's reliance on the economist Sir Alan Walters. Between 1985 and 1988, growth was well above the trend rate of 2.5 per cent a year, but by 1990 inflation had increased to 9.5 per cent and was becoming embedded in inflationary expectations (when prices are raised in anticipation of inflation and so inflation accelerates). The Lawson Boom was a classic example of a 'boom and bust' economic cycle: after the recession of the early 1980s, the late '80s saw rapid growth. This rapid expansion was caused by loose monetary policy and rising house prices being used as collateral for more loans and inflationary tax cuts, leading to unwarranted optimism. It all stemmed from the unjustified confidence of a Chancellor who believed that monetarism had killed inflation and driven out inefficient firms which, together with reduced union power and widespread privatisation, had performed a 'supply-side miracle'.

Nigel Lawson thought this supposed 'miracle' of the Thatcher government warranted tax cuts, as he believed that the consequent increase in aggregate demand would be absorbed by a growing supply of goods and services and therefore would not be unduly inflationary. As he said in his budget speech of 1988:

> The plain fact is that the British economy has been transformed. Prudent financial policies have given business and industry the confidence to expand, while supply-side reforms have progressively removed the barriers to enterprise.

The effect of these tax cuts was a fiscal stimulus that increased disposable income and consumer confidence and hence led to a rise in consumption. Indeed, the Lawson budget of 1988 is often referred to as the 'giveaway budget', although it should be noted that the Lawson Boom also significantly increased inequality, helped by the tax cuts for high earners. As this budget had followed on from the deep recession, Lawson believed that this meant there would be spare capacity, and so expansionary measures might be less likely to cause inflation. And yet, in 1985, unemployment was still over 11 per cent, much higher than earlier periods which had seen it around only 4 per cent. From 1986, the Chancellor made various expansionary decisions that culminated in an inflationary boom. This then had to be countered by contractionary policies to reduce inflation, as there is strong reason to believe, in both theory and practice, that the higher inflation is allowed to climb the more painful the measures then needed to reverse it. Consequently, the reversal of increases in aggregate demand caused a deep downturn into 1989.

The expansionary measures had included a significant deregulation of financial markets, allowing for increased competition and innovation in the banking and financial sectors, but at the expense of prudence and an increase in risky loans. Low interest rates and easier access to credit led to a surge in housing demand and hence a boom in the housing market. Property prices soared, contributing to wealth accumulation for many homeowners and hence creating a 'financial accelerator' as consumers could use the increased equity in their house as collateral to get yet more loans. Expansionary fiscal and monetary policy caused GDP to expand at a rapid pace, and yet none of this was perceived by the Chancellor as the economy dangerously overheating.

Interest rates at the time were still set by the Chancellor and not by the Bank of England, as is the case today. Then, in October 1987, there was a stock market crash. In just one week, 25 per cent of the value of the stock market was lost. The Chancellor was puzzled and worried about the macroeconomic implications of the crash, so he lowered interest rates further to avoid any slackening of growth; the economy did indeed continue to grow at a rapid rate, and the cut in interest rates furthered the momentum of the boom. By early 1989, the economy was growing at 5 per cent a year, which was almost double the long-run trend, but still the Chancellor was reluctant to dampen aggregate demand. Although interest rates were finally increased, this was only slow and limited. Again, this was partly because the Thatcher government was insisting that they had performed 'an economic miracle' that enabled a higher trend rate of economic growth. But it was also because Lawson, unlike Thatcher, was keen on aligning with the European Exchange Rate Mechanism and so didn't want higher interest rates to attract speculative funds to the UK that would raise the exchange rate for the pound sterling above an 'unofficial exchange rate' that he was intent on following, an exchange rate set by shadowing the German currency of the time, the Deutsche Mark (DM). All this allowed the rate of inflation to continue to increase, eventually reaching over 8 per cent in 1990. Faced with such high and accelerating inflation, the Chancellor felt forced to allow the Bank of England to raise interest rates. This contributed to a downturn of the economy in the late 1980s and early 1990s, culminating in a painful recession. This, in short, is a prime example of 'boom and bust'.

*　*　*

While the monetarist experiment had reduced inflation by the mid-1980s, many economists believe this reduction in inflation was then recklessly squandered by the Lawson Boom. Whatever the merits or demerits of the supply-side reforms, there was no 'supply-side miracle' that would allow aggregate supply to respond so strongly to an expansion of aggregate demand such that inflation could safely be ignored. Instead, despite the improvement in growth, the economy was allowed to overheat, leading to inflation and an unsustainable boom. Reversing this trajectory meant contractionary policies to counter accelerating inflation that then resulted in another painful recession. The experience of the Lawson Boom was a contributing factor to the argument that the Bank of England should be independent, so as to be free from immediate political pressures in the setting of interest rates. By the time Gordon Brown did make the Bank of England independent in May 1997 (discussed in more detail later in this chapter), there had also been movements in macroeconomic theory, suggesting that there are advantages to central bank independence and a stabilisation in prices that allows economic agents to optimise.

FROM MONETARY TARGETS TO EXCHANGE RATE TARGETS AND THE ERM

By the 1990s, monetary targets had been abandoned as an instrument of demand management and instead policy in the UK had shifted towards attempting to target the exchange rate. This was because managing the exchange rate was now seen as a key means by which inflation could be controlled, even if monetary targeting had not worked. A managed foreign exchange rate, known as a 'semi-pegged' exchange rate, was to be maintained. The idea was that if the exchange rate fell compared to major competitors then this was a sign that the UK's aggregate demand and costs were too high, hence increasing imports and reducing exports, and thus pushing the exchange rate down, thereby adding to domestic excess demand and pushing inflation above that of competitors. Previously, before the managed rate regime prohibited this, a fall in the exchange rate might temporarily restore UK competitiveness, but this was only ever a temporary palliative, as leaving the root problems of inflation and lack of productivity unaddressed meant the problems would return. Successive decreases in the value of the pound would make the UK worse off and so add to inflation again as imports became more expensive for UK residents.

When UK inflation rises above that of competitor countries – due to excess demand, say – then the exchange rate will tend to fall, as the UK will otherwise become uncompetitive. Raising UK interest rates to prevent the fall in the exchange rate has two strong anti-inflation effects:

- It reduces borrowing and increases saving in the UK economy, hence reducing aggregate demand and leading to price increases.
- As currency speculators buy pound sterling to take advantage of the relatively high interest rate, this raises the sterling exchange rate against other currencies and thereby lowers the price of finished imports and the cost of imported inputs to UK finished goods, and hence lowers inflation.

In practice, it was the Deutsche Mark that was shadowed by the UK in the European Exchange Rate Mechanism, which it joined in 1990. It was hoped that this would bring German post-war economic success in the form of higher productivity and stable growth with low inflation. The ERM had been set up in 1970 and was designed to bring about the convergence of conditions across EU countries necessary for the introduction of a Europe-wide currency, later to be known as the 'euro'. The ERM was originally designed to be similar to the Bretton Woods system, except that it was not based on any particular currency or gold. Member currencies were pegged to a central numeraire unit known as the European Currency Unit (ECU); the ECU was based on a weighted average of the participating countries' currencies set from 1979. But in a similar way to the Bretton Woods system, where all currencies were in effect measured against the dollar, the Deutsche Mark soon became the currency against which all other ERM member currencies were quoted. The advantages of the ERM were seen as stability, 'forced' competitiveness and the control of inflation, though in truth the policy seemed to work best for Germany. Stable exchange rates would allow the UK's exporting firms to plan ahead without worrying about large changes in the value of the pound that could wipe out their profits. This is important for such an open economy as the UK, which has a large international sector, and it was hoped it would encourage more investment and trade.

A near-fixed exchange rate system would mean ERM member countries would have to exercise discipline in controlling inflation as there would be no easy option to allow the exchange rate to devalue the currency if inflation reduced competitiveness. Instead, it was hoped that any fundamental lack of competitiveness must be tackled by producers through increased productivity and prices that maintain competitiveness. However, we can see from more recent experiences in the Eurozone that such a requirement does not necessarily translate into action, and if the currency markets think a currency's exchange rate is unsustainable then speculation will quickly cause enormous financial flows that put pressure on the exchange rate.

A big problem with maintaining a fixed exchange rate is that a country may lose control over its interest rate as it must match the interest rates offered by the currencies of other countries. That is, without capital controls to prevent international reserves being quickly exhausted, interest rates must be set so as to prevent large flows of speculative money, as these flows would otherwise change the relative prices of the different currencies through imbalances in the international supply and demand of currencies. In short, once in the ERM, to shadow the Deutsche Mark the UK interest rate was forced to closely follow movements in the German interest rate. Today, by contrast, the Monetary Policy Committee of the Bank of England sets interest rates in accordance with the UK domestic situation, but cannot also then control the value of the pound on foreign exchange markets without massive offsetting through currency reserves. In practice, without effective capital controls, controlling either the interest rate or the exchange rate means losing control of the other. Capital controls, interest and exchange rates are known as the 'impossible trinity' in economics.

The UK government became acutely aware of this policy dilemma during its time in the ERM. Monetary policy was effectively dictated by the actions of Germany in setting interest rates for the German economy, which happened to be the strongest economy in the ERM. The problem here is that one size does not fit all; the right interest rate for one country may very well be the wrong interest rate for another. Perhaps because of their experience of disastrous hyper-inflation in the 1920s, Germany is notoriously strict on inflation, but their stronger economy could bear higher interest rates set to keep inflation down, even if these interest rates were set higher than they needed to be. Because of this, the UK was also forced to keep interest rates undesirably high to keep the pound within the margins set for it in the ERM – particularly undesirable given the UK was back in recession. This did seem to keep inflation down, but many observers again argued that it only achieved this by keeping the UK economy chronically depressed, as seen with the high interest rates used by Thatcher to limit monetary growth.

Again, like Bretton Woods, the ERM framework obliged all members to help struggling currencies stay within the permitted bands of the pegged exchange rate. When the UK's exchange rate began to fall against the ECU, this should have required other countries to buy pounds and cut their own interest rates in order to make the pound more attractive to investors and speculators. In the event, such help was minimal, perhaps as it was recognised that any help given to the pound would be ineffectual in the face of massive global financial flows. Meanwhile, Germany was coping with the impacts of its East and West reunification, and as a consequence the country's interest rates were relatively high over the period 1990–92.

Despite the attempts of John Major's Chancellor, Norman Lamont, to disguise the Bank of England's efforts to prop up the pound, currency speculators became convinced that the pound would need to be devalued eventually, and so they continually sold the currency. Most famously, George Soros bet that the pound would be devalued, speculation that 'earned' him a billion pounds and the nickname 'the man who broke the Bank of England'. By September 1992, about the only buyer of pound sterling left was the UK government itself. Speculators become convinced that the pound was only going one way, and that was down. By selling the pound they could both help it on its way and realise a profit by moving into other currencies that would then rise in value compared with the pound.

* * *

Prime Minister John Major had replaced Thatcher as the leader of the Conservative Party in 1990, largely because of internecine party rows over the UK's attitude towards Europe. Major's new Chancellor, Norman Lamont, now Lord Lamont, quickly raised interest rates to try to protect the pound's value. During 'Black Wednesday' on 16 September 1992, interest rates were raised first from 10 per cent to 12 per cent and then to an astonishing 15 per cent. Lamont authorised the spending of billions of pounds of UK reserves in a doomed effort to keep the pound within the range allowed by the ERM. Of course, this only further convinced speculators that the UK had been abandoned by other members of the ERM. As certainty grew that the pound would devalue, the more it was sold, and this put further downward pressure towards devaluation. An estimated £6 billion to £7 billion was wasted trying to 'buck the market' in a futile attempt to keep the UK in the ERM. John Major even penned a letter of resignation to the Queen, which he was then prevented from sending by his colleagues. The irony is that after leaving the ERM, the UK's economic performance improved markedly. This recent history is, understandably, quite worrying for those who advocate rejoining the EU if we are obliged to join the Eurozone, which is not the same thing as saying we shouldn't rejoin.

THE GREAT MODERATION AND THE NICE PARTY

Leaving the ERM freed up the exchange and interest rates and seemed to lead to better growth, stability and the avoidance of re-cessions. With a new Conservative Chancellor of the Exchequer, Ken Clarke, at the economy's helm from 1993, the demand manage-ment of the economy shifted firmly towards using interest rates to manage the level of demand and hence indirectly control inflation. In normal times, interest rate levels can be more or less set directly by the Bank of England, the UK's state-owned central bank, dictat-ing the rate at which they will be used for the commercial banks. Hence, Chancellors – who are also politicians – often sought to have direct control over the Bank of England. They were always subject to the genuine temptation to use interest rates to manipulate the economy for political reasons (to boost the economy just before an election, for example, so that output and employment are increased before consequent inflationary pressures take over).

Now, the credibility of the Bank of England can be very important indeed for its effectiveness. To increase this credibility and make the bank more effective in influencing inflationary expectations, Gordon Brown's first act on becoming the new Labour Chancellor in May 1997 was to give independence to the Bank of England. That meant that the bank was tasked with using its control over inter-est rates – in principle, without interference from the Chancellor

– to keep inflation close to a target set by the Chancellor. That target has been set at 2 per cent since the bank was formally made independent. Though it's worth bearing in mind that despite 'independence' the targets in the bank's remit are set by the Chancellor, who also appoints the bank's governor and the external Monetary Policy Committee members who must be approved by the Treasury Select Committee. And the Chief Economist of the Treasury also attends the committee's interest-setting sessions as a non-voting member. Moreover, most Bank of England deputy governors are senior ex-Treasury officials. This may suggest a general hawkish bias in the Treasury, which is often evident in deliberations, though more balanced external appointments do in theory act to moderate this.

In the following years, similar policy arrangements across the UK, US and the EU of explicit inflation targeting being left to the central bank all seemed to work extremely well. As we saw in Chapter 1, this long period of apparent success from Ken Clarke right through to 2007 came to be known as the 'Great Moderation' or 'NICE' ('non-inflationary continuous expansion'). As the years of non-inflationary continuous growth ticked by, a 'new macro consensus' was becoming established in academic economics, a consensus that reduced the differences between many Keynesians and more neoclassical economists. This new consensus was based around the primacy of monetary policy over fiscal policy (that is, the use of interest rates over government tax and spending) as a demand stabilisation tool and the assumption of at least a short-run trade-off between inflation and unemployment that could be exploited, via the interest rate, to offset shocks to the economy. By contrast, trying to hold the economy above its 'natural growth rate' for any sustained period, or at least above its long-run equilibrium path, would lead to accelerating inflation. Many economists became confident that they finally understood how to prevent 'boom and bust'. Indeed, too many were downright arrogant. They believed they had learned that monetary policy, i.e. interest rates, should be used to keep inflation at low levels using gentle adjustments to keep the economy close to its trend growth without disruptive sudden changes in direction.

Despite challenges from some quarters – challenges which diminished as time passed and the economy continued to grow – Tony Blair's 'New Labour' government, elected in 1997, followed the 'New Consensus model' and did not revert to active fiscal Keynesian-style demand policy – that is, using the government's own budget of tax and revenues to attempt to 'fine-tune' the economy. Instead, New Labour declared it would adhere to Gordon Brown's 'Golden Rule' for its budgets: the fiscal rule was to keep current spending and revenue balanced over the economic cycle and allow borrowing only to invest in 'worthwhile' infrastructure projects that would benefit longer-term UK growth by, hopefully, expanding GDP and hence increasing the tax base, thereby paying for the investment. It was still accepted that aggregate demand could influence the level of economic activity in the short run and hence adjustments were useful for keeping the economy near to a 'non-accelerating inflation rate of unemployment' (NAIRU), but this was to be done through the Bank of England's interest rate policy, a monetary policy. The use of fiscal policy for demand management was not part of this 'new macro consensus'. It seemed at the time that such fiscal policy demand management was now confined to history's dustbin of outmoded economic ideas.

Reflecting this seemingly great leap forward in macroeconomic policy, the American economist Robert Lucas, in his 2003 Presidential Address to the American Economic Association, declared that the 'central problem of depression prevention [has] been solved, for all practical purposes'. Before the financial crash of 2007 which led to the Great Recession, eminent UK economists were echoing Gordon Brown's boast of having 'ended boom and bust' and senior policymakers claimed that they had 'cracked macro'. Consequently, the esteem of macroeconomists was riding high. The instability that had dogged capitalism for centuries seemed to have been conquered, a claim touted by the majority of 'modern macroeconomists' in academia and the Bank of England. In contrast, there were many economic historians and economists, wiser from history and experience, who were far more doubtful, the authors of this book included. As Philip Arestis and Andy Ross argued in their 2007 book, *Is There a New Consensus in Macroeconomics?*:

> The past fourteen years or so seem to have been a period of enormous success for Central Banks, but practice is running ahead of economic theory. So long as practice works, this may seem a problem for economists rather than governments. But experience shows that past consensuses turned out to have been based on inadequate or misleading economics, or at least the parameters of the real world changed, rendering them inoperable.

Optimism that this new consensus would be permanent peaked around the time that the US Federal Reserve's chair, Alan Greenspan, was described as 'the greatest central banker who ever lived' at the 2005 Jackson Hole conference – just a couple of years before the global Great Financial Crisis.

In truth, of course, much of the central bank's success in controlling inflation owed little to those institutions having masterminded the solution to periods of rampant inflation in the past, and more to the emergence of China and other nations into the world trading system, keeping prices low. Globalisation did help many billions escape poverty, but it also gave a sense of omnipotence to central bankers who remained extraordinarily relaxed as deregulation was happening all around them. In the case of the Bank of England, this was exacerbated by the way independence was granted, as most of its regulatory functions were split between it, the Treasury and the new body created after a series of mergers of prudential organisations into the Financial Services Authority (FSA).

DEBT AND THE GREAT FINANCIAL CRISIS

In truth, therefore, there had been a dangerously large build-up in debt going into and during the early years of the new century. Contrary to popular belief and most media coverage, this was not mostly government debt but private sector debt, owed by households and by financial institutions. Indeed, rather than an overhang of public sector debt being the problem, some economists argue that in effect there was a shortage of government debt to be purchased, and so banks began treating risky assets issued by the private sector as safe assets. In other words, it is argued that one of the primary reasons for the Great Financial Crisis was a global shortage of genuinely safe government debt.

Whatever the explanation, so long as asset prices kept rising and people kept spending, the party could continue: banks were making profits, this profit was providing tax revenues for the Treasury and the public and businesses were enjoying easy access to credit. According to an estimate by McKinsey (2018), the world's total debt (government, non-financial corporations and households) in 2007 amounted to 198 per cent of global income. Rising house and financial asset prices made the positions of those holding them look secure, and the asset inflation provided ever more collateral on which to secure even more loans. This was a 'financial accelerator' cycle of rising asset prices facilitating more borrowing, and hence more asset price rises and hence more borrowing, and so on. But this had created a massive 'debt overhang' – that is, the increase in apparent wealth was not being secured on an increase in real income. Such a situation is known as a 'bubble' because it can all change at terrifying speed, rather like a bursting bubble, when the expected income from assets fails to materialise or an increase in interest rates causes default. Then asset prices fall, consumers and business no longer have collateral to borrow, banks which looked secure no longer look secure, they find it difficult to borrow and now face both liquidity and the threat of insolvency if their total assets fall below what they owe or if they don't earn enough profits to operate. The fear of default on loans increases interest spreads, commercial interest rates charged to borrowers rise and lending falls, and so the demand for assets – already falling in value – falls too, threatening further insolvency. This then repeats and worsens the vicious downward cycle.

THE END OF THE PARTY

In 2004, the Federal Reserve began to tighten its monetary stance and so increased interest rates in response to an upturn in inflation, which was mainly from oil and commodity prices. This reduced the volume of borrowing and increased the cost of mortgages. House prices stalled and then fell. Some mortgage holders began to struggle to meet their mortgage payments, trapped by higher interest rates and falling collateral that prevented them borrowing to fend off rising debts. Even selling their houses could not now pay off the loans as house prices fell and many were thrown into 'negative equity', where the asset value of their house fell below the amount of the mortgage they owed. From mid-2007, serious debt default problems began in the US subprime mortgages sector. Credit expansion through new loans to provide mortgages for those on low incomes had been greatly encouraged by US policymakers. This led to huge volumes of mortgages having been sold to those who previously would not have been deemed credit-worthy enough to trust with mortgages, hence the name 'subprime'.

Rapidly, the over-inflated value of assets, created in effect by ignoring their real riskiness, became apparent. It also exposed the precarious positions of many banks, which had used leverage from short-term loans to fuel credit expansion into assets that could not be readily converted back to liquidity. Subprime mortgages, risky loans and many other dodgy and often fiendishly complicated financial instruments such as 'derivatives' had all been mixed together in 'securitised' packages of different types of assets, known as 'collateralised debt obligations' (CDOs). These securities were then sold widely across the financial sector. This made it near-impossible to isolate these 'toxic assets' as the bubble burst; it was as if some bad meat had been mixed in with good meat and then spread out into countless pies. No one really knew which were safe.

Financial institutions had packaged together bundles of good debt with bad debt and the rating agencies, who were paid by the financial institutions themselves, had endorsed these packages as 'safe'. The crisis and the tumbling prices of such assets made it plain that the assets were not safe at all and, given the huge volume of debts that had been created and sold on, it meant that even well-established financial institutions might not be safe. This fear and uncertainty in turn led to the asset value of famous and long-standing banks falling sharply, as they moved towards insolvency from positions that had, only months earlier, seemed secure. This is the difference between 'micro-prudence', where an institution looks safe based on current assets and liabilities, and 'macro-prudence', where unexpected shifts across all asset values can lead to many institutions suddenly becoming exposed to liquidity or a capital loss crisis.

The first banks to face complete bankruptcy were those that had been more reckless in the good times. Now, it is the case that banks generally make profits by borrowing short term (e.g. taking deposits) and lending long term (e.g. loans), which is inherently risky as at any time depositors and creditors may wish to take more money out of their bank than the bank can recoup from its loans. Major financial institutions had taken advantage of deregulation and the 'liberalisation' of the finance sector to fuel rapid but excessively fragile growth. They took on liabilities in the good times that they would be unable to pay in bad times. Northern Rock was one such bank that had built up massive short-term debt by borrowing in short-term money markets to finance long-term debts that they then sold on to other financial institutions in a process known as 'securitisation', whereby a range of debts were packaged together and given a current value. So long as Northern Rock could keep selling securitised long-term debt it could service its short-term loans. But by August 2007, as the global demand from investors for securitised mortgages had sharply decreased, Northern Rock became unable to repay loans from the money market and in September 2007 it sought and received liquidity support through the Bank of England's long-standing 'lender of last resort' facility, to replace the funds it was now unable to raise from the money market.

This led to panic among Northern Rock depositors, not helped by the widely published official term 'lender of last resort', which much of the public did not know was simply the standard term used for emergency loans from the Bank of England to commercial banks. Depositors feared that their savings might not be available should Northern Rock go into receivership. The result was a bank run, the UK's first in 150 years: long queues formed outside Northern Rock branches as depositors sought to withdraw their savings, and to do so as quickly as possible before others doing the same had exhausted the cash reserves of the failing bank. Even Bank of England support for the bank proved inadequate, and so by February 2008 Northern Rock had been nationalised in an effort to stem the panic. By then, the macro-imprudence that had been built during the Great Moderation, particularly from 2005, was overtaking even those financial institutions that had exercised more micro-prudence.

In September 2008, Lehman Brothers, a giant and well-established investment bank, collapsed in the largest bankruptcy of all time. Lehman had a massive $691.1 billion in assets. The shock was profound, sparking a meltdown of Western finance markets. In the days following, other financial giants, including American International Group (AIG), Washington Mutual and Wachovia also collapsed. Even such stalwarts as Morgan Stanley and Goldman Sachs slid toward the abyss. The Federal Reserve, the UK Treasury and other regulators were forced to step in, sometimes in conjunction with famous private investors, to rescue the system. Governments used nationalisation and direct injections of capital into leading private banks to stop the contagion effects.

Debates have raged about why the authorities, the Federal Reserve and the Treasury allowed Lehman Brothers to go broke, a course of action which contrasted starkly with their earlier active assistance in salvaging a series of other institutions. Most analysts would conclude, in retrospect, that letting Lehman Brothers go bust was a very big mistake indeed. It sent panic right through the banking sector; other banks, fearful of their own positions and the credit-worthiness of one another, ceased to lend to each other, and so the money markets froze. This left banks completely exposed as their asset prices continued to collapse, further threatening their solvency. Further bailouts and nationalisation followed; banks raised their lending interest rates to protect themselves against risk even as the Bank of England cut the rates at which it would lend to commercial banks. To reduce their debts, the commercial banks also cut back their lending.

The financial crisis had spread to the rest of the economy and the UK and the rest of Europe, along with the US, fell into a massive recession. The collapse of Lehman Brothers had in fact plunged most of the world into recession. The Bank of England had lost control of interest rates; even as the bank cut its lending rates to commercial banks, these banks were raising their own lending rates to reflect the increased risk of lending. The 'spread' between Bank of England policy rates and commercial rates increased sharply. With interest reductions no longer effective and approaching the 'Zero Lower Bound' for nominal interest rates (that is, the lowest point before interest rates would become negative), the Bank of England turned to 'extraordinary' or 'unconventional' measures, particularly quantitative easing, to try to counter the fall in aggregate demand caused by the financial crisis. As we saw above, quantitative easing in effect involves the central bank using newly created money to buy up assets, providing a supply of 'base money' which can be used to create additional credit and drive up the prices of bonds. This was intended to lower the yield on bonds and hence interest rates, with the hope that this would increase spending. It also creates wealth effects from increased asset prices and causes 'portfolio' adjustments as investors seek to spread some of their new financial cash wealth into real assets, such as capital expenditure. Quantitative easing undoubtedly injects some demand into economies, but its potency is disputed, and some say its main effect was to increase the wealth of asset holders and subsequently the volume of interest paid on government debt.

Overall, when world output and trade began to contract in the fourth quarter of 2008 at a pace similar to that of the early stages of the Great Depression, policymakers in the UK, US and elsewhere (including China) acted quickly to 'bail out' banking systems teetering on the edge of collapse, while simultaneously unleashing a fiscal and monetary blitz of 'whatever it takes'. In the event, the degree of international cooperation on coordinated demand stimulus by governments across the globe was impressive, serving to counteract plummeting private sector spend. The April 2009 G20 summit was a landmark event for agreeing on reflationary policies that limited global economic contraction, even though returning to pre-crash growth has proved elusive.

* * *

It became increasingly apparent that the deregulation of the banking sector that had accompanied the rebirth of free market macro policies in the 1970s, as encouraged by Thatcher's and Reagan's governments, had increasingly allowed banks to take risks and so create an asset bubble, often using exotic and highly complex financial instruments. This was particularly so from the beginning of this century. In the US, the Glass–Steagall Act was repealed in 1999. The act had been introduced in 1933 to separate retail banking from the riskier investment banking as a response to the crisis of the interwar Great Depression. In the EU, the long period of stability had led regulators to allow latitude for banks to estimate and manage their own risks, encouraged by the free market 'efficient market hypothesis'. This abstract theory asserted that financial markets factor in all knowable risk and hence asset prices merely reflect all available information. In addition to this increasing risk among regulated banks, banks were also engaging in more so-called 'shadow banking' activities: bank-like organisations were buying and selling securitised debt beyond the scope of the regulators and off the balance sheets of the regulated banks.

In short, banks had become less regulated and were increasingly engaging in higher risk activities; they reduced their capital buffers, increased their leverage – using other people's money to buy up assets – and hence increased their exposure to downturns. Meanwhile, with the help of complicated mathematical models – barely understood by many of the actors involved – they were reporting to regulators that their risks of insolvency and illiquidity were falling. It was extraordinary in this context that many bank oversight board members apparently didn't understand what the products their institutions were creating, investing in and selling were – and yet they obviously deemed them to be safe. Indeed, as the economist Hyman Minsky had noted, financial cycles of repeated crises may well be intrinsic to capitalism, as long periods of stability tend to lead to complacency by financial institutions and regulators and then to greater risk-taking by financial institutions.

These so-called 'Minsky cycles' may vary in in length but follow a repetitive pattern. After a financial crisis, such as in 2007, institutions and regulators are risk averse and so the supply of credit and speculation for assets of 'debts and bets' are, for a while, restrained. This produces stability and, during this phase, capitalist economies tend to experience steady growth. This stability then leads to growing confidence and the desire to take more risks to increase profits. Governments may well begin to encourage this to allow more economic growth and tax revenues. As confidence grows, investors and the financial institutions increasingly engage in speculative investments, particularly by creating new debts and borrowing. This leads to over-leveraging, whereby financial institutions and others take on excessive debt relative to their ability to repay it. This credit creation and speculation drives up the market value of the financial instruments created which encourages more credit creation and investment in these 'assets', further driving up the market price of the financial instruments. This 'financial accelerator', however, is ultimately unsustainable, as the market values of assets assume future real returns that will not be achieved. At some point there will be a 'Minsky moment': the speculative bubble bursts and holders of these speculative assets try to sell them off to limit their losses, leading to a sudden severe collapse in asset prices. A period of de-leveraging and tightening of regulations follows, as investors become risk-averse and sell off assets, and receive state support to cover their debts, leading to a period of instability and recession. The painful 'market correction' then realigns asset values with real returns once again, creating another period of stability. After a while, memories fade, confidence rises and the cycle repeats itself. Hence, the worry that financial markets are inherently unstable if left unchecked, creating the tendency for periods of economic stability to sow the seeds of future crises.

Much of the blame for the 2007 financial crisis fell on the 'reckless greed' of the bankers, and there were indeed deeply irresponsible behaviours on show, but it is more useful for the mitigation and prevention of future financial crises to look at the policies and vested interests that created a financial framework where 'bad behaviour' was not only rewarded but became an imperative for corporate survival. This is because, should a CEO fail to match the share price of competitors, he (it's usually a he) is rejected by shareholders. Hence, there were incentives for individuals and organisations in the banking sector to take risks and pocket early profits from selling risk on to others, regardless of the dangers of increased systemic risk. This is particularly so when financial institutions are so integral to the functioning of economies that state bailouts become a necessity, as has been seen in the West. That necessity raises the potential for 'moral hazard' – that is, the knowledge that financial institutions may be bailed out by the state increasing their appetite for risk-taking. The phrase 'banking on the state' has been used to describe the way banks took advantage of the fact that banking sector gains are privatised – with profit accruing to bank shareholders, managers and employees – while the losses are largely socialised as liabilities to the state.

The problems of aligning incentives to avoid systemic instability remains a thorny problem for central bankers; perhaps it will always be an inherent problem for capitalism. This is especially so when powerful interests are eager for profits while governments, who are eager for tax revenues, become convinced they could get more if only regulations were removed. As profit-seeking firms, banks may well trade off risk for profits beyond what is socially optimal, and individuals who receive bonuses are not generally required to repay them if in the future it turns out they took excessive risks. This emboldens profit-seeking individuals to go even further into excessive speculation. Even if a professional conduct regulator body, similar to, say, the General Medical Council, imposed strict limits on reckless behaviour, which is probably a good idea, there would still be the technical problem of distinguishing between micro-prudence and macro-prudence. For example, individual banks may look as if they have adequate capital reserves to weather a crisis, but in a crisis the value of assets across the board held by all banks may tumble. In short, the extent to which a crisis will expose the banks to risk is difficult to know in advance. In the meantime, when there's profit to be made and hence tax revenues to be had, there are strong incentives for individuals, financial institutions and the government to act imprudently.

*　　*　　*

It was noticed, most prominently by the late Queen Elizabeth II herself, that the majority of economists engaged in developing mathematical macroeconomic models had failed to anticipate the worst financial crisis since the Great Depression. In large part, this was due to neglect in incorporating the financial/banking sector into mainstream macroeconomic models. Nevertheless, the insights from the financial economics literature arguably played an important role in the response to the crisis, particularly in the form of liquidity provision through quantitative easing programmes. And in the immediate aftermath of the financial crisis, Keynes was suddenly back in fashion. The eminent biographer of Keynes, Lord Skidelsky, responded in 2009 with a book titled *The Return of the Master*. The late Alistair Darling, Gordon Brown's successor as Chancellor when Brown stepped up to become Prime Minister on Tony Blair's resignation, looked for both monetary and fiscal stimuli to fight the deep recession, and this did seem to lift the economy to begin a nascent recovery.

Nevertheless, at the time of the general election in 2010, the Labour government was blamed by much of the electorate, led by the populist media, for the global crisis. It was claimed that Brown had spent and borrowed too much, and this was partially true, but there was not a historically large deficit. As we have noted, it was the collapse of private sector rather than public sector debt that had caused the financial crisis. As the recession had led to a greatly increased fiscal deficit, mainly because of post-crisis falls in tax revenues, and because a smaller state is a long-held goal of the Conservative Party, the incoming Conservative and Liberal Democrat coalition under David Cameron and Nick Clegg made 'fiscal consolidation' its main priority. As such, from 2010 there followed a decade of huge spending cuts.

The subsequent extended period of flat-lining and then stagnant GDP led many economists to claim the Conservative Chancellor George Osborne – along with his close ally in advocating austerity policy, the German Chancellor Angela Merkel – were ignoring the lessons of Keynes. Osborne argued he was simply maintaining the confidence of the markets and so allowing the UK government to continue to borrow at low interest rates. He argued that not being strict on reducing the fiscal deficit would raise fears of sovereign default and inflation and hence cause UK interest rates to rise, making conditions much worse. Today, the central policy debate in economics still largely revolves around 'austerity' measures versus Keynesian stimulus, sometimes called the 'Austerians versus the Stimulards' debate. It's pretty much the same argument that was had in the 1930s, even if the analysis has developed in its technical sophistication.

RECENT NEGATIVE SHOCKS
While economists were debating the enduring effects of auster-ity, another global shock was waiting in the wings. The Covid

pandemic hit both the supply and the demand sides of the economy with a simultaneous and very large negative shock. It goes without saying that workers not going to work had a large negative shock on the supply of goods and services, and the loss of income and uncertainty had a large negative shock on demand. Both tend to decrease output, but the effect on prices and inflation was less certain, as a sharp decrease in supply tends to increase prices, but a decrease in demand will tend to decrease prices. In the event, governments responded by trying to put the economy into suspended animation or a state of deep freeze.

The UK government attempted to hold supply chains in place, prevent firms from collapsing and securely hold employment and contracts using 'furlough' payments (officially known as the 'Coronavirus Job Retention Scheme'). This scheme provided payments to firms, at 80 per cent of earnings, to pay their employees even though they were not at work, and to keep the firms afloat with loans and grants to businesses. In effect, the state was now paying the wages of some nine million workers in the private sector, in addition to those in the public sector. This would prevent the deterioration of the myriad connections and contracts that make up modern supply chains, and so limit the increase in unemployment, the idea being that the economy could simply be restarted again when the pandemic was over, rather like returning from an extended holiday. As a result, during the 'bounce back' when Coronavrius restrictions were lifted there was rapid, if short-lived, GDP growth.

Importantly, these furlough payments were not simply standard Keynesian demand management, which seeks only to mitigate fluctuations in demand and hence indirectly impact supply. Rather, the policy was a direct intervention into the supply side itself, to hold productive potential in place until the economy could be 'switched' back on. The obvious risk was that maintaining demand as output fell could spark inflation, especially as governments across the globe were running similar schemes. The Covid measures, also adopted in most other Western countries (except in the US) were successful in avoiding what history shows could have been a very sharp drop in output and too slow a recovery thereafter.

In the event, the Covid 'recession' started with a sharp fall in GDP in the first quarter of 2020. Looking at real GDP per head – the most meaningful measure, as it excludes inflation and population change – by the third quarter of 2020, GDP was already back to 94 per cent of the pre-Covid level and a year later it was above the starting level. Other comparable countries had had even better recoveries, although later ONS revisions cast considerable doubt on the extent to which the UK recovery lagged behind. Of course, the UK may well have had its unique economic features – negative impacts from Brexit and an exceptionally large service sector – and just returning to where we were still means a lot of lost output in the trough. The negative shocks of Covid, conflict in Ukraine, Brexit and possibly the fragile state of the Middle East have all added to the very serious shortfall in GDP since the Great Financial Crisis. And that was *before* the capricious President Donald Trump took to shaking up the world economy with tariff wars, causing huge fluctuations in share and bond markets.

The shortfall of GDP per head from what might have been expected before the crisis is now at least 25 per cent. This has had profound consequences for living standards and for the government's fiscal plans, as tax revenues are greatly affected by the level of GDP.

THE RETURN OF INFLATION

As the UK economy emerged from the Covid 'freeze', the question of inflation became more worrying. The combination of record fiscal deficits used to fight the pandemic and fears about the monetary impacts of the huge volume of quantitative easing used to fight the financial crash revived fears that inflation would again become a problem. To the surprise of many, this did not happen – at first. In the event, low inflation continued, leading central bankers to persist with historically low interest rates. But there had been serious disruption to many supply chains and hence shortages that tend to drive prices up; this was perhaps exacerbated by pent-up demand, including from 'forced' savings and furlough loans, released by ending Covid restrictions. A demand surge hitting a restricted supply caused inflation to rise to some 4 per cent, even before the war in Ukraine and sanctions on Russian energy supplies sent it much higher. The vast majority of economists also believe inflation in the UK has been exacerbated by Brexit, though by a considerably smaller factor than the war.

There was much debate as to whether this was a temporary rise in inflation, caused by demand surging with supply unable to fully respond, and whether the inflation would become incorporated into inflationary expectations, making it harder to bring down again. In the face of such uncertainty, the Bank of England's Monetary Policy Committee has a very difficult task in judging what to do with interest rates to avoid levels of demand that would cause inflation to rise above or below its target.

Before the war in Ukraine, the Bank of England had been reluctant to raise interest rates for fear of reversing the recovery, but as inflation rose to some 10 per cent the Bank of England felt it had to act, if only for its own credibility as an institution with a responsibility to control inflation. Such credibility helps to anchor expectations of inflation and so help prevent it from getting out of control; with trust in the central bank, economic agents are less likely to increase their prices for fear of higher inflation or reduce them for fear of deflation. If inflation persists or simply increases, then the Bank of England is likely to respond by raising interest rates. Each rise may be small, as the danger is that acting to head off inflation by depressing demand could prevent the supply side recovering and set off a wave of pessimism that would have negative effects on both supply and demand, and hence on GDP and employment. Also, as inflation is largely imported – via commodity and energy prices – using interest rates to reduce domestic demand may not do much to counter it.

Any rise in interest rates is likely to be cautious at first, as a negative supply shock will have real and unwelcome impacts. Even if a natural/neutral rate of interest does exist, the Bank of England will not know what it is and so is likely to adopt a gradual pragmatic approach, rather than attempting to aggressively restore the economy to an uncertain estimate of 'equilibrium', which could do more harm than good. Again, much of the inflation is likely to come through inflated import prices, and the Bank of England can't directly act on world demand, though by raising the interest rate it can increase the strength of the pound and so reduce the sterling price of UK imports, which lowers UK inflation directly in consumer goods and through reduced input prices.

Another worry was that although the initial impacts of furlough and reduced supply may be inflationary, the secondary impacts of this 'negative supply shock' in the medium and longer term could well have been deflationary, as a decrease in real income will tend to reduce consumption and discourage investment. It was the policy dilemma of the '70s all over again: with stagflation due to a large negative supply shock and output suppressed but inflation rising, do we use aggregate demand to head off recession or inflation? Of course, not doing anything at all could weaken the credibility of the Bank of England's commitment to control longer-term inflation by making it harder for the bank to 'anchor' expectations. So, central banks are likely to cautiously raise interest rates even at the risk of worsening an oncoming recession, while reviewing the evidence frequently to assess the direction of the economy and bearing in mind that inflation could become lower as energy prices fall and pent-up demand is inflated away.

The impacts on government borrowing were very large indeed, adding to the large increases in national debt during the Great Financial Crisis. During the pandemic in 2020 and 2021, the government borrowed more than at any time in history other than the First and Second World Wars, and then borrowed massively again to offset energy bills which soared due to the war in Ukraine which disrupted energy supplies, leading to higher prices for energy suppliers. National debt and the government budget deficit can be measured in various ways – some consider bonds held by the Bank of England, others don't; some factor in treatment of debts such as student loans, others don't – but however the debt is measured, the increase is striking. In 2005, the UK national debt was less than £0.5 trillion. After the worldwide financial crisis of 2007 and subsequent recession in 2008, it exceeded £1 trillion in 2011 and then was over £1.5 trillion in 2016. At the end of March 2024, national debt stood at £2.69 trillion. In percentage terms, the debt was only about 38 per cent of GDP in 2005, then in the wake of the crash of 2007 and subsequent recession, it doubled to over 80 per cent of GDP. At the end of March 2024, national debt stood at 97.7 percent of GDP, meaning the UK's debt was as large as its gross income. The tax burden, as a percentage of GDP, reached its highest level for more than seventy years. Given the UK's ageing population, unless there is more immigration and/or significant economic growth, the tax bill for social care, health and pensions is unlikely to see that percentage fall in the policy-relevant future.

THE 2022 MINI-BUDGET

The September 2022 mini-budget of Prime Minister Liz Truss's Chancellor Kwasi Kwarteng was widely denounced as 'reckless', a perfect storm that 'spooked' the markets. Against a background of rising inflation and slow growth, it incorporated inflation-boosting tax cuts without providing a convincing fiscal plan as to where the money to replace these tax cuts would come from. Instead, it made a very optimistic assertion that the tax cuts would stimulate growth and so provide revenue. This lack of credibility was exacerbated by denouncing 'Treasury orthodoxy', sacking the Treasury's well-respected Permanent Secretary Tom Scholar and circumventing the usual modelling of the budgetary impacts by the OBR. Subsequently, the IFS did its own modelling and found that the mini-budget would lead to a chronically accelerating budget deficit, but Kwarteng insisted that if anything he would go even further in cutting tax. Indeed, the National Institute of Economic and Social Research (NIESR) saw the political and institutional background as even more important than the state of the UK economy:

> Within days of Liz Truss taking office as Prime Minister, the Head of HM Treasury, Sir Tom Scholar, had been sacked. This move was seen by many as a direct challenge to the independence of the Treasury, particularly as the Prime Minister had made clear

in her campaign to become Conservative Party Leader that she wanted to change 'Treasury Orthodoxy'. In addition, she had also made clear in the campaign that she was going to open up the issue of Bank of England independence. And, finally, the Chancellor asked the OBR not to produce their independent forecast and analysis to accompany the mini-budget. The financial markets saw all of this as a clear message that the new Prime Minister and Chancellor were challenging/ignoring the advice of the very institutions that had ensured economic and financial stability within the United Kingdom.

The argument made for the mini-budget was that there was a need to break a low-growth, high-tax 'doom cycle'. Lower taxes were thought to increase incentives, and to free funds for investment and generally to stimulate growth. The market reaction to the mini-budget also had a lot to do with the Bank of England's plans to reverse quantitative easing. The Bank of England was holding approximately £838 billion in gilts and on 22 September, the day before the mini-budget statement, it confirmed that it would begin selling some of these to reduce the number of government bonds it holds. It is claimed by supporters of the mini-budget that this, rather than the Truss/Kwarteng mini-budget, caused the market reaction whereby liability-driven investment funds, including gilts and other fixed coupon assets, rapidly lost resale value. This forced the Bank of England to support the government deficit by instead purchasing more gilts and to assist pension funds that were already dangerously over-exposed by the fall in bond prices. Supporters of Truss point to yields subsequently returning to similar levels to before the mini-budget.

Critics of the Truss/Kwarteng mini-budget, on the other hand, argue that although the Bank of England is meant to be independent of the Treasury, the relationship between the two is far from secretive. Treasury officials warned about the consequences of Truss's plans, only for Truss to effectively sack the Permanent Secretary. With some £45 billion in unfunded tax cuts, the mini-budget could have unleashed a spiralling structural deficit. The evidence for lower taxes stimulating growth sufficient enough to fund such tax cuts is scant, so in effect, there was no credible business plan for budgetary prudence. Certainly, the market reaction was negative, the pound and Treasury bond prices both fell dramatically and the Bank of England had to intervene heavily to support bond prices to preserve financial stability, particularly as the bonds held by pension funds fell in value, forcing them to sell more bonds to meet their obligations which further depressed bond prices. Not surprisingly, the Conservative Party has more recently tried to distance itself from the mini-budget. The Conservatives will 'never again' put the UK's economic stability at risk by making 'promises we cannot afford', the shadow Chancellor Mel Stride said in his June 2025 speech.

The market reaction to the ill-fated mini-budget reignited debate about the validity of comparing the government budget to a household budget and populist claims that government had 'maxed out its credit card'. Is the government budget like a household budget or a credit-card that can be maxed out? The short answer is no, but the longer answer is that although a country with its own central bank can never run out of money per se, nevertheless by printing too much money it can run into severe problems. The real constraints are therefore not the amount of money, or even the budget deficit, but rather their consequences. That is a much more nuanced consideration, and an 'it all depends' type of situation.

* * *

A permanent fiscal deficit funded by increasing borrowing or printing money can lead to inflation, a trade balance deficit and higher
borrowing costs as bond prices decrease. In contrast, a temporary
deficit used for demand management during a recession may be
largely recuperated as the economy recovers. This approach can
also be funded in the future through investments expected to increase future tax revenues, which could be positively received by
the markets. Currently, that is a risky but much-needed strategy for
any UK government. An increase in borrowing that is to be used
for investing in infrastructure to increase economic growth (discussed further in Chapter 6) may also be seen as wisely planned
and judged akin to a private sector firm's borrowing to invest and
expand. A budget with permanent tax cuts funded by borrowing
and/or printing money, with no credible plan as to how to prevent
an accelerating budget deficit, is a very different thing, and that is
how the markets viewed the mini-budget. To break the 'doom loop',
investment, not unfunded tax cuts, is needed. The risk of increasing investment is that the desired returns do not materialise and so
leave only more debt. We consider the recent performance of the
Labour government in these respects in Part II of this book, but first
we'll look more closely at the sequence of shocks the UK economy
is still reeling from.

CHAPTER 4

SIX SHOCKS AND SEVEN PMS

Since 2006, economies around the world have experienced a sequence of shocks. The six biggest have been the Great Financial Crisis; the austerity of the 2010s; Brexit; Covid; the Russian invasion of Ukraine; and Trump's tariffs, in his first term and now in his second. A possible seventh could be potential knock-on impacts from the ongoing trouble in the Middle East, though this situation is still unfolding. Not only has the frequency of these shocks increased, but they now tend to be from the supply side of the economy (with the notable exception of austerity). Supply shocks are harder to deal with than demand shocks; as we've seen, the rapid recovery from Covid was only possible because massive fiscal spending was used to hold things in place until the pandemic passed, and generally measures to adjust aggregate demand can be achieved relatively easily compared to addressing supply-side shocks. It might be possible sometimes to try to 'wait things out' for supply shocks to pass, as central banks recently tried to do when post-Covid supply chain issues raised inflation, a policy they had to abandon as inflation then surged due to sharp energy price rises. But whatever central banks decide to do, managing aggregate demand alone doesn't repair a damaged 'real' supply side.

Once inflationary expectations become embedded in the

economy, inflation can be much harder to eradicate, requiring harsher rises in interest rates than if inflation were headed off earlier. In January 2022, the retired deputy governor of the Bank of England, Sir Charles Bean, voiced his opinion that the Bank had failed to act quickly enough to raise interest rates as increasing inflation took hold, and therefore had to move belatedly with higher interest rates than would otherwise have been necessary. If there is long-term damage – from such factors as natural disasters and environmental degradation, underinvestment in infrastructure, loss of relative national productivity, financial disruptions and uncertainty, loss of skills through prolonged unemployment and/or lack of training, loss of benign competitive forces, or sanctions and trade restrictions – then these things can't quickly be solved simply by managing aggregate demand. So, sadly, we do not see any policies that can achieve a rapid or significant increase in growth.

Monetary policy is comparably quick to enact and has 'less politics' involved than fiscal policy – it's easier and quicker to adjust interest rates than adjust the government's balance of tax and spend. Unfortunately, it is also comparatively arbitrary in its impact. For example, a rise in interest rates to ward off inflation works partly by making people poorer, particularly the young who are more likely to be net borrowers than older people with savings. Blameless people who are already struggling to buy a house may suddenly find mortgages increased beyond their means and business start-ups may fail to get off the ground. Using fiscal policy to manage aggregate demand, on the other hand, is relatively slow to enact and it can create fierce political opposition when certain expenditures are cut (as we saw with the winter fuel payments) or taxes changed (such as the inheritance tax on farmers). So, few economists now advocate using fiscal policy for 'fine-tuning' the economy. That said, many do still insist that it is more reliable than monetary policy for reflating the economy in times of very serious falls in aggregate demand. Keynes likened monetary policy to a string; it can pull the economy down but isn't good at pushing it up from a serious recession. Covid and furlough payments demonstrated that the state can be successful in using fiscal support to hold supply lines together, if it throws enough money at them quickly (and so tolerates some inevitable fraudulent claimants).

A large majority of non-partisan observers now agree that the coalition government's austerity, particularly during the initial period from 2010 to 2012, was a serious policy error that caused long-term supply-side damage. Even the fiscally conservative Permanent Secretary to the Treasury at the time, Lord Macpherson, admitted that, 'With hindsight we probably should have taken advantage [of low interest rates] and borrowed more when times were more stable ... and invested more.' Most would say he didn't need hindsight, as economists were warning at the time that a failure to invest in public infrastructure would weaken future economic growth and make the UK economy less resilient to shocks.

The decade of austerity cuts following the 2010s were unprecedented in scale. It was those public services that are least visible to the general electorate that were the most severely cut, such as social care, the justice system and prisons, but each cut has long-term consequences. Health spending did eventually rise but at the lowest rate ever for the NHS, and that spending was outpaced by the dire need for health services, particularly as complementary social care was so drastically cut. The level of public satisfaction with the NHS fell from its highest ever recorded level in 2010 to its lowest ever level by 2023. Local government spending was drastically reduced by a fifth, including draconian cuts to adult social care. Workers saw their real wages fall and benefits for the unemployed and low earners fell to levels well below comparable countries. Overall, in the aftermath of 2010 the UK saw the biggest fall in living standards since accurate records began in the 1950s (and arguably since the Napoleonic Wars).

The degree to which such spending cuts, particularly in investment across the whole public sector, did long-term damage to the UK economy is difficult to measure. What is certain is that the current state of the economy is very different from what it was expected to be when Labour was last in power. GDP per capita is over one fifth lower and the UK faces rising pressures from myriad factors: an ageing population; the lack and cost of social care; record queues for the NHS; unprecedented levels of working age incapacity and disability; strong resistance to any more cost-saving measures for pensions; the long fallout from Covid, including a fall in the employment of the over-fifties and the lost education during the pandemic; low levels of working-age benefits compared to other European countries; rates of destitution more than doubling in the last five years alone, as a result of benefit cuts and cost of living pressures; and, on top of all that, the need to address climate change. The harsh reality is that simply to hold the level of public services and welfare provision at their current depleted levels, let alone repair the damage and meet increasing demands, we will need more tax revenue. And all of this will be exacerbated if we also increase our defence spending as a percentage of GDP, which now seems a certainty.

There has recently been more tax collected from excess energy profit and a rise in corporation tax, but most of the additional tax revenues have come from freezing income tax and National Insurance thresholds in the face of inflation. This means that as nominal (money) incomes rise with inflation, millions more begin to pay tax or move into higher tax bands, even as real incomes fall. The phenomenon is known as 'fiscal drag'. The IFS estimates that an additional 2.5 million people will move up beyond the basic tax rate by 2027. Over the last thirty years, higher income tax bands are no longer reserved for the very rich; a third of the expected fall in household disposable incomes is because of increased tax burden.

Even so, shocks and low productivity growth have meant that tax revenues have struggled to provide the required revenues to keep up with expenditure needs. The IFS reports that the parliament from 2019 to 2024 was the biggest tax-raising parliament since records began, pushing UK tax revenues, but not tax rates, to historically high levels. Raising more tax remains a choice, and a tough one politically, but it is becoming more and more of a necessity unless there are further painful cuts to public services and welfare provision. By 2024, the tax take had reached a level not seen since the 1940s, when high tax was necessary for the war effort. Of course, it's not that US citizens 'enjoy' low taxes overall, as they have to pay for their health through other means. Quite simply, if we want public services as good as France, Germany, Spain or Italy, we need to pay more in taxes.

The UK economic and fiscal outlook remains highly challenging. A combination of sluggish growth prospects, an unprecedented rise in public debt, increasing demand for expenditures following previous underinvestment and higher interest on the volume of debts limits the fiscal room for manoeuvre of any Chancellor of any political persuasion. And yet still the UK desperately needs much better public infrastructure, not only in tangible investment such as energy supply and interconnectivity but also in human capital such as health, education and skills training. Investment is necessary to avoid locking in the slow growth that is the root cause of so many of our problems. A worry is that even if more tax revenue can be secured, it would mostly be swallowed up just by current needs, making it necessary to borrow or print money to finance public investment and to give fiscal rewards for private investment.

IS THERE A MAGIC MONEY TREE?

The phrase 'magic money tree' is a mocking parody of those economists who advocate something called 'modern monetary theory' (MMT). Such economists pick up on Keynesian themes further developed after Keynes's death by esteemed economist Lord Kaldor. Kaldor correctly saw that the supply of money is 'endogenous', not 'exogenous' like gold, which is limited in supply. In other words, money can be created at will and without limit by governments or their central banks and modern credit systems by the creation of bank deposits. Such deposits act as money through loans unfunded by previous deposits. In a sense, all anyone must do to prompt a bank to create new money is to have sufficient credibility that they will be able to repay their loan with interest. A central bank, such as the Bank of England, can simply create money with no limits by, directly or indirectly, giving new central bank deposits to the government to spend; its only constraint is the possible economic or political consequences of doing so. MMT economists therefore argue that the flow of causation isn't taxation funding government expenditure but rather government expenditure funding taxes. In a recession, such an approach has merit, but over the longer-term printing money can't create new, or divert existing, resources for the public sector.

If raising taxes to meet expenditure needs is so difficult, then why not just borrow or print more money? In an incident that is often cited by Labour's opponents, Gordon Brown's outgoing Chief Secretary to the Treasury, Liam Byrne, left a note to his successor in 2010. He scrawled, 'I'm afraid there is no money. Kind regards – and good luck! Liam.' The confidentiality tradition was not honoured and so, to Byrne's horror, his note was used relentlessly and repeatedly as proof of Labour's fiscal profligacy.

In short, printing too much money for too long will eventually cause problems. And, as we saw with the widely derided Liz Truss mini-budget, setting a course for a permanent budget deficit makes both the deficit and the economy worse. Debt is much higher now than in 2010 (as we have seen, it now roughly equals our national income). This is not a disaster in itself, but even based on current policies it would only stabilise rather than fall as a percentage of GDP. Given that shocks seem more frequent nowadays, it would be fiscally safer to claw back some 'fiscal space', given the correct response to shocks is often to spend a lot quickly. The higher the debt ratio, the worse the long-term consequences are likely to be, and the more unsafe it is for economic stability. The problem remains: cutting current expenditure is painful, with many false economies, and we do badly need to spend more on investment.

We have already printed a vast amount of money since 2007. It's true that, ultimately, the only constraints on printing more money are the real constraints imposed by the economy itself, such as inflation and loss of confidence in UK bonds and economic stability. In the face of such constraints, if printing or borrowing is used to build in a permanently increasing deficit that outpaces the growth of the economy then it will eventually end in a bad way. The good news on borrowing to invest is that, with a good business plan, credit can be secured and, if sensibly invested for growth, it can pay back a healthy surplus in time. Indeed, a perennial problem with so-called fiscal rules – those restrictions on fiscal policy set by the government to constrain its own decisions – is that they have led to Chancellors meeting them by leeching off their capital budget in order to meet their more immediate need for current spending. That is, under political pressure for immediate spending, they have cut investment and so decreased the future GDP that will be needed to pay for future spending.

The alternative, which is to constrain total debt, means that vital investment may be foregone to meet an arbitrary and self-imposed rule. That does not mean that fiscal rules are all bad, but they need protection from short-term political pressures to cut investment, so there is much talk of giving more authority to the OBR to include the potential from investment as an asset that counts against debt. As with the Bank of England being made independent of the day-to-day pressure from the Chancellor, giving the OBR more authority is a recognition that the harsh realities of economic forces often show little respect for democracy and care nothing for politics.

FISCAL AND MONETARY BALANCE

Helpfully, Prime Minister Liz Truss demonstrated exactly what a bad business plan looks like: sack respected Treasury officials, ignore the fiscal watchdog set up by your own party, fail to liaise budget announcements with the Bank of England, and borrow to cut taxes on the fanciful justification that it will cause a 'magic growth fairy' to spring into action. Unfortunately, given the debacle of the Truss/Kwarteng mini-budget, the UK might now have what has unkindly been dubbed a 'moron premium'. That is, the long-standing reputation of the UK for sound finances may have been eroded, which could now make it harder and more expensive to borrow. That said, just a year after the mini-budget and its subsequent reversal by

Jeremy Hunt, it was not clear if there had been long-term damage (unless, of course, one had taken out a mortgage at that time). The risk premium on gilt yields fell back to where it was prior to the mini-budget. Nevertheless, as Jagjit Chadha, director of NIESR, warned in oral evidence to a Treasury Committee in 2022: 'Moving ahead without proper scrutiny, whether it is by the OBR or experts, is an incredibly dangerous thing to do, particularly with the financial markets so keenly watching what we are doing.'

In short, the fiscal space is now more limited than it has been for many decades, but using higher interest rates to tackle inflation, much of it due to global rather than domestic factors, places disproportionate pain on some unlucky people. The good news for those who do wish to raise more tax is that, though we are set for the highest level of tax ever seen in the UK, it is still only middling by international standards. Also, total government revenues, which include both tax and non-tax revenues (such as the interest paid on student loans, foreign reserves and public corporations) are forecast to rise to about 42 per cent of GDP by 2028. That is historically high, but it's not an unprecedented level.

The bad news is that higher interest rates, which are intended to reduce inflation risk by bearing down on aggregate demand, are threatening to slow down the already sluggish-to-zero growth in GDP. Private borrowing is falling, the private sector is paying down debts rather than taking new credit and defaults on debt are rising. Well-judged investments can attract funding and turn an economy around, and that can be done by governments, but it is all made harder against a background of falling private sector aggregate demand.

Although fiscal policy is clumsy and slow as a means of fine-tuning the economy, it can be vital in a deep recession and for building long-term growth-enhancing infrastructure. Fiscal policy also sets the background in which monetary policy operates. Currently, the Treasury and Bank of England seem to be 'arm wrestling' over which of them sets aggregate demand, but the underlying fiscal arrangements can be made more equitable and less arbitrary than can be done for monetary policy. Fiscal policy can set the scene for aggregate demand management, while the greater speed and flexibility of monetary policy can then be used more effectively for more short-term adjustments and responses. An overly expansionary fiscal stance can be reined in by higher interest rates, and permanently very low interest rates are not necessarily a good thing as they can discourage saving and create property booms. It is also dangerous to allow interest rates to go too near the ZLB (Zero Lower Bound), as it means quick monetary responses to a negative shock run out of room to be lower, and a large reduction in interest rates can be a strong stimulus. Raising government expenditure, with taxation to offset the inflationary effects, can introduce more stability and reduce the work that interest rates have to do. More fiscal spend also allows interest rates to be that bit higher, which makes more space for interest rates to fall and is fairer to savers. In short, it is dangerous and inequitable to rely on monetary policy to do all the work, though fiscal policy is slow, cumbersome and often overly political. Getting the balance right with longer-term fiscal and shorter-term monetary policies is tricky but much needed.

*　*　*

The operational logistics of managing demand are tricky, but it is still a lot easier than addressing long-term structural changes. Money can always be printed, though not always without wider adverse consequences if the economy is near capacity and/or the markets are jittery. Fiscal stimulus is vital when the limits of monetary stimulus are reached, though it is clumsy and potentially politically toxic when used for temporary stimulus, especially when the fiscal handouts are later withdrawn. Overall, managing aggregate demand well can successfully ease temporary problems, and that is vital as in many ways the 'long run' is simply the sum of multiple 'short runs', but it is the supply side that brings lasting successes or failures in attempts to improve the performance of the economy. It is to that we now turn our attention.

PART II

CURRENT PROBLEMS

CHAPTER 5

THE STUPIDITY OF BREXIT

It is nine years since Britain voted to leave the European Union after a national plebiscite in which only 37 per cent of the registered electorate voted to break the existing trade, personal, social, educational and political links with twenty-seven other European nations. A transition period started at the end of January 2020 and the UK exited formally at the end of January 2021, but the change in perceptions and investment had already set in long before that. Immediately after the vote in June 2016, the Bank of England had to intervene with quantitative easing to calm financial markets which were caught by surprise. The pound itself fell sharply and by the time the UK formally left, it was still some 15 per cent down compared to pre-Brexit.

Since then, public opinion has shifted in the opposite direction, with many Brexit voters now ruing their decision. A poll in May 2025 showed 56 per cent of Leave voters saying it was wrong for Britain to leave the EU and only 2 per cent confirming their vote to leave. Some 53 per cent went so far as to say Britain should simply rejoin the EU, with 66 per cent expressing a wish for a much closer relationship than is currently on offer. Indeed, many commentators have called Brexit the biggest act of self-harm by a nation ever. It has caused countless issues with the treatment of Northern Ireland

– which is partly still in and partly out – and with other territories like Gibraltar. In short, it's a mess.

While Keir Starmer has made it clear that there is no question of Britain again embracing the core principles of the EU dating back to the days of the common market (namely free movement of goods, services and people), the economic data continues to show the enduring morale-sapping impact of breaking trade links with the UK's closest partners. Sadly, there has been only a limited 'reset' agreement between London and Brussels.

Much energy is now focused on stronger defence cooperation in the face of Vladimir Putin's invasion of a sovereign European state. But such cooperation was always mainly handled within the framework of NATO, causing confusion in the current European climate. Brussels, with the support of the European Central Bank, is offering support funding for increased arms expenditure, which the UK can tap into, but the UK is still lagging well below the NATO benchmark on defence spending.

THE SLOW PUNCTURE OF BREXIT

For economists, this all makes for a wonderful opportunity to see trade theory being put to the test in real time, despite its many negative consequences. The type of random, or not so random, controlled experiment which is unfolding before our eyes shows clearly that overriding the free movement of goods, people, capital and services reduces potential growth and is ultimately very bad for the consumer. And while the counterfactuals are usually difficult to calculate, no non-partisan economists are seriously challenging the OBR estimate that cutting trade links with Europe is reducing UK GDP by 4 per cent on a permanent basis. At a time when the government's mantra is 'growth, growth, growth', resetting relationships with the EU should be a top priority.

To be sure, so many economic forecasts on future trade are now thrown off balance by US President Donald Trump's erratic see-sawing pronouncements on trade. One also worries over the extent to which Britain's giveaways might annul the supposed benefits of any deal. Even after the latest agreement – still to be signed and sealed at the time of writing – the cost of selling a certain quota of UK-made Jaguar or Land Rover Discovery vehicles to a US customer will be at best 10 per cent higher than before. This 10 per cent tariff still applies to most goods that the UK exports and there are additional worries about how President Trump decides to deal with, for example, the pharmaceutical sector, with his renewed threats to raise drug prices for the NHS. The UK government celebrated securing a 25 per cent tariff for vehicles and the steel and aluminium sector under the renegotiated UK–US deal, but many UK cars remain more expensive in the US market. What's more, the new trade deal with the US will allow the US to export 1.4 million litres of bioethanol fuel entirely tariff-free, which is apparently the entire annual demand in the UK. This, according to UK fuel industry leaders, will wipe out up to 600 jobs in the UK bioethanol industry, a sacrifice apparently deemed acceptable to UK trade negotiators.

The government's own assessment of the trade deal made with non-European trade partners shows that the much bigger hit on GDP is from leaving the EU. It will weigh heavily on the UK's future hopes of growing its way out of its current economic slow-down. Granted, the UK has been able to strike its own trade deals with other countries, many of which had trade agreements with the EU, largely to make up for the fact that they were all void when the UK exited the EU. In some cases, as with Japan, these deals have been slightly strengthened. There have also been new trade deals with Australia and New Zealand, and now also limited deals with India and the US. But the impact of these on the economy is judged by the government's own official assessments to be minor, relative to the negative impact on UK–EU trade.

These deals are hardly all positive. The deal with the US is essentially damage limitation that leaves many sectors exposed to higher tariffs than before, while concessions in a number of areas may prove harmful to UK domestic producers, particularly for agriculture but potentially also for other manufacturing sectors. The trade deal with India – which allows Scotch whisky to be exported tariff-free, among other things – has been in exchange for easing immigration rules to allow Indian nationals to work in the UK without initially paying income tax, which labour market economists fear may lead to British employees being replaced by cheaper Indian ones. And, again, the overall impact of those deals on GDP is still likely to be minimal.

The truth is that the EU remains the UK's main trading partner, even post-Brexit. Despite new deals struck with other countries, the 'EU–UK reset' announced in 2025 will be the main way to improve the UK's trading position, and hence productivity and growth, which has remained lacklustre. It is not a question of tariffs – Brexit does not involve the EU imposing any tariffs on UK exports – but one of costly bureaucracy between the UK and the EU, including elaborate 'rules of origin' paperwork. The issue, therefore, has been the regulatory requirements and safety standards at the border, which have added to costs and discouraged many companies, particularly small- and medium-sized enterprises (SMEs), from exporting to the EU. Many of these have decided simply not to export at all.

In short, the real problem is 'non-tariff barriers'. These have also affected financial services, though the impact here has been limited as no other centre in Europe has been able to replicate London's robust ecosystem of support for these services, including lawyers, accountants, pension funds and asset managers. A move to a single capital market in the EU, when it comes, will, of course, be a challenge for London, but again it could offer greater opportunities for UK firms and skills. Hence the push for recognition of qualifications between the UK and the EU, which should have been pushed a lot harder than it has been by now.

Economists overwhelmingly agree that improving the ease of trading with the EU would have positive shorter-term impacts and help SMEs, whose buying from and selling to Europe has fallen significantly since Brexit. For example, Frontier Economics – chaired until recently by Lord O'Donnell and now by Dame Sharon White – produced a report in February 2024 for the campaign group Best for Britain, showing that deeper alignment with the EU on goods and services could boost growth by between 1.7 per cent and 2.2 per cent. The biggest benefits on the goods side, they found, would be enjoyed outside London, and specifically in the west Midlands, east Midlands, the north-east and Yorkshire. It is not surprising, then, that some politicians have called for a partial rejoining of trade, in the sense of asking to be allowed into a UK–EU customs union. This sounds attractive, but Turkey has been in a form of customs union with the EEC, now the EU, for decades. Turkey's deal has not allowed a single Turkish citizen to travel via visa or allowed Turkish firms to trade freely into the EU, as was possible for British firms when Britain was part of Europe. If Britain were to rejoin the customs union, the terms of that entry would have to allow for that.

We know that exports and imports encourage competition and innovation, and sectors which export tend to invest more than others, as a percentage of revenues, to keep up to date with technology and to ensure that they remain competitive. Sadly, exiting the EU has affected our ability to enjoy economies of scale and therefore the associated productivity increases. As a result, costs to consumers are higher than would otherwise have been the case, as such benefits do not accrue to the extent that they had done while the UK was a member of the single market. In recent years, prices in the UK have risen consistently higher on average than those in the Eurozone, while interest rates have also been higher, negatively affecting growth. Professor Adam Posen, a former member of the Monetary Policy Committee, has attributed some 80 per cent of the difference we see between the UK's and the Eurozone's inflation rate to Brexit.

After updated GDP figures were published days after the Chancellor's Spending Review in April 2025 – which revealed a better performance in the first quarter, largely because companies were trying to produce and sell as much as possible to the US before the extra tariffs came into effect – Labour ministers could be heard patting themselves on the back about the UK's being 'the fastest growing economy in the G7'. Yet, in real terms, UK goods trade volumes have grown just 1 per cent on their 2019 levels.

As mentioned, the main problem comes from so-called 'non-tariff barriers': time-consuming and sometimes complicated new paperwork that businesses must fill out when importing from and exporting to the EU. The goods exporting sector of the UK has been hit especially hard. Some recent studies suggest that UK goods exports are 30 per cent lower than they would have been if we had not left the single market and customs union.[1] Indeed, the working assumption of the OBR is still that Brexit in the long term will reduce exports and imports of goods and services by 15 per cent.

Brexit has also affected the UK labour market, a fact which is often overlooked in economic discussions. Britain had access to the wider European labour market pool when in the EU; the NHS, for example, sent two recruitment teams a year to Portugal, where nurses have a university-level qualification, to hire new nursing staff. From the 1980s onwards in the UK, there was a steady decline in apprenticeships as firms were released from their obligation to train the next generation of non-university graduate workers. Instead, many firms – in construction, for example – could hire workers from Poland and other former communist nations which maintained a historic tradition of apprenticeship and workplace-based training. If employers cannot access labour at the right price at the right time, their bottom line is hit.

BREXIT AND MIGRATION

Net EU migration to the UK was running at a yearly rate of between 200,000 and 300,000 during the 2010s, mainly from workers and students from the EU, but this has turned negative since 2021. The types of migrants who used to come were young and typically well-educated; they brought few dependants and had a better employment record than the British. Some 40 per cent of London's construction workers came from the EU, though many of these have now returned. These migrants were helping productivity and were also, on balance, net contributors to the Exchequer according to earlier OBR analysis. To fill the gaps, the Conservative government in 2023 granted 1.2 million visas and had some 900,000 new immigrants arrive that year from Nigeria, Pakistan, India, Sri Lanka, Ghana and other nations. Net migration might have fallen sharply to 400,000 in the year to June 2024, but is still considerably higher than the pre-Brexit average. The Brexit claim that the UK would solve its immigration problems by leaving Europe has turned out, *quelle surprise*, to be a delusion. Meanwhile, international students from elsewhere now stay longer in the UK, partly because of legislation change and the new trade deals with Australia, New Zealand and India; many will be allowed to stay even longer as part of new trade deals.

An important aspect of this is the extra cost to business of the new arrangements. The 'skilled visa' rules were tightened by the Conservative government before the election and the Home Office's own assessment is that the changes to the sponsorship arrangements for visas will cost business some £37.4 billion over the next ten years. That figure may increase as the government announced changes in salaries thresholds and visa fees in May 2025. If you add this to the costs from higher minimum wages, the increase in employer NICs and changes in labour laws which are expected to take effect over the next couple of years, this presents a grim picture for employers in the UK. No time has been more important for a proper reset with the EU than now, as geopolitics increasingly makes navigating national business more difficult than ever. Reducing uncertainty is a must.

Of course, Brexit made it considerably harder for UK citizens to live, work, travel and often retire in the warmer climes of southern Europe. Being a member of the EU had made it easy for British professionals, especially those in the service sectors such as finance, consultancy or tourism, to work in any city or town in Europe while enjoying many of the same rights as nationals of the country. It's unsurprising, then, that in the 2021 census 160,000 UK citizens had obtained Irish passports compared to 26,000 in the 2011 census, but this still leaves most Brits who once freely lived across the Channel unable to stay more than ninety days at a home they own in Europe, while now paying costly healthcare insurance. There have also been problems over passport control, with Brits having to pay for an electronic visa (similar to the US ESTA system) to travel to Europe, and Britain imposing a more costly variant for EU citizens coming to the UK. This is not great news for anyone; it's certainly not great for UK tourism or school visits from the Continent, which have declined sharply since the UK put up barriers to what was once an open border. Freedom of movement ended with Brexit, affecting tourists and business travellers alike. British passport holders can no longer use 'EU/EEA/CH' lanes at EU border crossing points, though this may change with the current 'reset'.

In truth, of course, many EU laws, so-called directives and other regulations have remained in place, as they were common-sense measures often proposed by the British government when the UK was an EEC or EU member. It was decided that getting rid of thousands of laws and replacing them directly with new UK ones would be too cumbersome, so the idea of voting them all out at once was abandoned. In any case, all firms involved in exporting must abide by the rules of the importing nation and the EU remains the UK's main trading partner. In other areas, the British government has sought to create its own regulations.

The Europe-wide chemicals industry, for example, adopted so-called 'REACH' regulations so all chemicals, paints and any products which had certain chemicals involved in their production, were produced safely and in line with consumer, worker and environmental production standards. The UK chemical and paints industry estimates the cost of replacing the EU REACH regulations will be around £2 billion. In the face of such expense, the firms concerned would undoubtedly be content to remain under the EU-wide regulations.

TAKING BACK CONTROL?

One of the claims made about Brexit is that it would restore parliamentary sovereignty over economic policy. But in truth, the subsidiarity element still ruled most laws in areas like tax and spending. Foreign policy was domestic, as were the rule of law and sentencing principles and guidelines, though these were still under the auspices of the European Court of Human Rights, which also had jurisdiction over migration issues. Countries like the UK with their own currency had more room for manoeuvre. That was one of the reasons why Gordon Brown was keen for Britain to remain outside the Eurozone and retain its own currency – the five economic tests undertaken by Brown to confirm this desire happened while both authors of this book were working for the government, and both partook in the analysis. Though we were paying for EU membership, much of that was being redistributed in terms of regional and cohesion funds, through membership of Horizon for our universities and scientists, for example, and through the Common Agricultural Policy (CAP) for farmers. Since Brexit, the UK government has had to pay subsidies to farmers directly instead of these coming through CAP. Britain was a net contributor to the EU budget but, in return, British farmers got higher farm support payments as well as access to the EU market.

Support for British regions has been cut since leaving the EU. In the 1990s, the drop in per capita income in Yorkshire following the great shake-out of the steel and coal industries in the 1980s was such that the entire region became eligible for EU funding to alleviate poverty and regenerate public infrastructure. Post-Brexit, this funding now poses questions for Whitehall and the Treasury, whose parsimonious rules often seem to favour the rich south over the poorer north. We know that spending should be prioritised to get the best value for money, and this spending can favour the south as monetised returns tend to be higher where people are better off financially. But as the gap between London and the south-east and the rest of the country has widened during austerity, and certainly since Brexit, the cost of 'levelling up' has risen sharply, and that brings with it its own difficulties at a time of constrained resources.

Britain has not left the Council of Europe which regulates common human rights obligations for all its member states. As such, Britain's decisions remain bound by the European Convention on Human Rights largely drawn up by British jurists, backed by Winston Churchill in his last period in office and now overseen by the Council of Europe. A delegation of UK parliamentarians makes decisions on EU-wide human rights legislation; some significant examples for Britain include the sanctioning of practices by security forces and the military in Northern Ireland during the 'Troubles' and the outlawing of beating children in British schools.

Today, there are difficulties over the rights of refugees, which have presented an array of political problems in the UK, as they have in many EU nations. The number of arrivals on small boats from war-torn regions, the slowness in tackling asylum applications and the perceived difficulty of community integration is heightening social tensions and deepening political polarisation. For some, these highly complex issues have been reductively bundled together as an outright attack on 'foreigners'. Even Keir Starmer said Britain needed to avoid becoming a 'land of strangers', though he later apologised for this Enoch Powell-like phrase. Clearly, for many voters, the UK withdrawing from the EU is not enough. They want a total rupture from any legal obligations that come from membership of a partnership organisation that has 'Europe' in its title. As we have seen, from an economic viewpoint, such a demand is completely nonsensical.

CHAPTER 6

ALL YOU NEED IS GROWTH?

We've often heard it said that all economists care about is gross domestic product or about economic growth, as growth is usually reported as synonymous with an increase in GDP. But this accusation simply isn't true. Speaking personally, we've never met an economist who believes that GDP is the only thing that matters (and we've met a lot of economists). Indeed, all introductory economics tomes are at great pains to explain why GDP is an inadequate measure of economic welfare. We do however accept that, with notable exceptions, economics as a discipline does not give sufficient attention to vital issues like the environment. In addition, we recognise that GDP is biased towards aggregating the transactions of individuals rather than capturing the value of collective needs and wants, and, yes, that policymakers are often prone to putting GDP above all else, though sometimes they may have good reason to do so when fiscal and societal problems look grim.

WHAT IS GDP?

So, what is GDP? A standard definition is that it is the monetary value of all finished products, goods and services produced within a country over a period of time (usually a year or a quarter of a year). It's immediately obvious that this leaves out things that have no monetary value. Indeed, if we all swapped housework with our neighbour and paid each other the same then it would do nothing but boost GDP. As it is, all this 'household production' isn't itself reflected in GDP, which is part of the reason why women still don't get a fair representation in GDP. GDP focuses solely on things that have monetary cost or price – not the environment, relationships, unpaid caring or any other form of nurturing. Only a non-economist who doesn't understand GDP, therefore, could regard it as a comprehensive measure of social welfare.

The weakness of GDP (or Gross National Product, which is simply GDP plus some incomes earned abroad) as a measure of welfare has never been more eloquently expressed than by Robert F. Kennedy some fifty years ago:

Gross national product counts air pollution and cigarette advertising, and ambulances to clear our highways of carnage. It counts special locks for our doors and the jails for the people who break them. It counts the destruction of the redwood and the loss of our natural wonders in chaotic sprawl. It counts napalm and counts nuclear warheads and armored cars for the police to fight the riots in our cities. It counts Whitman's rifle and Speck's knife, and the television programs which glorify violence in order to sell toys to our children. Yet gross national product does not allow for the health of our children, the quality of their education or the joy of their play. It does not include the beauty of our poetry or the strength of our marriages, the intelligence of our public debate or the integrity of our public officials. It measures neither our wit nor our courage, neither our wisdom nor our learning, neither our compassion nor our devotion to our country, it measures everything, in short, except that which makes life worthwhile.

And it can tell us everything about America except why we are proud that we are Americans.

All of Kennedy's observations are true, but none of them surprise an economist. It is fair to say though, as Dame Diane Coyle has explained with such insight, that not even economists or national income accountants have kept up with just how far GDP has drifted from measuring all that is productive in the modern technological age.[1] Coyle shows how, on the one hand, the digital transformation of work and leisure is enabling human creativity and satisfying new uses of individuals' time, while, on the other, creating dangerous concentrations of money and power. This has allowed technological advances to create new oligarchs and the most powerful corporations the world has ever seen, which challenge cherished notions of freedom, democracy and the power of the state:

> There is a feedback loop between events (like the crises from 2008 on), politics and economic ideas; political priorities shape what is measured, and the measures in turn define ideas about the economy and thus political choices. Articulating a new political economy, if it is indeed starting to emerge, will require a different framework of economic statistics. The underlying structure of the economy and society is changing with the dual transition in general purpose technologies, zero carbon energy and the ongoing digital and information revolution.

* * *

In an effort to avoid so-called 'double counting', GDP only includes 'finished products'. For example, if the value of steel used to make a car is, say, £1,000, then as this is included in the price of the finished car it would be double counting to add together both the price of that steel and the price of the car. This example is straightforward because, as far as we know, steel is always an 'intermediary product', an input into something else. But what of the food we hurriedly eat to fuel us as we work at producing these finished products? Perhaps we should separate out accounting for the food we really enjoy eating, or, alternatively, count only the food that fuels our body during leisure time? Obviously, that would be impractical. What about the transport we use just to get to work to produce finished products? What about the mindless entertainment and alcohol we might consume to de-stress from the effort involved in working to produce finished products? Are the health and counselling needs that arise from the stress of work also intermediatory products? Is defence expenditure a finished product or merely a 'regrettable necessity' needed to protect our country so that we can make and enjoy finished products? A finished product is defined as 'something that is wanted for its own sake', but it should be clear by now that this immediately plunges us into murky philosophical waters. In short, because of myriad conceptual and practical problems, GDP excludes and includes many things that should or shouldn't be counted as productive activities, let alone as welfare measures. All that said, it still doesn't mean that GDP is unimportant. Indeed, for managing aggregate demand and for estimating tax take it is indispensable.

CIVIL SOCIETY

It surprises many people, your authors included, to hear that while estimates of spending on illegal drugs and prostitution are included in GDP, the work of volunteers isn't. GDP doesn't pick up what is now collectively lumped together under the name 'civil society'. Civil society refers to the myriad connections that exist between individuals and institutions outside the private and public sectors, which could be as informal as mutual support WhatsApp groups or simply helping the neighbours. More narrowly, it comprises the formal organisations that provide the infrastructure for such connections, from charities to trade unions and from housing associations to social enterprises. Without civil society, the UK would be unrecognisable and a considerably worse place to live; the organisations that make up the sector and the people working within them are fundamental to maintaining and improving our quality of life. As such, its omission from GDP seems to deprecate the good work done in civil society, including work undertaken by millions of volunteers. Although GDP methodology is constrained by international rules, the broad 'levelling up' initiative pledged to introduce a civil society 'satellite account' dedicated to collecting data on the sector, and there have also been attempts to give charities and volunteers a bigger role and more recognition. We hope these efforts eventually succeed.

When he was Prime Minister, David Cameron promoted his vision of the 'Big Society'. He emphasised 'community empowerment', giving local communities more say over local decisions and services; 'social action' to promote volunteerism and philanthropy; and 'public service reform' to encourage a diverse range of providers, including charities and social enterprises, to deliver public services. However, as his Big Society initiative coincided with the unprecedented slashing of public expenditure by George Osborne, it was largely regarded as a slightly ironic euphemism for cutting public services. That is a pity, as civil society can sometimes be the Heineken of public policy, reaching parts of society that neither the public nor private sector can reach. Government and commerce lack the local knowledge, relationships with the community and understanding of the challenges faced by people that civil society bodies possess.

More recently, Lord O'Donnell, the former Cabinet Secretary, announced the final report of the Law Family Commission on Civil Society in January 2023, which he had chaired on behalf of Pro Bono Economics. Lord O'Donnell felt strongly that governments had done too little to foster and promote the public benefit that civil society can bring, claiming, 'Successive governments have neglected charities for too long, and our country is the worse for it.' Recognising this, early in 2024 Pro Bono Economics hosted a 'Civil Society Summit' for seventeen shadow ministers – including Sir Keir Starmer, Yvette Cooper, Wes Streeting and Bridget Phillipson – along with 150 civil society leaders, to discuss the different ways in which the social sector might work alongside a future Labour government. The Cabinet now includes eight members with charity sector experience, a fourfold increase on the previous government. This doesn't guarantee the 'reset' Keir Starmer has promised, but the government has instructed the Department of Culture, Media and Sport to set up a new 'Civil Society Covenant', working closely with key civil bodies, including the National Council for Voluntary Organisations (NCVO) and the Association of Chief Executives of Voluntary Organisations (ACEVO). Its ambition is to work 'hand in hand' with charities to harness their innovation, dynamism and trusted community reach. None of this is likely to show up in the GDP numbers, but if the initiative is successful, it will show up across a much broader 'dashboard' of wellbeing indicators.

Despite this effort, the Labour government has put 'growth, growth, growth' of GDP as its paramount target, even though everyone knows there is more to life than GDP. Again, that certainly doesn't mean that GDP should be ignored, but the special thing about fostering and harnessing the power of civil society is that it doesn't just help those in material need. It also makes both the helped and the helpers feel more included in their communities, and, for the majority of us, helping others makes us feel more fulfilled as human beings.

WELFARE 'DASHBOARDS'

For all the obvious criticisms of GDP as a welfare indicator, efforts to construct a single 'alternative' accepted measure of wellbeing have failed. Human wellbeing is just too complex and multifaceted, and any weighting of the things that contribute to it will depend on perspective and the purpose of the index. That is why the ONS has sensibly decided to take a 'dashboard of indicators' approach to measuring wellbeing.[2]

The wellbeing dashboard the ONS provides is described as an 'overview of wellbeing in the UK' on an individual, community and national level that considers change across fifty-nine measures of wellbeing, grouped by ten topic areas. How you might weight them is up to you, but they cover: personal wellbeing, life satisfaction, feelings of happiness, anxiety, and sense of purpose; relationships, including quality of relationships with family, friends and community; health, both physical and mental, as well as life expectancy and self-reported health; what we do, including employment, volunteering, and leisure; where we live, including housing quality, access to green spaces, and crime rates; personal finance; education and skills, and satisfaction with the educational system; the economy, including GDP, along with inflation and employment rates; trust in government and participation in democratic processes; and the environment, air quality, biodiversity and access to natural resources. In short, there is a whole lot more to wellbeing than just GDP.

GDP MATTERS

Even in a relatively rich country like the UK, having more GDP is important. In spite of this, as the 'Easterlin paradox' has made clear since the 1970s, it's not so much that an increase in GDP per head makes us all happier. The 'paradox' is that at a point in time richer people tend to be happier than poorer people, but, over time, as populations grow richer, they do not grow happier. This is mainly because relative income – your income compared to others – is more important for happiness than your absolute income. Hence the joke about the employee who says to their boss, 'I know you can't give me a pay rise but how about cutting the pay of my colleagues?' And so, the Easterlin paradox is often cited to claim that GDP growth is unimportant for wellbeing. While it may be correct that, in the long run, income growth doesn't make individuals with adequate and above standards of living happier, per se, it is incorrect to say that GDP doesn't matter for the wellbeing of a nation.

Firstly, to say that more income doesn't permanently make you happy is not the same thing as saying that you don't want more income. A dramatic and bleak turnaround this century has meant that today's young people cannot assume that they will be better off than their parents. In the ten years between 1997 and 2007, real disposable income in the UK rose by almost 30 per cent; in the seventeen years to 2024 it rose by only a little over ten per cent. Paul Johnson of the IFS reports that we've had the slowest growth in earnings and in income per capita for perhaps two centuries.

The stalling of the economy has meant the 'left behind' fell further behind as incomes stagnated and public services deteriorated.

The major increase in economic inequality over the last thirty-five years or so has come from wealth inequality; to tackle economic inequality we need income to become more important in relation to wealth. Without this, wealth is largely determined by who one's parents happen to be. In addition, slow growth, with all its associated discontent, breeds radical politics. While the Treasury fretted about sovereign debt during the Great Recession, austerity was seriously eroding social capital. This created a fertile ground for racism and anti-establishment sentiments, which the hard left and the far right remorselessly exploited for their own, often hidden, agendas. It was in this context, supported by the usual tabloid masters of misinformation, that the Leave campaign hoodwinked their way to Brexit. All of this has simply added to the difficulty of balancing taxes with public expenditure; without growth the interest on our debt is harder to meet, making it a drain on public finances.

It's also important to remember that GDP matters greatly when it comes to having a say in the global community. Generally, the bigger a country's GDP, the more influence it has in the world. That is why the UK is no longer the world's superpower, and the US and China are.

Although it would be nice to include more of life's important things in the measurement of GDP, it wouldn't necessarily help pay the Chancellor's fiscal bills. At the end of the day, volunteering, wildlife, clean air and wellbeing don't add to tax revenues, which need monetary incomes. Meanwhile, demographics, increased care and health needs, interest on debt, infrastructure investment and rising defence expenditures are only going to widen the potential gap between public expenditure and tax revenues. Almost two decades of depleted public services and infrastructure, along with cuts to public expenditure, mean it's little wonder that Labour is hoping for growth to boost tax revenues. To pay for public services we ultimately need tax revenue and for more tax revenue we must have higher tax rates, which would be politically very painful. Only growth will ease the pain.

CAN GDP CAPTURE THE OUTPUT OF NEW TECHNOLOGIES?

Dame Diane Coyle has been the leading economist considering whether the changes to the outputs of modern economies are adequately captured by current measures of GDP. She has authored a series of fascinating and insightful books on the subject, from her 2014 *GDP: A Brief but Affectionate History* through to her most recent books *Cogs and Monsters: What Economics Is and What It Should Be* (2021) and now *The Measure of Progress: Counting What Really Matters* (2025). As she rightly says, 'The more AI reshapes business and daily life, the more glaring the gap between the actual economy and official economic statistics will be.' And so, with ever-deeper insights and updates over a decade of research and analysis, she reveals how out of touch GDP is becoming with the services made possible through modern technical advances, such as artificial intelligence and the use and abuse of resources. This increasing gap between what is measured and the whole gamut of technically advanced production challenges how meaningful our current measures of GDP and productivity actually are. Coyle says:

> Productivity gains may correspond to time saving in production or higher quality in products and services provided – for in addition to the standard, intuitive metric of labour productivity, we should look at the productivity of the other inputs too, including output per unit of carbon and other resources, and per unit of time.[3]

This brings us on to an important question that we'll return to in the next chapter: is economic growth compatible with protecting the environment? We must first dispel a common misunderstanding that we so often hear in the call for 'prosperity without growth'. As we saw above, GDP is a flow of economic activity; it is not a stock. With the same technology and composition of output, a constant flow of GDP means the same level of emissions and damage to the environment, and so to reduce the rate of damage, GDP would have to be reduced, but this would only slow the rate at which CO_2 is emitted. Anti-growth voices do seem to dim somewhat when growth is sluggish, as the immediate and pressing economic and social implications of low growth appear.

*　　*　　*

The evidence is that growth is fostered, though not guaranteed, by a variety of complementary factors: investment in capital, both physical and human, through education and skills; research and development, and the diffusion of innovation; free trade; the right demographics and a healthy labour force; and strong institutional frameworks. All of these are also closely related to policies for increasing productivity (discussed in Chapter 8).

It is a truism to say that there is more to life than GDP. Though it is true that economists as a profession do not typically pay enough attention to exploring and highlighting environmental concerns, it is certainly not true that GDP is unimportant. A 'dashboard' of indicators might be a better approach for monitoring welfare, but such a framework is harder to summarise and digest. What is certain is that a reduction in GDP would greatly add to the UK's already considerable problems.

CHAPTER 7

ENVIRONMENTAL IMPERATIVES OR GREEN WILD GOOSE CHASES?

We hear from advocates of green policies that a transition to green energy would make us better off while creating many jobs. Conversely, from sceptics, we hear that going for net zero carbon emissions is going to make us all worse off and will cost us jobs. The truth, as is so often the case, is somewhere in between. In the longer run, it is certain that a modern economy could operate entirely on renewable and non-nuclear power, though unfortunately that happy state has yet to be reached. As is now widely accepted, the global environmental emergency won't simply go away if ignored; the weight of evidence is clear, and we are already a long way behind on what needs to be done globally. We need to act urgently and that will require some economic pain, though not, as we will argue, futile economic and political suicide.

The claim of a scientific hoax, of a clandestine conspiracy of 'scientific crooks' all around the world, largely propagated by fossil fuel shills, is simply ridiculous. Of course, the scientists could all be wrong about human-driven (or 'anthropogenic', if you want to sound scientific) climate change. As economists we don't need to have an opinion on whether it's real, and that's all it would be anyway: an opinion. As lay persons, we accept that it is a real threat, but all we need to know as economists is that an overwhelming majority of climate scientists, the actual *experts* in the field, report that anthropogenic climate change is a very big problem indeed. We must take them seriously and factor into our own discipline the weight of that scientific opinion.

We also need scientists to tell us *how much* climate change is likely to affect the globe, so that we can properly estimate the costs and benefits of mitigation and adaption, and therefore better understand and advise governments. That was the influential 'business case' approach that economist and academic Nicholas Stern put into mainstream debate in his landmark Stern Review in 2006. Scientists warn that climate change increases extremes of weather, raises sea levels and destroys vital parts of our biosphere. It is also estimated that the annual mortality rates caused by human-made air pollution in the UK are roughly between 28,000 and 36,000 deaths every year, with all the associated costs for the NHS.[1] As global patterns of weather change, so will the range of temperatures across the globe. Heatwaves, droughts and floods will become more common and could even make some regions effectively uninhabitable. Speaking of the US, Mark Gongloff of Bloomberg wrote in July 2025:

> The latest evidence comes from Bloomberg Intelligence, which this week estimated that climate-related disasters have cost the US economy at least $6.6 trillion in higher insurance premiums, cleanup spending and other expenses over the past twelve years. Adjusted for inflation, that makes climate disasters already twice as expensive as the Great Depression's $3.3 trillion in losses over the same time frame.[2]

Climate change could even cause a 'great march north' as climate refugees seek more temperate climes. If all that isn't enough, there is also the threat of catastrophic positive feedback loops, such as the melting of permafrost releasing greenhouse gases, and of decreasing ice cover reflecting less sunlight back into space. Worryingly, the tipping points for positive feedback loops are very uncertain, and all the while there is the ever-rising concentration of CO_2 in the atmosphere, which is increasing every year by around two parts per million (ppm); this is now at over 420 ppm compared to the 275 ppm pre-Industrial Revolution. Meanwhile, the world's increasing use of renewables isn't even close to stemming the increasing demand for fossil fuels. In the face of such existential threats, it isn't surprising that many voters, not just those who sit down to block roads, worry deeply about climate change, despite the propaganda from fossil fuel interests.

In response to these concerns, the Labour government has set an ambitious target to achieve overall 'net zero' carbon emissions by 2050, building on what the previous Conservative government had set out to achieve (though, before the election of July 2024, the previous government had rolled back on dates for achieving targets in areas such as banning sales of petrol-powered cars and the granting of new North Sea oil and gas licences). The Labour government has also increased its own capital spending and support on carbon capture and storage and on new nuclear capacity, hoping the private sector will follow, though the private sector will undoubtedly need further reassurance that renewables will not remain more expensive than their zero marginal cost of production suggests.

The goal is to reduce greenhouse gas emissions to as close to zero as possible, with any remaining emissions offset by measures such as tree planting or carbon capture and storage. Labour have also pledged to the net decarbonisation of the UK power supply by 2030, which is five years earlier than the previous target. We can't comment on net zero by 2050 – as who knows what new technologies might come along – but we are confident in saying that net zero of the UK power supply by 2030 is, to put it bluntly, pie in the sky. It simply won't be achieved, and going for such an unrealistic target is most likely to add a lot of expense compared to a more moderate target. Moreover, so far one can be forgiven for thinking that Labour's plans aren't consistent. Before the election, for example, Labour dropped its long-standing commitment to spending £28 billion a year on green projects, citing the difficult fiscal position it had inherited. The worry, of course, is that climate change doesn't just hang about waiting until you find the money to tackle it, and the central message of the Stern Report was that it's cheaper to act on climate change sooner rather than later.

To add to the mixed messaging, Labour had said 'Yes' to a new runway at Heathrow and 'No' to new drilling for North Sea oil. The economic case for Heathrow is strong: the airport is now full, and expansion would have significant economic benefits not just for London but for the UK as a whole. On the other hand, more capacity means more flights and more emissions, which doesn't seem compatible with a net zero target, even considering all the talk of miraculous new aviation fuels. In fact, emissions from aviation have doubled since 1990, even as total UK emissions have halved. In an altogether contrary decision, Labour had pledged not to grant any new licences for North Sea oil production, even though such a decision will have a negative economic impact for the UK and won't directly make even a slight dent in total global emissions, which are what matter for global climate change.

In fact, even if the UK shut up shop completely – not something any economist would advise, let alone a politician suggest – it would only reduce global greenhouse gas emissions by less than 1 per cent. Meanwhile, China, the US, India, the EU27, Russia and Brazil together account for over two-thirds of all greenhouse gas emissions. China has committed to net zero by 2060, but, despite some amazing technical advances, its domestic record on curtailing fossil fuel expansion so far is poor, though its extensive investment in electric vehicles is expected to dent fossil fuel use at some point soon. The US now has Donald Trump as President, of course, and one of Trump's first actions was to pull the country out of the international Paris Agreement to reduce emissions. India has not committed to net zero until 2070, and again has a poor record in this regard; it is forecast to grow its emissions for longer than other big and populous countries/regions, despite the adoption of new technology. The stark truth is that although renewable energy is scaling faster than ever, global energy demand is rising even faster. The outcome is that, rather than replacing fossil fuels, renewables are just adding to the overall energy supply as it expands to meet an ever-growing demand.

The OECD, in a recent policy paper, recommended a 'dual policy shift'. The first imperative, they suggest, should be to seriously rethink how economic progress is measured (something we touch on in the previous chapter about GDP) and then to better align it with climate goals and wellbeing, a discussion which has exercised economists for some time.

It would be very welcome if technology gave us more ways to bypass what is likely to be a difficult period of transition. Many countries greatly envy the living standards we enjoy, and it would be immoral for the West to insist that others stay so much poorer than us, especially as most of the greenhouse gas already in the atmosphere was emitted by rich countries. The truth is that whatever the misgivings and fantasies, the modern world is not going to embrace subsistence as a lifestyle, so GDP will continue to grow no matter how much orange paint is sprayed by protestors. The only feasible way out of the dilemma is investment in technology for a global decoupling of GDP and emissions – yes, a 'technological fix'. In the same way that the world could not possibly sustain its current population without science – indeed, most of us wouldn't be here at all if we had to rely even on early twentieth-century medicine – so a technological fix could harness modern innovation. It's reasonable to question the point of the UK sticking its neck out now to punish itself economically for the tiny difference it would make to global emissions. And if technologies are needed to solve the problem and reduce emissions, to keep us within the two degrees of temperature rise that the globe can bear, then pushing for more technological innovation is a must.

WHAT ABOUT THE COUNTERFACTUALS?

A recent report from the Carnegie Institute suggested that Europe is warming at 50 per cent faster than the rest of the world. There are two main reasons for this. The first is that we are close to the Arctic, which is melting rapidly, and Europe is seeing the effects of this on its temperatures. The second reason is more surprising: Europe is cleaning up pollution faster than other parts of the world, leaving the Continent with less of a protective layer in the atmosphere and so allowing the sun's rays to penetrate with less inhibition. So, tackling one issue has had unintended consequences, partly offsetting progress elsewhere.

It's a similar story with the rise in sea temperatures. Thankfully, this rise is still just at the surface rather than penetrating all the way through to the seabed, but as heat stays on the surface it then rises to the wider atmosphere and makes heating worse. Again, the rise in that sea surface temperature is attributed to a considerable extent to new regulations that are aimed at reducing CO_2 emissions from the fuel mix used by cargo vessels, tankers and commercial shipping more generally, which has again deprived the sea of a layer of sulphur that had tended to limit the ability of the sun's rays to penetrate.

Of course, the main argument for the UK pressing on with its net zero target is that, particularly as the world's first industrial nation, the country is well placed to demonstrate that an alternative path to economic growth, one not dependent on fossil fuels, is not only feasible but is part of a world-leading economic strategy. The problem is that the UK's clout internationally has been much reduced since Brexit, while it has been pursuing contradictory policies with different short- to long-term aspirations, a problem faced by democracies worldwide. The promised Labour strategy, for example, is to go hell for leather for growth while simultaneously dramatically reducing greenhouse emissions.

It is true that, historically, carbon emissions are strongly correlated with GDP, because more GDP has needed more energy and hence more burning of fossil fuels, but this correlation is no longer an iron rule when higher incomes are achieved. Many countries have now managed to achieve economic growth while simultaneously reducing emissions. They have 'decoupled' GDP from CO_2 emissions, and that's even when consumption of imports from abroad are included. Indeed, in contrast to GDP being the villain, it seems that green projects are something that richer people are more likely to feel they can afford. The World Bank reports that since 1990 the UK has seen GDP per head increase by around 55 per cent while CO_2 emissions per head have fallen by about 60 per cent.

Allowing for importing products that, in effect, export our CO_2, it's still around a 40 per cent reduction in emissions per head. In 2024, renewables accounted for 41 per cent of total UK energy consumption compared to just 27 per cent in 2021.[3]

To make its ambitious net zero targets seem more plausible, Labour has set its targets in terms of carbon production in the UK, but as we have just noted, because of imports this is largely meaningless as our consumption of carbon is much higher. Meanwhile, globally, there is no convincing evidence that the increase of carbon in the world's atmosphere is going to slow anytime soon. So far, all the renewables of all the rich countries are dwarfed by the increases in energy demand from fossil fuels, which is persistently at about 80 per cent of the world's energy. The prospect of seeing little to no impact on climate change while suffering from self-imposed higher energy costs is increasingly unattractive to many voters, and hence politicians. In April 2025, average UK energy prices rose by another 6.4 per cent, meaning an average household cost of £1,849, which is £600 more than three years prior. And all the while, fossil fuel's powerful vested interests use their profits to fund propaganda to undermine the public resolve to do something that would change the dangerous path we are already too far down.

A LOT OF COP BUT NOT MUCH COP

The UN-led Conference of the Parties (COP) aims to contain global emissions through brokering emission cuts by rich countries who will also be obliged to provide funding and finance for the green development of poorer countries. Unfortunately, the cuts are only for domestic carbon production and not consumption, and the financial transfers are far too small to entice a green development path for poorer countries. The COP process asks countries to sign up to emission reduction targets in an international and legally binding agreement. However, the US, Russia and China are not going to allow international bodies to legislate on their domestic affairs, and the major growth in emissions is now coming from India, Southeast Asia, Nigeria, the Middle East and North Africa – not the EU or the US – with China still the world's biggest emitter of CO_2. Poorer countries demand that richer countries put in large sums, but rich countries don't feel they can face their electorates with such a proposition. Add to this stalemate the 'drill, drill, drill' stance of the US under Trump (who has effectively wrecked his predecessor's pledges on emissions and paused most climate funding), Russia's need to increase oil and gas outputs to shore up its war-strained economy and China and India continuing their heavy reliance on coal, and the prospect of reduced global emissions anytime soon looks bleak.

Clearly, whatever successes the UK may have had with decoupling, it has not made a significant difference to the global situation. Yet the government is persisting with its emphasis on meeting domestic targets and putting faith in an eventually successful COP outcome. To be fair, despite its shortcomings and much reneging on promises, the COP process is currently the only show in town globally for talks on emission reduction, and it may well now be locked-in institutionally by those who are directly or indirectly employed by, or simply profiting from, the COP process and its subsidies. Sadly, it seems unlikely that COP alone will save the day, today or tomorrow.

WHY HAVEN'T RENEWABLES SWEPT FOSSIL FUELS INTO HISTORY?

In addition to decarbonising the UK power system by 2030, the

Labour government also aims to double onshore wind, triple solar power and quadruple offshore wind by 2030. It seeks to invest in carbon capture and storage, hydrogen and marine energy. Labour claims that plans for a green transformation will power economic growth, boost employment and bring cheaper energy bills for consumers and businesses. Wouldn't that be lovely, if true. Our high energy costs are damaging for our remaining industrial sectors and, in addition to deindustrialisation, contribute to volatile inflation, rising fuel poverty and apply generally downward pressure to living standards. The promise of cheaper energy prices from a transition to renewables rests heavily on the claim, so often heard from the green lobby, that renewables are now much cheaper than fossil fuels ('Ten times cheaper', Ed Miliband, Labour's rather evangelically green Environment Minister, used to say, though he no longer claims such a high ratio). Nevertheless, if renewables are dramatically cheaper than fossil fuels, then why would governments, let alone COP, need to convince anyone? The economics of the market would simply sweep away fossil fuels in the same way that internal combustion engines replaced steam engines.

While it's certainly true that producing energy from wind and solar is much cheaper than fossil fuels, the problem is that all that investment has to be paid for, and there's a costly sting in the tail. It's expensive not only because of the renewable energy installation but because provision must be made for when the sun don't shine and the wind don't blow. Renewable energy storage is currently too expensive to reliably fill the gaps in the weather, and with much greater reliance on energy-intensive AI and data storage, the need for guaranteed energy supply becomes ever more important. All this means that renewable energy must be increasingly backed up with reserves of alternative sources of energy as its own capacity increases. The problem here is that these back-up sources are, in effect, made far more expensive when they aren't used constantly, because the capital cost per unit of energy is then made so much higher. To better understand this, simply imagine the total cost per unit of electricity of a gas-powered power station that is expensively built but only used for one day every few months. To top it off, higher interest rates increase the cost of capital investment. The outcome is that these energy sources aren't less expensive when everything required is factored in. That is why policy, rather than the economics of competitive costs, will have to drive the transition to green energy.

WHY IS UK ELECTRICITY SO EXPENSIVE?

The UK has been closing nuclear and coal power stations for decades now, relying instead on gas and the growing output of renewables. For the first time since the 1970s, the UK is now a net energy importer. The result is that it now has some of the highest energy prices in the developed world, a fact that weighs heavily on production costs. In 2023, in the US, one kilowatt hour of industrial electricity cost about 6.5p. For Sweden, the figure was 8p. For France, 18p. And the UK? Almost 26p. Industrial electricity in the UK is priced at more than double the OECD average, and more than any other comparably rich country. That noted, don't be fooled by the fossil fuel shills who claim this high price is mostly because of 'green levies'. It isn't. Obviously, green levies do affect prices, but the high price of our electricity has much more to do with the fact that the UK is now very dependent on imported gas due to mismanagement of our mix of energy supply. We've also allowed our gas storage facilities to massively decline while failing to invest in the storage of electricity from renewables. Indeed, so inadequate is its capacity for electricity storage that the National Grid pays wind farms to shut down when it can't cope with surplus supply. In 2024, the UK spent £1 billion on payments to wind farms so they would turn off their turbines during particularly windy periods, as we lack the infrastructure, including power cables, to deal with the electricity being produced.

Within the UK's crazy pricing system, the price of electricity is determined by the most expensive supplier at any time supplying to the national grid. So, when the national grid has a shortfall, there is a bidding war, and this leaves the private gas suppliers with tremendous monopoly power. Seeing as consumers have no alternative, these companies get away with charging very high prices. It is this 'marginal cost', the cost of the extra bit needed, that sets the price of electricity, not the average costs. That means that even if we were to get 99 per cent of our energy from wind and the remaining 1 per cent from gas, the wholesale price would still be set by that last 1 per cent from gas. Crazy. Indeed, despite receiving less than a third of our electricity from gas, it contributes to 98 per cent of UK wholesale prices. In short, despite our heavy investment in renewables, we are as dependent as ever on fossil fuels for pricing. To make matters worse, some producers are holding the network to ransom by insisting on extraordinarily high margins or they'll shut off power to the grid.

As the price of electricity is dominated by the cost of gas-generated electricity – most of the time, our most expensive source of electricity – our prices are high when the price of gas is high, with our current electricity storage capacity being far too small to store the volumes of energy needed to ride out fluctuations in gas prices. Hence, the UK's industry electricity prices are also among the highest in developed economies – higher than in the EU and around four times the price of the US. The result is that UK energy-intensive industries remain globally uncompetitive. We have not invested enough in renewables, but going for an unrealistic target of net zero by 2030 will only increase costs, as it strains supply chains, drives up the cost of infrastructure and parts and front-loads the costs to ensure everything is ready at once. It also reduces economic growth by increasing medium-term costs, and as costs rise the UK becomes even more uncompetitive, causing the closure of more of its energy-intensive industry and hence causing a shift to imports – using cheaper and dirtier energy. So, the UK's dash for net zero could even increase global emissions.

THE GREEN WAY FORWARD

Clearly, the situation is far more complex than many green evangelists or fossil fuel shills would have us believe. But there are some suggestions that should be considered as we face up to a warming planet.

Domestically

Companies who exploit monopoly power as marginal providers when selling gas at peak moments should simply be nationalised, preventing them from exploiting our inadequate energy infrastructure at peak times. That infrastructure needs to be invested in, with more emphasis on energy storage rather than just new renewable suppliers, to balance out supply and demand and prevent the bizarre practice of having to pay renewables to stop supplying electricity when the grid can't cope. Although nuclear power used to be expensive, once all the costs were accounted for, there are now cheaper nuclear options with new modular reactors. Even better, the private sector seems willing to provide these reactors in the medium term. The drive for better-insulated homes and businesses is also still urgent and cost-effective, and the UK is lagging behind the rest of Europe in our use of heat pumps.

The current pricing regime tries to match supply to demand, rather than the other way around. This could be addressed by differential pricing dictated not only by place but by time. This will become more important as the use of electric vehicles increases. Schemes by suppliers that incentivise homes and businesses to use off-peak electricity should be encouraged. Local pricing rather than a uniform national price could be used to decrease NIMBYism and to encourage heavy users of electricity to move nearer to renewable energy sources, which also reduces the cost and complaints about cables and pylons. We should also go back to the pre-privatisation 'bulk supply tariff' practice of relieving industrial high users of electricity of much of the capital costs of electricity supply, something the Labour government seems to have made a start on. This really would make renewals cheaper for industry, but without substantial subsidies it could mean higher prices for households. On the other hand, driving energy-intensive industry away through our high prices will dump more of the capital costs of renewables onto consumers anyway. One way to mitigate this would be for GB Energy, the new state-owned renewable energy investment authority, to be empowered to buy and run green generators to bypass the current wholesale market and sell more affordable power to consumers.

However, the UK doesn't have a comparative advantage in producing parts and materials for green infrastructure. This is reminiscent of when polyester was hailed as the future of Britain: though it was invented here, production quickly moved to other countries (an idea we return to in Chapter 11). The jobs will be in installation but not manufacture, and so it won't help our balance of trade. The same applies to nuclear, but as it is currently the most reliable constant source of green energy, it has to be an important part of the mix until technology moves on.

In the meantime, costs of production will remain high compared to international competitors, hampering investment and growth. The government, in its industrial strategy (discussed at length in Chapter 11), has vowed to further reduce those electricity costs by rethinking its green levies and the other network charges it imposes on businesses and extending its subsidies. How that will be paid for, and whether the policies of reducing costs to high energy users and extending subsidies to many more (as is intended over the coming two years) will have the desired effect, remains to be seen.

Internationally

Costly, and often ultimately futile, gestures of decarbonisation by artificial politically driven deadlines are not the solution to climate change and biodiversity degradation, which, short of a nuclear war, are likely the biggest existential threats we face. Governments must heed the weight of scientific opinion, but not by forcing through unrealistic policies that unnecessarily raise resistance to green transition and fracture already weakened cross-party consensus. The well-funded, often clandestine shills of fossil fuel interests are only too eager to exploit such policy failures. The UK should eschew grandstanding promises and unrealistic and ultimately counterproductive targets. Such targets that measure only domestic carbon production and not overall consumption of carbon drive a particularly unhelpful dynamic.

Our universities are world-class; we can and should lead the world by investing heavily where we have a comparative advantage in science. We can profit from this science and from educating scientists, while demonstrating the overall public good of advances in electricity generation and storage, energy efficiency and, quite probably, the potential of hydrogen. The UK can continue to proselytise globally with some credibility, but distinguished economist Sir Dieter Helm advises that instead of putting all our green eggs in one COP basket – by seeking an elusive top-down agreement among the unwilling – we should seek to advance a bottom-up 'coalition of the willing'. Sir Dieter argues that there are enough global electorates who are sufficiently concerned about the environment to suffer short-term pain to set in motion an alternative to the COP top-down 'all the ducks in a row' approach.[4] Sir Dieter's proposal is for a 'make the polluter pay' carbon border adjustment mechanism (CBAM) for the bigger items in energy-intensive trade. This adjustment will equate a carbon price/tax both domestically and externally; the dynamic is that the coalition would drop the CBAM for those countries that export to them if they follow suit by also imposing a similar domestic carbon tax. The incentive would then be for those exporters to impose their own carbon tax and so enjoy the revenues for themselves. In short, the scheme could align individual incentives rather than attempting to restrain countries, as with COP.

The global case for addressing the climate and environmental emergency is overwhelming. Sadly, despite impressive advances, the world is still a long way off course in the essential goal of reducing emissions. Even as the world reaches new milestones for low-carbon sources – renewables, together with nuclear, provided over 40 per cent of the world's electricity generation in 2024, according to a report by global energy think tank Ember – the truth is that there is not sufficient time left, nor the desire and political will, to dramatically reverse industrialisation.[5] But a green future is possible. We *will* be able to achieve a green transformation and sustainably maintain living standards for rich countries, while raising living standards for poorer countries, but we are not in that green future yet. The hard truth is that there will be some loss of potential GDP; this is a necessary sacrifice to invest in new infrastructure and incentivise the green technological advances needed to reach a sustainable future.

*   *   *

Pretending this can all be done with artificial targets and timescales is counterproductive, both environmentally and politically. Nations going it alone won't convince global partners to follow suit and the restrictions and timescales of the COP process offer only a forlorn hope. 'Clever' schemes for taxing carbon can get bogged down in bureaucracy and lose sight of the actual goal, but making the polluter pay is the right way to make us live within our environmental means. There are important steps that we can follow domestically, particularly those that will reduce the burden of high electricity costs for our industry. Internationally – and thinking internationally is vital if our efforts are to succeed – the UK should be engaging with the EU and all willing countries to be a leading partner and champion for a 'coalition of the willing' and its incentivised spread. Rich countries should be heavily investing in green science, for both profit and for wider sharing for the public good. Investment in renewable projects that do not strain supply chains, credibility and political consent is a good thing. For, unless we succeed in our global mission to tackle climate change, the consequences are likely to be very nasty indeed. The world would have to kiss goodbye to sustainable GDP and to a way of life that has benefitted billions of people and could benefit billions more.

CHAPTER 8

PRODUCTIVITY AND
WHY IT MATTERS

The Nobel Prize-winning economist Paul Krugman once said, 'Productivity isn't everything, but in the long run it is almost everything.' Some basic arithmetic shows he is right. In the long run, the prospects for our standard of living, wages and profits, public services and wealth for redistribution all depend on what happens to productivity and hence the size of the 'national cake'. That is why Martin Wolf, senior economist at the *Financial Times*, says, 'The most important economic problem the UK confronts is long-term stagnation of productivity.'[1]

But what exactly is productivity? Productivity is essentially how much you get out from what you put in: the amount of output from the input used to produce it, although the productivity of the population as whole – including those not providing inputs to production – is also an important determinant of living standards for all citizens. In GDP terms, productivity is the value added to production by the nation's inputs to production.

There are two main ways to measure productivity, though both are problematic. The first, 'total factor productivity', is the most difficult. This attempts to measure the value added by capital and labour combined, but it turns out that measuring capital is very tricky indeed, and even when we get to an acceptable measure of total factor productivity it is only really an 'unexplained residual'. So, we shall instead concentrate on 'labour productivity', remembering that capital investment is vital to increasing this too.

Labour productivity is simply the output per worker, or, alternatively, the output per hour worked. In practice, such a measurement is not so straightforward, and measuring per hour worked or per worker can yield drastically different results. For example, many workers will be part-time, seasonally employed and/or working overtime, and what counts as full-time differs across countries. Comparisons of measures of productivity between sectors and between groups of workers are often distorted by these differences. Women, for example, tend to do more part-time work than men and less highly paid overtime, either because they don't work in particular sectors or have other responsibilities that make it difficult to do so. Surveys are normally used to keep the measurements up to date, but these were disrupted by Covid and their resumption has not been smooth. The Bank of England itself, among others, has warned that the ONS Labour Force Survey in the UK cannot give accurate coverage of developments in the labour market, and this makes it more difficult to estimate how to set monetary policy.

PUBLIC SECTOR PRODUCTIVITY?

Unsurprisingly, measuring public sector productivity is even more problematic. Should we judge the productivity of a prison by how many criminals we can cram into a cell or a school by the size of its classes? Obviously not. The World Bank has offered a definition: 'Public-sector productivity measures the rate with which inputs are converted into desirable outputs in the public sector', while adding the understatement: 'Measuring productivity in the public sector can be tricky.' Yes indeed, largely because public services are not weighted in value by the market, or are only offered in heavily distorted markets such as for nationalised railways, and lower pay for many public service workers such as nurses and care workers does not mean that their productivity is lower. As such, measuring public sector productivity is still very much a 'work in progress'. In the UK, although the percentage of the workforce employed in the public sector has fallen from some 28 per cent to 18 per cent over the last forty years, it is still a very significant chunk of our economy, and so an important part of the productivity picture.[2]

It might be hard to measure, but this does nothing to change the fact that productivity is central to the economy's performance, competitiveness and our living standards. Unfortunately, we haven't fared particularly well in these regards. It is true that many Western nations have seen a noticeable fall in productivity growth since the financial crisis, but the UK has arguably suffered disproportionately. This is partly due to the UK's leading international position in banking and finance and also because of the hit to various high productive industrial sectors as a result of austerity, followed by Brexit, Covid and recent geopolitical conflicts.

In fact, data for the last year or so suggests that the UK's lacklustre productivity performance continues. In truth, much of the issue in the public sector stems from areas such as the NHS, though a big injection of funds by the Labour government over the course of the rest of the decade could see a difference in treatment and outcomes. If more money is spent on scanners, equipment and research and development more generally, we could see some boosts to productivity over the coming years. However, there is always the worry that if targets such as reducing NHS waiting lists are the main priority, Goodhart's Law may apply here too and other areas might suffer as staff concentrate their efforts on meeting the new targets.

POPULATION AND PRODUCTIVITY

The more efficiently a nation's resources are deployed, the higher productivity tends to be. Essentially, more GDP means more can be shared out for wages and profits, and there are more tax revenues for welfare support and pensions, health, education, law and order, defence and myriad other public services. Of course, for any population size, the higher the proportion of people working in activities that count towards GDP, the higher productivity per head will tend to be for that economy. That's why, for richer countries, an ageing population is becoming a break on productivity per head. If productivity per worker increases but the proportion of people in full-time paid work in a population falls, then GDP per head for the whole country could be unchanged or could fall. In the UK, where the percentage of the population over sixty-five years of age is set to rise for the next forty years or more, this is likely to act as a partial brake on living standards, although this has largely been offset by people working until an older age as life expectancy increases.

So far, the number of people in employment in the UK has risen since 2000, even with the birth rate falling below the death rate, largely because more people are working past sixty-five and because of immigration providing a supply of younger workers. In November 2024, the official employment rate was just under 75 per cent; in 2011, it almost dropped below 70 per cent. From that trough the employment rate started to climb at a relatively fast pace, peaking in early 2020. After a significant number of the over-fifties dropped out of employment during and after Covid, the employment rate has since recovered, though it has to be admitted that the official statistics have been somewhat shaky.

The impact of immigrant workers on growth and productivity varies a lot depending on which employment sectors they enter. As most are in healthcare and social work, the impact is less on measured productivity because of the relatively low pay compared to entry into high-skilled, better-paid private sector jobs. Whether high levels of immigration will continue in the future, despite a pledge from politicians to cut the numbers of net migrants, is debatable. But the costs of that migration are much higher for businesses now that there is no longer freedom of movement from the EU, given the UK's exit from the single market. The Home Office recently released research that estimates that there is likely to be some £37 billion of extra costs to businesses over the next ten years. At the same time, getting more UK-based workers to participate in the labour market is becoming more difficult. Although inactivity by UK workers has generally been low against comparable international averages, other countries have been catching up with the UK, and the UK and the US are the only countries where inactivity rates have risen since the end of the pandemic.

Immigration both reduces the dependency ratio – the number of retired people that each worker in effect supports (discussed in the next chapter) – and increases productivity per worker through increased competition and the skills they bring. It is not a 'Ponzi scheme' of ever-increasing immigration, as those poor at maths might claim. In fact, immigration could merely provide a better balance of workers to the retired – but, for this to be the case, of course, various conditions must be met. The economy also needs skills which perhaps should not, for both political and social reasons, come entirely through migration. As part of this, we need far more emphasis on vocational training, not just on higher education and universities. Better and more reliable infrastructure, together with a stable and transparent regulatory regime for fair and open competitive trading in which efficient firms can thrive, will also help drive growth and productivity.

*   *   *

A significant problem for the UK and other advanced economies is that the preconditions for improving productivity are not in place. As we have seen, many advanced economies have experienced a drop in productivity growth since the financial crisis of 2008. Germany, in particular, has faced a severe negative shock from the end of its reliance on cheap energy imports from Russia. Germany's previous rejection of nuclear power and the lack of sustainable alternative options are currently hampering growth in the country and hence having a drag effect on the wider EU.

Worryingly, recent movements towards protectionism and deglobalisation – accelerated under President Trump's second administration but already evident during his first – threaten global growth and productivity, as protectionism moves production away from where there is a comparative advantage to less efficient national industries. The UK has also fared poorly since the Great Financial Crisis: indeed, if UK output per head over the previous fifteen years or so had continued rising by 2 per cent per annum – which was being achieved before the financial crisis – instead of the anaemic growth of just 0.5 per cent, then GDP by 2024 would have been almost 25 per cent higher. Such growth would have made a tremendous difference to where we are now.

WHY HAS THE UK HAD SUCH POOR PRODUCTIVITY GROWTH?

This poor productivity is partly due to the legacy of the decline of the traditional sectors discussed in the first chapter, but also because of North Sea oil and gas depletion and vetoes, a slowdown of technological advances in retail, and, of course, the impact of the financial crisis on the financial sector. However, the problem is still broader than that. In particular, the UK has lagged woefully behind other G7 countries in investing in gross fixed capital formation (GFCF) – that is, in investment in physical assets including buildings, machinery and infrastructure. GFCF is a major determinant of long-term growth, and the UK's GFCF as a percentage of GDP has been consistently low compared to other G7 nations. Physical capital is one thing, but the concept of capital in economics is much wider than just physical capital. It includes the 'human capital' that is also vital to productivity: investment in education and skills, as well as the physical and mental health of the workforce. Also, 'intangible capital' including basic science, research and development, software, IT and now, perhaps very importantly, artificial intelligence. The state has an important role in encouraging capital formation; in many successful countries, the state acts as a co-investor with the private sector, and as a funder, enabler and risk-taker.

In addition to lower capital investment, the impact of austerity from 2010 onwards also saw a substantial shift from the workforce being employed to being self-employed. Again, there are measurement issues, though it is generally agreed that productivity is lower for those who are self-employed compared to when they were in employment.

Openness to trade and access to large markets allows economies of scale and hence higher productivity. This has, of course, been affected by Brexit. Despite the EU–UK Trade and Cooperation Agreement, there are now considerably higher barriers for UK exporters than when we were in the customs union and the single market. These barriers affect not only finished products but also the supply chains that allow international specialisation and hence the efficiency benefits of comparative advantage. Many smaller firms have simply stopped exporting to the EU as a result. Despite a desperate attempt to strike new deals outside the EU, the UK has reduced its trade intensity as a percentage of GDP. This is likely to depress long-term productivity, growth and prosperity. The Labour government recognises that reducing barriers to our nearest giant market, the EU, would be a boost for growth and productivity. Although wary of opposition and calls of 'betrayal' from the popular press, the government is attempting to reset our economic relations with the EU through a review of the Trade and Cooperation Agreement.

CAN WE DEREGULATE OUR WAY TO GROWTH?

The institutions of a country are an important determinant of productivity and hence growth. In addition to investment and technology, growth requires social contentment with the system of justice, the rule of law and clear property rights, a stable macro environment, effective competition policy and avoidance of stifling regulation and red tape. Fair competition is also a boost to the efficiency and innovations that can improve productivity, though the magnitude of its effect is disputed and hard to measure. Despite the Labour government prioritising growth above regulations – with the promise to back 'the builders not the blockers' – on many aspects of regulation, the UK doesn't seem all that restrictive in the first place. According to the OECD, the UK is the second-least regulated developed economy in product regulation globally, and fourth-least for employment legislation. Indeed, the World Bank rates the UK one of the world's best places in terms of ease to do business. Deregulation requires attention to detail, for it covers a wide variety of different industries and contexts, which is why broad-brush 'cut the red tape' campaigns have stalled or, worse, exposed why the regulations were there in the first place.

Following Rachel Reeves's first Mansion House speech as Chancellor on 14 November 2024, Mariana Mazzucato, professor in the economics of innovation and public value at University College London, argued on the BBC's *World at One* that deregulation to encourage investment wasn't really the issue for UK growth, as we are about as regulated as most countries in Europe. She is essentially correct. But regulations should be examined line by line, as some matter more than others. And the truth is that we are regulating more in most areas, not least for diversity and environmental reasons, but also just to keep up with what goes on in other countries.

The UK is similar to the EU on gender and diversity legislation, though the EU is moving faster to legislate in favour of quotas and enforcement. Otherwise, the UK is tougher than the US on environmental issues, food and other areas, largely as part of its attempt to stay more in line with the EU to ensure tariff-free trade continues. And, during the last Conservative government, environmental targets were increasing and have continued to increase at pace with the new Labour government, which will add to industry costs for the short- and medium-term.

Labour's builder-backing deregulation of property development planning regimes could make a difference. If it leads to more housing being built, then that should also increase labour mobility, and labour being able to move more freely to where it is most productive will increase GDP if other things remain constant. Elsewhere in the economy, the Digital Markets, Competition and Consumers Act became law in May 2024. This gives the competition regulator powers to stop the major players from abusing their monopoly positions and/or breaking consumer protection laws. The EU is also pushing hard in this direction and already imposing major fines on digital firms for anti-competitive practices. Labour is moving ahead with reforming workers' rights that will add costs to many businesses operating here. The costs are significant; the government's own impact assessment puts the cost at up to £4.5 billion per annum once fully implemented.

* * *

The finance sector is, of course, of major importance to our economy. It made sense for Rachel Reeves to follow up on the previous government's plans to redirect and reform local authority pension funds, and to encourage pension funds and insurance companies to buy more UK companies' shares as a percentage of their overall portfolio. But these measures will take time to take effect and, in most areas, we have pretty much followed international norms, for example with the Basel rules (a part of the Basel III framework) on capital requirements for the financial sector, which have all been progressively strengthened in response to the financial crisis.

But listing requirements in the UK have probably been too severe. A few weeks after the general election, the Financial Conduct Authority (FCA) announced some relaxation in the rules to bring

Britain further in line with the US and presumably therefore attract more IPOs (when a private company offers its shares to the public for the first time on a stock exchange), as well as potentially increasing the valuation of companies here. New categories of shares are allowed to give more voting control to original owners, even if share ownership is diluted because of an IPO or further fundraising. The regulator admitted that the changes add to the risks but argued that they 'will better reflect the risk appetite the economy needs to achieve growth'. Perhaps this is the aim. It is true that the risk appetite in the UK is below that in the US though it has tended to be higher than that in Europe.

Requirements of briefings and consultations by the board for some company activities and plans have also been reduced, causing some consternation among activist shareholders worried about the diminution in the quality of company governance. In addition, the City must hope that the easing of some regulations – including the lifting of the EU-wide bankers' bonus limit by the Conservatives when in power, which Labour has not reversed – may also increase the UK's attractiveness in the eyes of international talent. Barclays is the first bank reported to have moved from the two-times basic income limit for bonuses to ten-times basic pay. And this comes at a time when the mean pay of FTSE 100 CEOs rose by £500,000 to an average of £5 million last year. Median FTSE CEO pay stands at 120 times that of the median full-time worker: not a great look, but it makes the UK appear pretty competitive internationally.

Given the bad reaction to the 30 October 2024 budget measures by businesses, Rachel Reeves in her Mansion House speech added the requirement for financial regulators to also have growth of the economy as a part of their remit. She seemed to be trying to reassure the City that she is determined to support investment in the

UK through a multitude of means and does not plan on reversing some of the earlier deregulatory measures introduced by the Conservatives. The Labour government is going further still, with such measures as loosening regulations on private equity and hedge funds.

We'll have to wait to see if the new deregulations work, but they are not without potential worries. In 2022 – before the latest deregulatory measures – Sir John Vickers, the architect of banking reforms designed to prevent a repeat of the 2008 financial crash, said of the lessening of financial regulation:

> The competitiveness of the whole economy needs banks that are extremely well-regulated with very strong capital buffers, and properly structured banks … It does not need chiselling away at those protections for the rest of the economy, which could rebound on us very badly … We saw that clearly fifteen years ago, and let us not forget the costs of that, that we're still living with.

As memories of the last financial crisis fade and growth falters, the temptation is always for the government, under pressure from powerful voices in the City of London, to increase risk for short-term gains. This path, however, can all too easily lead to the privatisation of profit, the socialisation of debt and increased inequality.

AI, OR WHY THIS TIME IT'S DIFFERENT

John Maynard Keynes – yes, him again – predicted in his essay 'Economic Possibilities for our Grandchildren' (1930) that technological advancements and increased productivity would end the basic economic problem of wants exceeding means. It would mean, he envisioned, a future where people would be freed from economic constraints to focus on higher moral and intellectual pursuits. Keynes was clearly premature in his prediction, and, sadly, probably overly high-minded in his aspirations for our species. Interestingly, he summarily dismissed the work of Karl Marx, whose predictions he was so determined to thwart. Marx had defined the capitalist epoch by its 'commodification of labour', where the bulk of the population – the 'proletariat' in Marx's words – had no means of sustenance other than by selling their labour power to those who owned the means of production: the capitalists. Now, let's undertake a thought experiment by borrowing an idea from a different thinker entirely. Stephen Hawking's 'singularity' is defined as the point at which artificial intelligence surpasses human intelligence and works on itself in a feedback loop that rapidly reaches the limits of technological possibilities to produce a technology that can do all that a human can do and much more (except perhaps feel emotion, but that's another conversation). Imagine such an option being available to a capitalist: an android that never tires or complains, doesn't ask for wages or argue and is far more productive and cheaper to 'employ' than a human. This might not sound like it's coming anytime soon, but it is certainly the direction in which we are heading.

Futurist Roy Amara's 'law' of technology could well apply here. He says, 'We tend to overestimate the effect of a technology in the short run and underestimate the effect in the long run.' Predictions of impending mass unemployment in the 1970s following the application of microprocessors turned out to be wildly inaccurate. That said, AI is changing things already, in some fields in a hugely transformational way, and the feedback loops into more advanced AI are only likely to accelerate the pace of technology. This isn't only in the production of things: it is optimising supply chains and helping with the performance of routine professional tasks, such as drafting documents and analysing medical diagnosis information.

Yuval Noah Harari, in his work *Nexus: A Brief History of Information Networks from the Stone Age to AI*, argues that information networks have always shaped human societies and perceptions, from religious beliefs and political systems, through to the invention of the printing press, mass media and now digital algorithms. He warns us that the rapid advancements in AI now pose unprecedented existential threats: algorithms that track us and analyse what stimuli we respond to are already reshaping public perceptions and interactions, algorithms that may soon know more about what drives us than we know ourselves. That's before we consider the vast potential for the creation of fake news and images.

As mere economists, we have no expertise in such futurology, but it is plain to see that the economics of a society where a large percentage of the population is simply not needed by employers would look markedly different to our own. The implications for inequality are frightening, unless a socioeconomic system can be found that prevents a widening disparity between mega-rich tech giants and the new 'left behind proletariat'. Marx was surely right that profound changes in the means of production tend also to precipitate profound social and political changes. So far, technology has created more jobs than it has destroyed; in this sense, the Luddites were correct to fear for their own jobs, but they couldn't have been expected to foresee the myriad jobs of the future. How would we have described to people of the nineteenth century the role of cabin crew, digital designers, motorway assistance mechanics, call centre workers, or the jobs created indirectly by the wealth from increased productivity due to modern technological advances, such as travel agencies, financial advisers, fast food servers, car salespersons and so many more?

This time, though, it could be different; rather like horses, we might eventually lose our place altogether in the production process. Perhaps, as Keynes suggested, the age of humans as 'beasts of burden' will also end, and we will then be valued simply for being humans. Would an android stand-up comedian be as funny? Could AI poems be as poignant? An electronic mentor as inspiring? Could android performers fill Wembley Stadium? Would robot carers be as comforting, and would you trust them with your kids?

Stephen Hawking couldn't provide even an approximate date for when his singularity might occur. No human can, and nor can AI. We can't know for certain if any of this will happen as predicted, or even that we will still be around to see it happen. Perhaps, like the Industrial Revolution, it's the way to a better epoch, though it could again invite cruelty for so many along the way. Are we now, by lacking effective international safeguards, caught in an AI whirlpool whisking us to our own destruction? Certainly, whatever the rhetoric about safeguards, the AI international arena currently seems to be focused more on competition than cooperation and caution. Of course, we can't ignore the pace of AI and its implications for productivity and our international competitiveness. Compared to President Trump's 'Stargate Project' – $500 billion investment in AI infrastructure with more pledged already – combined with his 'Genius Act' to support and regulate cryptocurrencies and stablecoins, the UK's own bid to become an AI superpower, though boosted by recent investment pledges by US tech firms, looks rather puny.

However, what we do know is that so far productivity has not gone up in leaps and bounds despite huge advances in technology.

It has certainly had an impact on the speed of communications, in improving connectivity, on health procedures and slowly also on health outcomes, while also creating all sorts of concerns about privacy, intellectual property rights and security, both personal and national. But the main result, no doubt, has been in massively enriching a handful of technology firms and their founders and shareholders. Beyond this, it has done very little for measurable productivity. The substitution of cashiers at supermarket pay points by self-service machines that buyers use independently has passed the job of being a cashier to individuals who are less well equipped to perform these duties and who – if you followed the principle of division of labour, which happens for a very good reason – could be doing something worthwhile, rather than becoming cashiers. It enriched the firms that cut costs but the opportunity costs to individuals are therefore immense. We could all be earning through using our expertise rather than becoming ersatz cashiers or any of the other jobs which firms now pass on to us. Perhaps those costs that are cut will then filter down to lower prices – but usually they just mean more shareholder dividends, many to overseas holders of shares.

WAITING FOR THE SINGULARITY

AI could change everything, though capitalism has proven extremely resilient through constant transformation and adaptation. We will defer to futurologists and creators of science-fiction when it comes to predicting the nature of a new epoch that could still be decades away, but we recognise that it could be transformational, perhaps for the worse, if we fail to implement sufficient regulations. Certainly, at the time of writing there is an AI race among global powers rather than a spirit of containment. In the meantime, however, there are more immediate and pressing concerns for economists and politicians to worry about. As we have seen, even with all the technological advances in IT over recent decades, there has not been any AI revolution in productivity; it is still rather the case, as quipped by Nobel Laureate Robert Solow, that 'you can see the computer age everywhere but in the productivity statistics'.

It is also obvious that unless we keep up with competitors and boost our productivity then there will be no hope of meeting Labour's ambition to have the highest sustained growth in the G7. Peter Kyle, Labour's former Secretary of State for Science, Innovation and Technology, acknowledges that this is an imperative in his department's rather scattergun 'AI Opportunities Action Plan' of January 2025. The plan states, 'It is hard to imagine how we will meet the ambition for highest sustained growth in the G7 – and the countless quality-of-life benefits that flow from that – without embracing the opportunities of AI.'

Politicians and others are dangling the promise of AI in front of the electorate as the facilitator of a 'reimagining' of the public sector. In this promise, AI has the potential to streamline bureaucracy, improve NHS efficiency and perform new services such as the intelligent matching of some of the nine million or so 'economically inactive' citizens with more productive roles. Some of the rhetoric about AI today is reminiscent of Harold Wilson's 'White heat of technology' speech from back in 1963. It is true that technology was crucial in driving the change in global supply chains that have transformed the world economy, but it happened over decades rather than overnight. Similarly, in the 1950s the application of mainframe computers to banking was thought to be a threat to thousands of banking jobs. That didn't happen: in fact, the workforce in banking and finance expanded considerably, largely because the technology made possible so many new financial services. The technology, that is, *transformed* jobs rather than reducing them. This time, of course, it may indeed be different, but an overall loss of jobs in either the private or public sector anytime soon is not a foregone conclusion.

PAIN BEFORE GAIN

Since the Industrial Revolution, many skills have been replaced by new technologies. The handloom weavers in the Industrial Revolution lost their livelihoods to mechanised weaving technologies, such as Edmund Cartwright's power loom, invented in 1785. The internal combustion engine destroyed so many jobs for grooms and blacksmiths maintaining horses used for transport. Robots have replaced many assembly line workers. Digital payment systems finished off mechanical cash register producers. Today, AI is increasingly used even for medical diagnosis. The list of potential applications keeps growing rapidly. This will mean job losses in many areas; as Milton Friedman liked to emphasise, capitalism is a system driven by both profit and loss. Joseph Schumpeter famously used the phrase 'gales of creative destruction' to describe how, in free markets, new giant firms come along to drive even the most established businesses into administration.

In capitalism there are always losers as well as winners; it's the Darwinian process at the heart of the system's wealth-creating power. Though, as Professor Mariana Mazzucato points out, the deep science used by modern technological giants in the private sector has often relied on state-sponsored science. For example, the technologies commercialised in smartphones – such as GPS, touchscreens and voice recognition – were all funded and developed by public sector institutions. Often, government bears the risk in the development of science and tech before it is commercially investible. Any sound industrial strategy should have a rigorous assessment of the risks that should be borne by government and the risks it should leave to individuals and businesses. What is likely to be different about AI is the pace of this process. It has the potential to rapidly precipitate a transformation that may take our species to a new epoch.

As no one can accurately predict how many jobs will be displaced by AI, the estimates, even those concerned solely with the UK, vary widely. The projections range from an 'apocalypse' for the number of jobs humans are left to do to an increase in jobs as new fields of activity are made possible. The Institute for Public Policy Research poses several scenarios. The first is that there is no reduction in the number of jobs, if the right policies are enacted, and a strong boost of 4 per cent annual growth in GDP. At the other end of the scale, they describe a whopping eight million jobs at risk in a process of 'full displacement' without government intervention. The Tony Blair Institute suggests only between one million and three million private sector jobs displaced by 2050, which would be quite modest compared to the UK's average annual job losses of 450,000 over the past decade. As we have emphasised, despite much hyperbole in either direction, all such projections are highly speculative. What we can't deny is that we are already seeing the impact of AI on thousands of jobs and that this time the change in technology might be transformative.

But the benefit will only come if there is proper dissemination of AI knowledge. What we are instead seeing is that most benefits coming from AI are confined to big firms. In the majority of cases, these firms still have a long way to go in ensuring that all staff partake in this digital transformation and enhance productivity in a substantive and sustainable way. A recent Eurostat survey shows that only 12 per cent of smaller firms use at least one of the AI tools available, while 40 per cent of larger firms have adopted these, potentially making it harder for smaller firms to compete.[3] Competition, of course, is one of the main ways in which productivity improvements across the economy are brought about.

THE FUTURE OF UK AI

The launch of China's DeepSeek not only shows that AI can be much cheaper than expected, but also that the US AI giants – such as Microsoft, Google, Apple, Meta, IBM and Nvidia – are not going to have things all their own way. In fact, if we can muster enough funding, then, potentially at least, Britain is well placed to do well from the AI race. We are the third largest AI market in the world. Our science base is very strong, with world-class universities in AI including Cambridge, Oxford, Imperial College London and University College London. We are home to pioneering AI firms like Google DeepMind, ARM and Wayve (though these are all very London-centric). We have a large public sector with which to procure, demonstrate and house AI infrastructure. Of course, we also need to attract the world's top talent in AI, and international competition for top talent is fierce (and this task has been significantly complicated by Brexit). We need to design our immigration system to attract, rather than deter, graduates from overseas universities producing the world's top AI talent. We need to find the funding for AI research and development and to train new talent to better supply the industry with the leading personnel it will need. Of course, that all takes money, and the UK alone is not going to be able to match the resources or the capabilities of the US and China. So, given the poor business ratings of UK capabilities in many high-tech and AI areas, working with other countries is going to be a necessity.

DO WE TRUST AI?

While we now use technology with largely reckless abandon for all manner of social purposes, trust in institutions and players in the markets has dropped. A Digital Trust Index produced by Thales assessed how much trust there was over the handling of personal data based on a 2025 survey of 14,000 consumers in fourteen countries. It found that trust was low in most sectors:

- News and media organisations: 3 per cent.
- Supply and logistic organisations: 4 per cent.
- Social media: 4 per cent.
- Entertainment: 5 per cent.
- Retail: 5 per cent.
- Transport: 6 per cent.
- Hospitality: 7 per cent.

There was some hope for the banking sector, with trust at 44 per cent – one assumes because the sector benefitted from the belief that higher regulation improves security. And, for the public sector with government organisations, trust was at 41 per cent.

For all industries, demonstrating how data is protected from cyberattacks is key. Yet the Department for Science, Innovation and Technology's Cyber Security Breaches Survey showed that though firms' highest risk factor seemed to be cybersecurity, the percentage of boards having a specialist cybersecurity expert on them appears to have fallen from 38 per cent in 2021 to 27 per cent in 2025. Greater transparency for customers on what is done with their data appears to be key.

*   *   *

In terms of this technological revolution, the UK spent a while playing catch-up but is now performing relatively poorly again in productivity terms, and investment will be vital to turn this around. Currently, the IFS points out that the OBR has consistently been too optimistic in its projections for productivity growth. And, as economist Paul Johnson notes, if the OBR cuts its current forecasts for productivity, even bringing them halfway to most recent experience, then a big fiscal gap opens – and that was before Trump's onslaught on the global economy.

CHAPTER 9

IMMIGRATION: WHY CAN'T WE GET IT RIGHT?

The ironic thing about right-wing populist politicians who complain about 'cancel culture' and insist they are prevented from having an 'honest debate about immigration' is that they clearly feel free to talk about it ad nauseum, and usually in a very distorted way. As do much of our press who seem only too keen to feed xenophobic and racist myths, with some scattered compassionate stories to show that they aren't really exploiting racism after all. Another common myth is that widespread opposition to immigration only began with or was 'provoked' by 'open door' immigration under Tony Blair's Labour government, even though the proponents of that view also frequently praise Enoch Powell's infamous 'Rivers of Blood' speech, which preceded Blair's premiership by some thirty years. Going back still further, in response to the migrants from the countries Britain had made part of its empire, the first immigration controls were introduced by James Balfour in 1905. Two years earlier, a Royal Commission on 'Alien Immigration' voiced a fear of newcomers who live 'according to their traditions, usages and customs' and who would be 'grafted on to the English stock'. In short, these ongoing debates aren't a new phenomenon, despite how heated they have become in the current climate.

In the 1980s and '90s, when asked if there is 'too much immigration', around 70 to 80 per cent of the public said 'yes'. This century, it's been nearer a 50/50 split at times, but, of course, it makes a big difference how the question is asked. If asked specifics such as, 'Should we have fewer immigrants for nursing, social care, doctors, and as students?' then the public seem much more favourable towards new arrivals. The public also seem more concerned with continuing flows than with the immigrants already here: it was those areas with the lowest percentages of immigrants that were most likely to have voted for Brexit. Fluctuations generally correlated with the level and nature of media coverage rather than with the actual numbers of immigrants; public attitudes towards immigration have in fact tended to soften this century.

Total immigration numbers have had an exceptionally high peak since 2022, though the numbers seem to be subject to substantial revisions and may well have been distorted by the problems of measuring movements post-Brexit and post-Covid; by entrants from Hong Kong and Ukraine due to exceptional circumstances in both cases; and by a big influx of international students. That said, 2023 saw net migration numbers reach 904,000 – the highest in British history, driven by the 'catch-up' from Covid, the war in Ukraine and, of course, Brexit. Although, if spread out over the longer term, it stayed around the net amount of 250,000 and is now forecast to fall back quite sharply to around that level, partly because higher immigration will later be followed by a higher number of immigrants returning to their home countries.

Most notably, post-Brexit, with the ending of freedom of movement from the EU and a 'level playing field' for non-EU migrants, we have seen a dramatic change in the composition of immigrants. As we saw earlier, while EU immigration has turned net negative since we left the EU, non-EU immigration has increased greatly. In terms of the 'racial hierarchy' of preferences of the UK public, at the preferred end of the scale are white, English speakers from European and Christian countries, while the least preferred are non-white migrants from non-European or Muslim countries.[1] In the past, a majority of migrants who came via both work and study visa routes have seen their visas expire and thus were not expected to have stayed in the UK permanently. For non-EU migration, the distances from their homeland may well mean this 'international commuting' is harder, and so, again, Brexit may have achieved the opposite of what many Leave voters hoped, as long-run net migration depends not just on immigration but also on how long migrants remain in the UK. The difference between EU and non-EU wages is also probably a stronger staying factor. These rather predictable changes in the volume and specifics of immigration patterns since Brexit do seem to confirm the claim that many Leave voters simply 'didn't know what they were voting for'.

The majority of this non-EU immigration is for work or study. And, as said, the public seem less bothered about students, which could be fortunate as our universities rely so heavily on foreign students for both money and talent. The previous Conservative government had already made it harder for international students by mostly banning the bringing of relatives and reducing the number of courses eligible to enrol foreign students. So, with the increase in work-related immigration accounting for almost half of the growth in non-EU immigration, and if we exclude students, visitors and refugees, then the percentage of visas for work is about four-fifths of legal immigration.[2] To meet their pledges to reduce even legal immigration, the government is already tightening the criteria regarding immigration for work, which is likely to conflict with both the 'growth, growth, growth' ethos and the public debt ratio reduction agenda of the Labour government.

Of course, there is so much public confusion and misinformation about immigration: the numbers of arrivals, the categories of legal immigrants and the distinctions between legal, illegal and refugees. There is also ignorance regarding the rigorous research on actual impacts, as well as myths around crime and a plethora of damaging 'replacement' conspiracies. Such a context is clearly fertile ground for politicians, if so minded, to exploit xenophobia and anti-immigrant myths. It often seems that the weaker one's evidence base, the stronger one's opinion. The rhetoric has certainly changed through the decades, however. Explicit racism was a dark hallmark of Powell's 'Rivers of Blood' speech but is no longer publicly acceptable – except on parts of social media – and so populist politicians have shown their supporters how to use 'slippery racism'. This includes misleading sweeping statements about immigrants stealing jobs, lowering wages and causing unemployment, or, contradictorily, 'only coming here to claim benefits'.

With such widespread debate and media coverage, immigration is certainly a social and political issue, but surprisingly for non-economists (if they deign to listen to the experts at all), it is considerably less of an economic issue. With so much press coverage of small boats and of vile crimes by non-whites leading to vilification on social media and the fear held by many of losing one's cultural heritage, it is not surprising that immigration is a social and political issue. Indeed, so strongly do some people feel about immigration that when confronted with the evidence on economic impacts they become angry rather than reassured. Whether their fears are rational or irrational, in a democracy politicians ignore the electorate at their peril. That said, responsible politicians do not stoke division. Edward Heath, as leader of the Conservative Party, threw Powell out of his shadow Cabinet for doing just that. Today, in contrast, we have politicians even within traditional centrist parties vying for the anti-immigrant populist vote.

THE ECONOMIC IMPACTS OF IMMIGRATION

As this book is about economics, we'll put aside the sociopolitical issues and consider immigration's economic impacts, which turn out to be mostly rather modest. Immigration certainly improves the lot of the legal immigrants who overwhelmingly come here to work for a better life, but, of course, there are instances of workers being displaced by immigrant workers (though other factors, like buying imports, can do the same). There is also some evidence of lowering wages, particularly for other recent immigrants, and immigration no doubt has consequences for administered wages such as in health and social care. But overall, the unemployment rate and wages have been, to the best of available evidence, very little affected by immigration. There have been studies that found immigration has a 'significant' impact in lowering the wages of the lowest paid. This greatly excited much of the press and some politicians, so much so that the lead author of the most definitive report, Sir Stephen Nickell, felt obliged to explain that the word 'significant' in this context was merely a technical term, as the actual effect was 'infinitesimal'.[3]

Of course, no political party is in favour of illegal immigration. It leads to exploitation of illegal workers, undermines the legal minimum wage and has security risks. It is also politically damaging. Being seen to be 'cracking down' on illegal immigration – even though the reality of doing so is much harder than is commonly supposed – is a way of reducing public fears about immigration.

Unfortunately, despite seemingly simple remedies from politicians, only the ill-informed and the gullible believe there are easy solutions (the clue is largely in the name 'illegal'). All this has nevertheless resulted in tougher anti-immigration measures in the UK and elsewhere, such as the EU and the US.

But even legal immigration is widely perceived to be a burden rather than a blessing. And it is easy to point to categories of immigrants – such as non-working dependents and the lowest paid – who are likely to be a net fiscal cost. But the weight of research, however, suggests that the immigration we saw while still part of the EU boosted the UK's fiscal coffers and productivity. That said, there is room for reasonable people to disagree about research methodology and there is no single 'correct' estimate of migrants' fiscal impact.

Different studies make different assumptions about the net contributions of immigrants. Not everyone will agree on what are the correct assumptions to make: should this be a snapshot in time or a longer-term assessment throughout a whole life? Do we count the children of immigrants who will only be working later in life? But to put all this in context, the impeccably impartial Oxford Migration Observatory notes that 'OBR forecasts have generally estimated that higher net migration leads to lower deficits and debt, because migrants tend to be of working age'.[4] Before we get too excited about that, it also points out that 'regardless of the differences in methods, studies typically find that the fiscal impacts of migration represent less than 1 per cent of GDP'. That said, even 1 per cent is around £25 billion, so on occasion immigration may help the Treasury meet its own fiscal rules. To the extent that migrants can be recruited to do lower-paid jobs in our public services, such as healthcare, there is no doubt an indirect fiscal saving because of this lower cost of provision, even though it doesn't show up as a saving on the accounts.

Opponents of immigration often ironically accuse economists of not understanding economics. Armed with a rudimentary grasp of 'demand and supply', they assert that it's obvious that an increase in the number of workers must lower wages. However, immigration is not a straightforward supply and demand matter. Although large labour movements are likely to cause adjustment spikes, there is nothing in economic theory that says that immigration must lower wages. In truth, supply and demand (but particularly supply) is far more complicated and conditional than non-economists think and even many courses in economics teach. The conditions required to meaningfully draw a supply curve are technical, stringent and usually put millions of demand and supply relationships together in simultaneous interaction, as in a real economy. This means the theoretical possibilities for outcomes become endless and are quite often counterintuitive. Even more rudimentary economics tells us that if immigration did prevent money wages from rising then it might also keep down prices and so prevent real wages being eroded by inflation. Moreover, immigration increases not only the *supply of* labour but also the *demand for* labour when immigrants spend their wages.

*   *   *

There are two broad economic perspectives that people tend to take towards immigration. Some view the economy as a 'zero sum game', where one person's gain can only come from another's loss. For them, there is a fixed 'national cake': the more people who have access to the cake, the thinner the slices must be for everyone else.

Others, and this includes economists, see the economy as an engine that needs fuel. Immigration is part of that fuel, and so when the engine goes faster it can drive everyone along that bit faster. Now, it should be obvious that a bigger population doesn't necessarily mean lower living standards, as generally a bigger population just means a bigger economy, and there are no vacancy signs on desert islands announcing, 'High wages paid – we just can't get the staff!'

Although immigration usually leads to an increase in GDP, it doesn't necessarily lead to a higher GDP per head. In fact, reports for Parliament based on long-term data do not find significant impacts on GDP per head from immigration. More recently, the rate of increase in real GDP per head has slowed and the population has increased at a faster rate than the volume of output produced. So, for example, in the second quarter (April to June) of 2024, real GDP per head was 0.6 per cent below its pre-pandemic level, while total real GDP was 2.9 per cent above its pre-pandemic levels. It must be said that detecting the impact of immigration on GDP per head is complex; there are, no doubt, dynamic effects that cannot be captured. For example, immigration may well punch above its weight in the labour market, because it tends to go to where there is a demand for labour and as the precise skills mix required is not always available locally. This helps prevents the labour shortages that can slow economic growth. There is also good reason to suppose that immigration can improve the all-important productivity of an economy. In short, merely comparing immigration levels with changes in GDP per head doesn't tell us what GDP per head would have been if there hadn't been that level of immigration. That is, it lacks a strong counterfactual, but there are reasons to suppose GDP per head might have been considerably lower without the increase in immigration.

IS BRITAIN FULL?

It is often claimed that there is no room for more people in Britain. And indeed, the ONS reports that the UK population is projected to grow by almost five million over the next decade, reaching 72.5 million by mid-2032. The driver of this growth is certainly migration, as the 'natural' change in the population – the difference between births and deaths – is projected to be around zero. Given such remarkable statistics, it's understandable that many people may think Britain is 'full', particularly as the population tends to crowd together. A third of the UK population lives within 100 kilometres of London and over half live within a narrow metropolitan population 'snake' – a highly concentrated area of urbanised residential, economic, cultural and educational hubs – which stretches from around London to the Midlands. With over four-fifths of us living in cities, the UK is one of the most urbanised countries in the world. Though we have an overall population density of about 277 people per square kilometre, this is less than Japan with some 333 people per square kilometre, Belgium with 376, the Netherlands with some 425 and far less than Singapore with a whopping 8387 people per square kilometre. In a list of the 194 universally recognised countries in the world, the UK is in the early thirties – in the top quartile, but far from top tenth. And, given that we crowd together in cities, less than ten per cent of the UK's land is urbanised, as used for residential, commercial, industrial and other built-up purposes.[5]

SERVICES AND INFRASTRUCTURE

Rumours about immigrants getting preferential treatment over British citizens in the provision of services and housing are common in the press and on social media. While there are some special arrangements for refugees and detained illegal immigrants, it is because they have no access to the NHS in the normal way of British citizens. *Quelle surprise!* Preferential treatment tales about immigrants invariably turn out to be a myth. One common version of the myth is that local authorities prioritise social housing for immigrants. In short, they don't. There is no prioritisation according to applicants' nationality or immigration status, though it might look like that sometimes: the criteria for allocating social housing vary across local authorities but, naturally, a higher risk of homelessness or pressing welfare needs can move applicants further up the queue. Some migrants are bound to have characteristics that would give them a higher priority, but overall, the 2021 Census of England showed that migrants were under-represented among social renters. Much is made of immigrants making it harder for British citizens to buy houses, but the foreign-born are less likely to be homeowners, and occupancy of rented accommodation is at a higher density. The research is inconclusive, but best estimates are that a 1 per cent increase in the population increases house prices by about 1 per cent. To put that in context, from 2000 to 2023, the UK population increased by about 16 per cent, while the average house price increased by 265 per cent.

It is certainly true that if public services and infrastructure are not maintained and expanded then the 'national cake' argument might begin to apply. But there is no intrinsic reason why infrastructure should have more of a problem adjusting to population growth through natural increase than it would adjusting to moderate immigration. As we have seen, immigration largely pays its own way fiscally, so the issue has more to do with moving additional funds to areas of population growth and making policy choices to pay for services and infrastructure. Indeed, immigration, if it raises productivity and/or growth and significantly reduces the ratio of national debt to GDP, might make it easier to find the money.

But didn't we say the fiscal contribution of immigration is modest? Yes, the absolute contribution of immigration to the public finances is relatively small, but here it is the ratio of debt to GDP that matters. If I owe £1,000 and I earn just £10,000, that is a pretty big problem, but its less of an issue if I earn £100,000. The point is that even if the amount of fiscal contribution is relatively small, a boost in the working population can increase GDP and hence cut the debt-to-GDP ratio. Without immigration, a declining population can make it harder to reduce the debt ratio, as there will still need to be spending on social services, such as care for the elderly, the NHS and, of course, pensions. Immigrants are also overrepresented in the provision of precious public services; this is an area where availability of immigrant labour can keep down the cost to taxpayers while also hopefully raising productivity.

WHY DO WE NEED MORE IMMIGRANTS?

The percentage of the population of working age is projected to rise from about 64 per cent in mid-2022 to just over 65 per cent in mid-2032, before falling again to just over 64.2 per cent in mid-2042. That doesn't seem at all alarming, but the change in the composition of the non-working population is something of an age time bomb. By mid-2032, people of pension age are projected to account for a higher proportion of the population than children. Children are expensive in terms of education and welfare, but on average the elderly cost the state more per person because of their healthcare, pension and social care requirements. This shift in the population towards an ageing society is a significant challenge for public finances in many rich countries. Net migration is projected to be the only source of population growth in the UK over the next twenty-five years, and although the total dependency ratio of non-working age to working population is kept down by the fall in the birth rate, the age dependency ratio – the ratio of people of pension age to the working population – will rise over the next forty years and more. By 2050, it is projected that one in four people in the UK will be aged sixty-five years and over, a sharp increase from almost one in five in 2018. That could potentially cause difficult tax increases for those who are working, though predicting the effects is far from straightforward. It depends on such things as who is and isn't working, life expectancy, the nature of work and contributions and on the volume and nature of immigration.

For a start, projections are not the same thing as forecasts and the assumptions based on current trends can change significantly over time. In particular, people are working until later in life and so continuing to contribute economically for longer than previous cohorts. To allow for this, the ONS proposed the 'Active Dependency Ratio' (ADR), which calculates the size of the economically inactive population against the size of the economically active population. It turns out the ADR is roughly twice that of the so-called Old Age Dependency Ratio. This is because it includes people of working age who are economically inactive and people of pensionable age who are economically active; the number of people of working age who are economically inactive, it turns out, is far larger than the number of economically active people of pensionable age. The years between 1992 and 2017 saw the ADR improve despite the population becoming older, because many were working past sixty-five, more women were participating in the labour force, particularly at older ages and on a part-time basis, and closer to our point here:

there was high immigration. The problem is that although the ADR is projected to increase at a slower rate than the Old Age Dependency Ratio, it is also projected to increase significantly over the next forty years.

The point is that immigration can act to slow the rate of increase in the ADR. It is sometimes claimed that this is akin to a 'Ponzi scheme' as immigrants will also age. It isn't. Not only will many immigrants leave again and so not retire here, but the maths is simply wrong. For example, the age distribution is heavily affected by 'baby boomers' from a surge in births after the Second World War and the long-term decline in the birth rate, so immigration could just smooth the sides of the population pyramid. The ONS projects that, similar to the Old Age Dependency Ratio, after some initial fluctuation, over the next forty years or so, the projected ADR will increase twice as quickly under zero immigration than under high migration. Under the high migration scenario, the ratio would reach around 627 by 2067, while under zero migration it would be 710.

In short, immigration can offset the possible economic impacts of an ageing population, and the higher the migration, the greater the effect. As intimated, there are many uncertainties, and the ratio may well increase beyond 2067, but then forty years is rather longer than most policy horizons as so much can change in the economy in the interim. And as Kevin Daly of Goldman Sachs points out, the key question for the incumbent population is whether employment falls on a one-for-one basis with changes in the working-age dependency ratio. Given people are working until later in life as life expectancy increases, Daly rightly says, 'While raising official retirement ages can help address the fiscal challenges of government pensions in an era of growing life expectancy, it doesn't seem to be an essential requirement for people to extend their working lives.'

A general belief is that positive net immigration can stave off some of the decline in the short to medium term, particularly if immigrants over time adopt the fertility rate of the host nation. This has given rise to nativists who believe that larger families should be actively encouraged, with incentives imitating the tax and other direct subsidies that exist elsewhere. There is no proof though that such incentives work over the long term; even places with cheap and abundant childcare and extended parental leave seem to have seen little impact on fertility rates. Finland, for example, has one of the lowest fertility rates in Europe despite an environment that appears to be one of the most conducive to guaranteeing more children per family.

THE OBR'S FISCAL ESTIMATES

As we have seen, there is more than enough complexity in the projected demographics alone, but the complexities multiply when we try to combine them with the likely economic outcomes. Uncertainties include changes in the pension age; the level of participation in paid employment of the population; trends in the volume of net migration; the types of immigrants; productivity and life expectancy; fertility rates; provision and use of public services; taxes and public spending; interest rates on national debt, visa and health insurance fees; changes in growth; eligibility for welfare support and much more. As most immigrants tend to be of working age, it is not surprising that immigration has short-term fiscal benefits. Long-term estimates over the lifespan of an immigrant are harder to estimate.

Luckily, we have the OBR to try to sort through all the variables and arrive at the most reliable estimates possible. The OBR estimates that a migrant arriving at age twenty-five and earning the UK average salary has a more positive lifetime fiscal contribution than a UK-born worker on the same salary, but low-wage workers had a negative lifetime fiscal impact. Again, the possibility of the indirect fiscal benefits of lower-wage immigrant workers contributing considerably more value than their wages suggest isn't considered, as the counterfactual is so problematic. As so often, a cost benefit analysis on the indirect fiscal and wider economic contribution of lower-paid public sector workers would be useful.

With the current immigration regime, the OBR forecasts that higher net migration leads to lower deficits and debt. At around 350,000 and adjusting for likely consequent increases in government spending, the forecast is a net reduction in borrowing of £13.1 billion, with debt 2.5 per cent of GDP lower by 2028. In the longer term, with net migration at 245,000, the OBR projects that higher net migration would reduce debt as a share of GDP by 30 per cent by 2072/73. This is all welcome for the Exchequer, but none of these economic benefits are sufficient to reverse the UK's fiscal direction and prevent debt from rising from around 100 to 300 per cent of GDP over the next fifty years. And, longer term, many immigrants will likely stay in the country and retire, so the OBR concluded that higher migration reduces the fiscal challenges of an ageing population *over a period* rather than resolving them permanently. That said, half a century of reducing the debt-to-GDP ratio will be a tempting economic prospect for many governments, and money spent wisely now is worth more later. It's no mean feat, however, to convince the burgeoning Reform demographic that that their pensions, elder care and health provision depend rather a lot on immigrants.

*　*　*

There aren't really any economic reasons for cracking down on the levels of legal immigration currently expected. As we have seen, immigration largely pays for itself while significantly reducing the debt ratio. It alleviates the rise in the dependency ratio, particularly along a longer policy horizon. It brings entrepreneurial vigour and improves productivity, while helping control inflation by increasing the flexibility of labour supply, thereby allowing lower interest rates. It reduces bottlenecks in the labour market and provides skills that are in short supply, such as in housing and construction, vital to investment for labour mobility and fixed capital formation. It ensures the provision of public services is possible at a lower cost, and although it doesn't seem to directly raise GDP per head much, there are good reasons to believe that GDP could be significantly lower without it.

In short, the 'problem of immigration' is sociopolitical rather than economic. Though immigration is expected to fall by itself from its post-Covid spike, the government will no doubt take credit – even more so if it can 'stop the boats', arrivals of which account for a fairly small percentage of immigration (despite the tabloid hysteria). It will say it has immigration under control, even though legal immigration is already heavily controlled by, in effect, a points system and identification of labour shortage. However, even net immigration at 250,000 per year won't be enough to prevent the projected long-term rise in the ratio of government debt to GDP and the consequent fiscal pressures. It would, however, mitigate that rise and bring other economic benefits that will help taxpayers and growth.

Currently, the main parties mostly parrot the press stance that immigration is a major and pressing problem. This reinforces much of public opinion that immigration is an unalloyed bad thing and is consistently too high. It is perhaps understandable that politicians are fearful of losing votes to populist sentiments, but vying with each other to crack down on immigration simply reinforces such populist beliefs. If you see immigration as the number one problem, then why not vote for the party that says it is the number one problem? As progressive parties will never be as anti-immigrant as their main opposition parties – and the Conservatives and Reform could feasibly tire of splitting their vote and come together in coalition – Labour badly needs to recognise the economic benefits of immigration. After all, immigration will fuel its growth agenda and improve public services. In the face of ill-informed anti-immigrant populism, choosing another strategy seems to be reasonable and certainly more moral.

Despite some mischievous claims by certain politicians, no one wants illegal immigration. The public very much want to feel reassured that their borders are being controlled, but progressive parties could do much more to counter the myths and to explain the benefits of legal immigration. That includes countering the non-economic myths too, such as immigrants being responsible for a record violent crime rate; in fact, the crime rate has more than halved since its peak in 1995, two years before Tony Blair was elected. The evidence is that areas of higher immigration have higher tolerance of immigration than areas of lower immigration and that public opinion is strongly influenced by press coverage. Policies that actively promote personal interactions with people from different backgrounds, as happens casually every day across London, highlight the social benefits of legal immigration, thus making the topic less toxic. This would allow a more enlightened government political access to the economic benefits of visas and immigration.

CHAPTER 10

INEQUALITY MATTERS

Inequality is an issue that so often lies at the heart of political discourse. It can take different forms, including social, physical and, our focus here, economic. Economic inequality can itself be measured in several different ways. Economists, along with other social scientists, record and attempt to analyse inequality by income, wealth, gender, ethnicity, region, disability; they do so nationally, internationally, intra- and intergenerationally.

Some financial inequality is a good thing, particularly if it provides incentives that spur people into being productive and innovative. A general rise in living standards can bring more inequality: no economist would want to undo the Industrial Revolution, for example, though it hugely increased inequality. A major problem, of course, is that not everyone can access opportunities to work that improve their financial position. Moreover, there is a huge weight of evidence that suggests high levels of inequality are personally and socially corrosive and can lead to more extremes in politics. When the public thinks that inequalities are large and, crucially, unfair, this undermines their faith in political and economic systems as a whole, creating an opportunity which populists with hidden agendas can exploit.

INCOME INEQUALITY

The most vivid picture of income inequality is still provided by the 'Pen's Parade' concept from 1971. Jan Pen, a Dutch economist, envisaged a parade of people in the UK organised so their income is proportional to their height. Those of average income are of average height, those of half the average income half the average height and so on. The marchers are arranged in order of income, with the lowest incomes at the front and the highest at the back, and the whole parade passes the observer, who is of average height, in an hour. What the observer sees is mostly a parade of tiny people with some unbelievably tall giants at the very end. The first marchers can't be seen at all: they include the owners of loss-making businesses who are in effect walking beneath the ground. Soon people appear above the ground, but they are tiny, and for the next five minutes the observer sees people who are only inches high. These are people with irregular work, along with a few retirees. After ten minutes of watching, the start of the full-time labour force appears. They are about half-average height, and there are a lot of them. About halfway through the parade the height is still only about five feet. It takes some forty-five minutes of parading before the marchers are the same height as the observer. Even at that point, the height of the marchers is only increasing slowly. The final six minutes is where things begin to go sky high, and higher. The people with earnings in the top 10 per cent begin to pass: professionals such as senior civil servants, doctors and lawyers some twenty feet tall. Then, moments later, corporate executives, bankers and stockbrokers at fifty feet tall, then a hundred feet then 500 feet. The final few seconds are completely bizarre:

The scene is dominated by colossal figures: people like tower flats.

Most of them prove to be businessmen, managers of large firms and holders of many directorships and also film stars and a few members of the Royal Family. The rear of the parade is brought up by a few participants who are measured in miles. Indeed, they are figures whose height we cannot even estimate: their heads disappear into the clouds and probably they themselves do not even know how tall they are.

Of course, it would be misleading to think of the top incomes as being an entirely stable group of individuals across time, but a clear majority of those who find themselves in the top 1 per cent can expect to remain there for several years, while it's a relatively narrow group of individuals who can ever expect to find themselves within the top percentile. And of course, Pen's Parade of 1971 is a long time ago: the share of income going to the top 1 per cent has increased considerably since then.

The IFS has highlighted how income inequality has risen over time: in 1961, the top 1 per cent of the population had a 3.66 per cent share of household income (net of taxes and benefits). By 2020, that share had more than doubled to 7.78 per cent, and that's only on recorded income. In fact, since 1980, the share of income earned by the top 1 per cent in the UK generally rose to almost 15 per cent in 2007, before the financial crisis. Among other factors, such as the technological displacement of industrial sectors and globalisation, the rise of financial services and renumeration in the City of London has also been a major factor in increasing income inequality. And our strong financial sector may well have had a 'Dutch Disease' effect – the phenomenon where revenue from a new natural resource or foreign currency leads to the crowding out of other sectors – by raising the foreign exchange rate above what it would otherwise be, for example, and so reducing our general international competitiveness and by absorbing much of our brightest talent. Of course, that doesn't mean that the City of London isn't important for our overall economy.

The 1980s saw a sharp rise in income inequality, which has largely not been reversed. In 2021/22, 37 per cent of UK total disposable household income went to the 20 per cent of people with the highest household incomes, compared to just 8 per cent of disposable household income that went to the lowest 20 per cent of people. London had the highest Gross Disposable Household Income (GDHI) per head in 2022 where, on average, each person had £32,330 available to spend or save, which compared with the UK average of £22,789, while the north-east had the lowest, at £18,388. At the more local level, Westminster was the area with the highest GDHI per head at £69,058, over three times the UK average, and Leicester had the lowest GDHI per head at only £15,075. And all this is before we note how difficult it is to get a complete picture of top incomes, as it is almost impossible to obtain accurate data on tax-evading incomes. For example, back-of-the-envelope calculations, based on studies that used leaked data such as the Panama Papers from 2016, suggests that around 8 per cent of the income going to the UK's top one per cent may be in undeclared, and hence unrecorded, offshore tax-haven holdings.[1] Many substantial gifts and inheritances also go unrecorded. All that said, the most striking increase in economic inequality over the last thirty-five years has been in wealth inequality.

WEALTH INEQUALITY

Not surprisingly, wealth inequality is much greater than income inequality. This is partly explained by age, as wealth tends to accumulate over a lifetime, peaking in the early sixties age group. Housing wealth in particular is increasingly concentrated among older age groups; research published by the IFS reported that 36 per cent of those born in the 1980s were homeowners by age 30, compared to 55 per cent of those born in the 1970s and over 60 per cent of those born in the 1960s and 1950s. The overall picture is much more than just an age effect though. The ONS has estimated that the wealth held by the top 10 per cent of households in Great Britain was about five times greater than the bottom half of all households combined, and that by 2023, the richest fifty families in the UK held more wealth than half of the UK population, comprising 33.5 million people. The Equality Trust reported that if the wealth of the super-rich continues to grow at the rate it has been, then by 2035 the wealth of the richest 200 families will be larger than the whole of the UK's GDP.[2]

All that said, valuing wealth is notoriously problematic, and in March 2025 the IFS and ONS found errors in previous official statistics regarding wealth distribution, to such an extent that the IFS concluded that they do not provide a reliable picture of total household wealth or of the inequality in wealth between young and old. Inaccuracies aside, there is no doubt that wealth inequality is now the major component of economic inequality, but it's worth considering some of the other forms of inequality in more detail.

REGIONAL INEQUALITY

We saw in the first chapter how the legacy of the Industrial Revolution and the British Empire led to regional inequality, exacerbated by the direction of the economy favouring financial and other services in the mid-twentieth century. 'Levelling up' hasn't even started to dent these regional disparities. Indeed, 46 per cent of those with incomes in the top tenth of one per cent live in London, despite Londoners only making up 13 per cent of UK adults. For the extremes, the Resolution Foundation and Centre for Economic Performance's 'Economy 2030 Inquiry' reported that in 2019 the income per person in the richest local authority of Kensington and Chelsea averaged £52,000, 4.5 times the income per person in the poorest local authority of Nottingham at £11,700 per annum.

INTERNATIONAL INEQUALITY

The Equality Trust records that the UK has high income inequality compared to other developed nations. Data from the OECD shows that in 2022, the UK had the ninth-most unequal incomes among thirty-eight OECD countries. Thinking internationally, you may be wondering how Elon Musk would figure in Pen's Parade. His annual income is tricky, as it varies so much with his net worth, but if we use his net worth in relation to the average UK height for men, then he would stand approximately 13,200 kilometres tall. Amazing, though still short of the 56 million kilometres or so he would need to reach Mars.

ETHNIC INCOME INEQUALITY

In 2020/21 and 2022/23, the highest median weekly incomes (after housing costs) in the UK went to people from Indian (£582), then white (£570) and Chinese (£523) communities. The lowest went to people from Pakistani (£345) and Bangladeshi (£304) communities. Data from 2016 to 2018 shows that median total wealth for a household headed by someone white British was £314,000, compared to only £34,000 for a household headed by someone from the Black African community. In light of this, there are calls for mandatory ethnicity pay gap reporting for organisations with over

250 employees to get better data, but this is unlikely to happen given the current emphasis on deregulation.

GENDER INEQUALITY

The ONS reports that the median gross hourly pay for full-time employees (excluding overtime) was 7 per cent less for women than men in April 2024. Data for the period between 2018 and 2020 suggests a 35 per cent pension gap in median private pension wealth between women and men. Around 80 per cent of those in the top 1 per cent of income receivers are men. Clearly progress towards gender equality has been slow and there is much more to do.

One welcome development has been that feminists and the #MeToo movement have been major forces in recent years in pushing for gender equality across all walks of life. It has been encouraging that the movement has influenced boardrooms in myriad ways. There has been an astonishing increase in the numbers of senior politicians, business leaders, film and other arts executives leaving their posts after reports of sexual harassment in the workplace. Some widely reported offences took place a long time ago and are only now being reported and actioned due to the shifts in gender power and our social norms.

There has also been an increase in the number of women in boardrooms. The percentage of female representation on FTSE 100 company boards by the end of 2021 was 44 per cent. In 2022, Ursula von der Leyen, the President of the European Commission, expressed her hope that a ten-year-dormant 'EU gender balance in the boardroom' directive – which set quotas for board membership of 40 per cent for non-executive women directors in listed EU firms – would be pushed forward. France seemed to be supportive; Germany was against it, its view being that it should be left to individual states to decide and implement best practice in this area. Nevertheless, its own mandatory quotas established some five years ago meant that the German figure had already reached the directive's ambition. Overall, the EU gender equality index, which measures gender disparities, still shows a significant deficit, and has been stuck at roughly the same level since around 2015. Only around 5 per cent of the *Forbes* Global 2000 companies are run by women.

In the UK, we have certainly seen many women in high places, including our first ever female Chancellor (all three of the great offices of state below the Prime Minister are now held by women) and women heading three of our most influential independent think tanks: Helen Miller at the IFS, Ruth Curtice at the Resolution Foundation and Bronwen Maddox at Chatham House. Sadly, history tells us that more general progress on gender equality will need government intervention, which is one reason why von der Leyen asserted, 'To have a critical threshold of women on boards, you need a legal [framework] nudging companies in the right direction.' She is right. The sad truth is that most of the progress made in regard to women's social, political and economic positions over the last century or so was not from market forces but from government legislation that either gave women rights – voting, access to contraception, property rights, access to education and employment, maternity pay – or abolished restrictive laws, easing the path to labour participation.

Sadly, in many parts of the globe, as the World Bank regularly reports, restrictive legal obstacles remain, depriving women of the economic empowerment necessary to achieve equal status in society, for them and their families. Even in the West, where legislative obstacles have now more or less been removed, the system remains suboptimal. Women often work below their skill level, or part-time to accommodate their multiple roles, often including shouldering the lion's share of looking after children and other dependents. The result is that, in the UK, weekly average earnings through a woman's lifetime are still some 30 per cent less than men's and their pension wealth is just a fifth of that of men. This is because there are barriers of a different kind, including difficulties in re-entering the market full-time after giving birth; lack of financial and entrepreneurship sponsorship; lack of role models and career advice; as well as lack of transparency over decision-making and openness about pay differences. Women have reduced choices in their careers once they have children, with mothers enjoying considerably fewer networking and mentoring opportunities while often suffering from conscious and unconscious bias, which is difficult to call out. They also commute shorter distances and move less for jobs, which reduces their choices and gives their employers more power over them. ONS analysis found that only 36 per cent of the gender pay gap could be explained by identifiable factors such as age, occupation and length of holding the post. Surveys of sectors that tend to attract highly educated women at entry level such as the legal profession show a prevalence of sexism that discourages women from staying and/or applying for the top jobs. The hiring process is also often skewed against women if the hirer is a man, as the tendency is to choose people who are similar to oneself – if the boss is a man, they are more likely to hire another man.

The result of all this is that the gender pay gap persists, with women over-represented in low-paying occupations, which are those now most at risk of being automated through AI. All this also puts women in more danger of falling into poverty, while the economy loses out on their talent. None of this makes any economic sense at all; it is clearly a massive market failure. Sadly, if anything, we are now seeing a reversal of progress, aided by President Trump's trampling over DEI initiatives in the US and affecting companies dealing with the US.

WHAT CAN BE DONE ABOUT GENDER INEQUALITY?

There are all sorts of relatively simple ways to mitigate gender imbalances when hiring: anonymous CVs that hide the applicants' gender, ensuring that enough women are in any shortlist (or perhaps even drawing up women-only shortlists) and having a woman make the hiring decisions. Many firms do try a combination of such measures. For example, the civil service is deliberately much more diverse on gender, ethnicity, sexual orientation and disability. However, as of 1 January 2025, only thirty-one companies of the Forbes Global 500 had a woman CEO. In the UK, the number of female CEOs in the FTSE 100 stood at a paltry eight. This is not much to show in terms of progress for women's emancipation and economic empowerment, despite all the noise around the issue.

Even when at the top, women have to fight to be taken seriously, as Mary Ann Sieghart covers in her book, *The Authority Gap*. Women like Christine Lagarde, head of the European Central Bank, and former German Chancellor Angela Merkel swapped notes about being conscious of this, and both felt they needed to be extra-prepared for meetings to be more than just on top of their brief.

So, what can extra legislation do? Firstly, it should serve to encourage cultural change, with consequences for non-compliance. Legislation already developed or under consideration includes shared paternity leave with the same benefits, which would mean that mothers would no longer have to bear so much of the 'motherhood penalty' of the pay gap widening for years after giving birth. We should also enshrine into law the right to greater flexibility in working hours and practices for all. This would be good for women and men alike in managing work-life balance; as we found during the pandemic with working from home and currently evolving hybrid models, such flexibility may also help raise productivity. Additionally, in some Nordic countries, people have the legal right to find out what others are earning. We are trying a limited version of such a policy in the UK, with impressive results. See, for example, the furore at the BBC when it was made public that the wages of female presenters were often only a fraction of their male colleagues', even though they were generally perceived to be doing the same job. Information asymmetry is a major market failure, and such remedial actions can only help.

In the boardroom, more and wider use of quotas would help. Unfortunately, box-ticking on numbers of women doesn't seem to do much. There is no evidence that adding a couple of female non-executive directors to a traditionally all-male board does much to change organisational culture, but women certainly need to be in positions of power on the board. The good news is that the focus is beginning to shift in the UK and elsewhere towards mandatory quotas which extend to below board level. It is women in senior executive positions within a company that can make the biggest difference to company culture, as well as being the main way of demonstrating that company culture has moved forwards.

INEQUALITY, DISABILITY AND INCAPACITY

According to Department for Work and Pensions' data from between 2020 and 2023, households with a disabled family member had a weekly median income (after housing costs) of £478 compared to £602 for households with no disabled family member. There is also a growing body of research on 'intersectional inequalities'. This is because many of those who are most likely to be in deepest poverty experience overlapping discrimination and intersecting types of inequalities. For example, someone might be disadvantaged in the labour market by ableism, racism and sexism simultaneously.

In 2025, Labour faced strong push-back on its proposals to reduce the welfare spend that goes to those registered as disabled or with an incapacity to work (not that we have a benefit system that is remotely generous or lavish by international standards). These proposals included a tightening of eligibility for Personal Independence Payments (PIP), scrapping the Work Capability Assessment and making PIP the gateway to receiving the Universal Credit (UC) health element. For new claimants, the rate of the UC element would be reduced and for existing claimants frozen until 2029/30. If these reforms went ahead, they would have represented the biggest cuts to disability benefits since the austerity of 2010. It is important to note that PIP is not an 'out of work benefit'; it is aimed at meeting some of the extra costs from being disabled, whether one is in work or not.

Not surprisingly, these proposals were met with abject horror by many. For example, the Rowntree Foundation estimated that some 400,000 people would be pushed into poverty. The Foundation also commissioned a poll that showed 58 per cent of respondents thought the proposals were a bad decision, with only 32 per cent saying they were a good idea. Significantly for Labour, opposition to these reforms was found to be particularly high among those voters who were most important for Labour's election victory in 2024.

Perhaps Labour's leaders have too readily believed the populist press, who insist that hundreds of thousands of people get cash handouts for claimed 'living and mobility costs' which they don't deserve. The government says it is addressing 'spiralling economic inactivity, with 2.8 million people locked out of work due to long-term sickness', but more recent data, reported by *Financial Times* journalist John Burn-Murdoch, suggests that much, if not all, of that post-pandemic surge in economic inactivity may be illusory.[3] One major reason to believe his account is that the usual source of data on economic activity and inactivity, the ONS, has been in a mess post-Covid. Burn-Murdoch's analysis of an alternative source of longitudinal data does not show anything like such a rise in economic inactivity. His analysis is also in line with findings from the Resolution Foundation, which reported that the inactivity rate in 2024 was roughly the same as in 2019. A second reason is that international studies show that, in Burn-Murdoch's words, 'the waxing and waning of health-related benefit caseloads is almost always driven primarily by changes to incentives and stringency in different parts of the benefit system, rather than by changes in people's health'. This may well explain why changes in the number of claimants of health-related benefits show a much higher correlation with changes in the benefits system than with surveys of the population's underlying health. All this suggests that policies aimed at the incentives in the benefits system can have a strong effect on the level of state spending on health-related benefits.

In fact, the IFS noted that the thrust of the proposed changes tilted the welfare support away from those who are disabled and towards those who are unemployed without an assessed disability, who would get a small uplift. This is intended to bring incapacity benefits back in line with the level of unemployment benefits that they have outpaced. So, for some people with health conditions, work incentives will be strengthened by reducing their income. For the 4.5 million households who are on UC but do not get a health-related benefit, there will be a weakening of the incentive to find work. The fiscal risk is therefore that those whose incentives are weakened will be the group most able to respond to financial incentives, while stronger incentives are targeted at those who are most likely not to be able to work regardless of the incentive.

The immorality of hurting the vulnerable who are unable to help themselves is glaring, but another moral and practical dilemma arises from tightening the PIP eligibility criteria. There have been far too many disgraceful past decisions when, in effect, targets were set for taking people off benefits and innocent folk were left in appalling situations through harsh decisions. It is also the case that when assessment criteria change, the way claimants approach the assessment is likely to change too. Previously, governments found that such behavioural adaptation has meant they saved much less than they hoped they would. This causes the dilemma: if the PIP eligibility criteria is too harsh there will be many horrific incidents of appalling treatment but if it can be more easily met there will only be relatively small savings.

Why risk the political flak from cutting benefits to those currently disabled and making it harder for people claiming disabilities to claim? Critics of the Labour government say it was an ill-conceived panic measure designed to clear some fiscal headroom under the Chancellor's own fiscal rules. The more rational reason is that the percentage of adults on either health-related benefits or out of work incapacity benefits, or both, increased from 7.5 per cent of the working-age population in 2019/20 to 10 per cent in 2023/24. The IFS reported that this represents a 38 per cent growth in the number of claimants in just four years. The average age of claimants also fell sharply. The number of new disability benefit awards made to under-40s grew by 150 per cent, with 37 per cent of new claims now primarily for mental health conditions, up from 28 per cent before the pandemic. The ONS reported that 2.8 million people were out of work and classed as long-term sick, one of the highest rates of any G7 country. This had driven up spending on working-age health-related benefits from £36 billion in 2019/20 to £48 billion in 2023/24. As the forecasts were for yet more runaway costs – with estimates ranging from £63 billion in 2028/29 to the government's own claim that it will hit over £70 billion by 2030 and the IFS even suggesting £100 billion – the government felt it had no choice but to try to stem the tide of disability and incapacity spending.

A key concern will be not only how much reductions in payments hurt but how humanely any cuts are achieved by any new eligibility criteria. Importantly, as pointed out by many concerned organisations in the field, people who could potentially enter the labour force often need support rather than fiscal coercion. Indeed, Starmer's ministers all say that the intention is not to harm the disabled but 'to free them from a life of dependency'. But it does seem premature to reduce support for the out of work disabled before a new support system is in place to help and encourage employers to keep those who are struggling on the payroll, especially during a major review on such matters, led by former John Lewis boss Charlie Mayfield.

Also, importantly, investment for those with mental health issues needs to be an integral part of any strategy to contain spending. Support services for adult mental health have been decimated ever since the 2010 austerity measures, with more than two million people currently waiting for mental health support. It may well require higher spending in the shorter term to provide support for those wishing to find paid employment; in other words, an investment programme, not merely a cuts programme. The urgency, as we have seen, appears to be driven in large part by the need to meet self-imposed short-term fiscal rules. That is no way to run an investment programme, let alone influence decisions that will have profound impacts on so many already disadvantaged people.

INTERGENERATIONAL INEQUALITY

Despite a general rise in living standards, there have been decreased opportunities in many respects for younger people. For the first time for many decades, the younger generation cannot expect to be better off than their parents. Home ownership, a major factor in intergenerational wealth, roughly halved for young people in their twenties and thirties between 1995 and 2010. It has risen a little since but is still much lower than in the mid-1990s. Young people from lower income households are particularly likely to feel they don't have much of a chance in life. Research published by the International Longevity Centre UK warns that the 'intergenerational contract', whereby older generations in effect support younger generations in return for their future support, is under mounting pressure due to demographic changes, low economic growth and rising inequality.

CHILD POVERTY

The evidence is clear that a healthy start in life is a major factor for success as an adult. This is not just about altruism, morality or even the savings in fiscal spend that better-equipped citizens bring. It is about hard-nosed economic growth, too. Currently, only 68 per cent of children in England are deemed 'ready to learn' when they start school, a measure of development that includes being able to sit still, share with others and do basic numeracy. Alleviating child poverty reduces the barriers that prevent more children becoming productive higher-paid workers as adults. It also provides the opportunity to develop and harness the latent creative and entre-preneurial talents of many more children, talents that are the key driver of long-term growth. Damningly, then, the House of Lords Library has reported that the number of children living in poverty is rising. In 2024, the government estimated that 4.3 million children, or 30 per cent of all children in the UK, were living in relatively low-income households after housing costs in 2022/23.

Back in 1998, the Sure Start scheme was set up by the Labour government under Chancellor Gordon Brown. It aimed to give children the best possible start in life by improving childcare, early education, health and family support. Sure Start started life with a £450 million investment into the development of 250 children's centres; it was then expanded considerably, which perhaps led to the centres becoming too dominated by better-off parents rather than the target families that the original designer of the scheme, a civil servant called Norman Glass, had envisaged. Early results were mixed, but the IFS reported that the Sure Start programme reduced hospital admissions and saved millions for the NHS alone. As with so many longer-term investments, the upfront costs are justified only if they are allowed to continue to fruition.

By contrast, it was an inexcusable decision to continue with the two-child cap on family allowance. Lifting the cap could lift a quar-ter of a million children out of poverty and reduce the severity of poverty for another 850,000 children. The evidence is that despite populist appeal, the cap does not affect fertility rates, it just increas-es hardship. There would almost certainly be long-term economic return from lifting the cap; economists have suggested that even the relatively small short-term fiscal saving claimed by the government will be trivial given the wider fiscal costs of poverty.

WHY INEQUALITY MATTERS

Almost everyone would agree that there should be a minimum threshold for living standards below which no one should drop, but it is worryingly common to think that the level of inequality does not matter for a healthy population and society. Free market think tanks and lobbyists such as the Adam Smith Institute and the Institute of Economic Affairs argue that the focus should be on addressing poverty rather than inequality. They also argue that gender inequality reflects individual choice, which is a specious argument, as being a biological woman isn't a choice and the drive to have children is far more complex than a binary choice – plus, it takes two to tango. In fact, there is an overwhelming weight of evidence that societies with lower levels of inequality also tend to have better overall wellbeing, including lower rates of mental illness, obesity, violence and imprisonment. Many of these correlations are eloquently summarised in the 2009 book *The Spirit Level: Why More Equal Societies Almost Always Do Better* by Richard Wilkinson and Kate Pickett. Even when poverty is controlled for, the effects of relative inequalities on health and wellbeing remain clear. This, combined with the complex moral reasons, is why we need institutions to promote upward social mobility, to restrict the power of monopolies and to ensure, as much as is feasible, that every citizen gets fair treatment.

ECONOMIC INEQUALITY AND TAX

It might seem a contradiction to say that the overall tax rate in the UK is at a record high and yet most taxpayers are not paying a higher percentage of their income in direct taxation than in the past. It is, however, true. The tax take as a fraction of national income is at record levels, but average earners are facing lower levels of direct taxation than for many decades. The basic rate of income tax has come down from 35 per cent to 20 per cent over the past fifty years. The tax-free allowance is being squeezed by fiscal drag – that is, inflation eroding its value and dragging more people into paying income tax – but it is still not historically high. The IFS reported in 2024 that someone on £35,000 per year, about the average for those working full-time, would have an income tax and National Insurance bill about £2,000 lower than someone would have on the same real earnings back in 2010. At the end of 2024, the overall tax burden was higher than at any time since 1950. Nevertheless, the direct tax take from an average earner was at its lowest for half a century.

The answers to this apparent paradox include the impact of in-flation on VAT and increased revenue from corporation tax, but to a large extent it's down to a combination of income growth and freezing of tax thresholds, and fiscal drag which has helped bring in more tax from the rich. While average earners have seen their tax bills fall, the reverse is true of high earners. Back in 2010/11, only 6 per cent of the adult population paid the higher or additional rates of income tax. Today, it's over 13 per cent and is predicted to hit 15 per cent by 2028/29. In 2010/11, the top 10 per cent of taxpayers paid 54 per cent of all income tax. This is now around 60 per cent. The top 1 per cent pay almost 30 per cent of all income tax now, up from 25 per cent in 2010 and 21 per cent at the turn of the century.

We shouldn't have too much sympathy for the rich, though. From Thatcher to the Great Financial Crisis, their percentage of tax con-tribution rose despite the tax regime becoming more favourable towards them – only because they were becoming so much richer. The past fifteen years have seen a combination of the very rich con-tinuing to pull ahead from the rest of the population and higher tax rates being imposed on them: until 2010, the top tax rate was 40 per cent, but it's now 60 per cent on incomes between £100,000 and £125,140 and 45 per cent on incomes above that. They also have less scope to pay into their pensions to avoid tax.

All this has meant that we have come to rely more on the tax paid by top earners, and we do badly need their tax contribution. The truth is, though, that if the UK wants to move closer to the higher tax regimes of EU countries to fund public services, then middle earners will need to pay more tax too.

TAXING THE RICH

We can still tax the rich more. We've seen throughout this book that wealth is increasingly consolidated in the hands of the wealthy: the top 1 per cent of adults received 15 per cent of fiscal income in 2018–19, fiscal income being a broad measure that captures most income sources but notably excludes capital gains and untaxed incomes. Their share is more than all the bottom 55 per cent of adults put together. Overall, direct taxes (which include income tax, National Insurance contributions and council tax) lower income inequality. Higher-income individuals pay a greater share of their gross household income in direct taxes compared with poorer individuals, though a smaller percentage in council tax. Despite being broadly progressive overall, we do need a comprehensive reform of our tax regime, as top incomes are not currently taxed enough. It's a need that is common across many developed economies, but it's particularly so for the UK, which is second only to the US in inequality within rich countries. While taxes on personal income are progressive on average in the UK – the top one per cent of UK adults pay 34 per cent of income tax, almost exactly the same share as is paid by the bottom 90 per cent – average tax rates are unequal across the different types of taxes. That is because tax depends not only on the level of income but also on the sources of income.

Income from business and capital is taxed at a lower rate than income, a particular issue for inequality as the top 1 percent, especially the top tenth of that one per cent, are more likely to get their income from business ownership. Business income, from self-employment or from closely held incorporated businesses, is considerably more important for the top incomes. High-income wage earners work disproportionately in financial services and high-income self-employed work, particularly in partnerships in professions such as accountancy and legal services. This matters hugely for tax rates. In 2024, the UK's overall combined top (statutory) marginal rate on employment income (including employee and employer NICs) was over 53 per cent when adjusted for National Insurance. But company owners can access a rate of just 27 per cent on income taken in the form of capital gains, which falls to zero if the realisation of gains is deferred until death, and even when accounting for corporation tax, dividends are taxed at a lower combined rate than employment income. UK company owner-managers commonly take most income as dividends rather than more heavily taxed salary. Alongside avoidance opportunities, business owners also have much greater scope for evasion, including by under-reporting their business incomes or inflating their costs. In short, company owner-managers have a strong tax incentive to pay themselves in capital gains or dividends rather than in salary and there are few rules to stop them doing it.

Unlike with the basic rate of income tax, it is doubtful that raising the top rate of tax on salary and wages would raise more revenue, largely because of the options open to switch the income to lower taxed sources. Many high earners can easily shift, reclassify and under-declare taxable income through their own businesses, making it harder to raise revenue by increasing income tax rates. HMRC's central estimate is that a 1 per cent increase in the additional rate of income tax, which is paid on income above £150,000, would raise only £90 million, which is a trivial amount compared to the total value of tax receipts of £840 billion in 2024/25. This is because the increase would apply to a relatively small group who would seek to avoid the additional rate; the rich are particularly well placed to be 'tax slippery'. That said, we should note that the personal allowance – the amount of income that can be received before any income tax is charged – is withdrawn at a rate of 50p for each £1 that an individual's income exceeds £100,000. As a result, those with incomes between £100,000 and £125,140 already face an effective 60 per cent marginal rate on direct income tax. All this means that to raise more revenue from the top, the government would need to raise rates of tax on business and capital incomes. In fact, highly-paid executives get a lot of attention, but they do not form the bulk of top earners. In 2018/19 the total remuneration paid to CEOs of the UK's 100 largest public companies was just over £450 million, whereas the total wage income received by the top one-tenth of the top one percent was £37 billion.

It is often argued that lower taxes on business and capital are needed to encourage enterprise and investment, but this argument assumes that the rest of the tax system remains unreformed, and the evidence of lower rates of tax on business incomes relative to labour income suggests that they are poorly targeted for addressing market failures anyway. It also ignores that there is a very strong tax incentive to work as a self-employed person or company owner-manager rather than as an employee, and so a large portion of UK closely held companies have no employees other than the owner and carry out little or no investment activity; such ownership would not be deterred by substantial increases.

With a reformed tax base, there would be a strong case to align tax rates across different sources of income to raise more revenue from the highest incomes. The effect of raising the top rate of direct income tax would be different if elements of the tax base were also changed. The government could increase taxes on dividends, capital gains and/or self-employed profits and raise additional revenue. Additionally, if rates of taxation were similar across the different types of income, then people would be less responsive to higher rates of income tax, and so the top rate of employment tax could be increased to gain more tax revenue that way, too. Of course, if pushed too far, all tax revenue from the top incomes could be lost if they leave the UK. However, this phenomenon has not been as prevalent as our media's obsession with celebrities portrays; some wild estimates in the past have turned out to be bunkum, though recent estimates from some sources suggest 'rich flight' may now be a more serious issue.

There are many top earners working in finance and professional services in London who enjoy strong location advantages from being in such an important financial hub, which means that companies and their workers would be very likely to stay in London, even if taxes were higher. As we have noted, business owners are the major component at the top of the UK income distribution and would be much less likely to emigrate than celebrities.

As we have seen, to align the tax rates on business income and employment income, some of the former would have to increase by a lot. Capital gains going to business owner-managers are taxed at just 10 per cent up to a lifetime limit currently at £1 million, or just over 27 per cent when corporation tax is accounted for. And so, capital gains tax rates would have to be increased substantially, to over 42 per cent, if the overall top marginal rate is to be aligned with the combined rate on employment income. Increasing capital gains tax rates could lead to some people delaying the realisation of gains in order to benefit from the 'forgiveness' of capital gains tax at death. And so, removing that relief would raise both current revenue from capital gains tax and the revenue potential of higher capital gains tax rates.

Moving on, Class 4 National Insurance contributions are paid by self-employed individuals in the UK whose profits exceed a certain threshold. The top marginal rate on self-employment income could be aligned with that on employment income if the additional rate of Class 4 self-employed NICs was increased from 2 per cent to 8.4 per cent. And equalising the top marginal rate of tax on dividends with the top rate on employment income would only require a small change from just over 38 per cent to 42.5 per cent.

In short, tax reform could increase these top rates of income tax and close the gap between overall tax rates on dividends, capital gains and self-employed profits with those on employment income, thereby closing tax escape routes for the rich and bringing in much-needed tax revenues. Undoubtedly, those on the right would say that this would discourage risk-taking, saving and investment. But, as the IFS-led Mirrlees Review of tax in 2011 argued, this trade-off could be largely avoided if the tax base were reformed.

To understand how this can be done it is useful to distinguish between normal and excess returns. Excess returns are called 'economic rent' in economics jargon, while a normal return is what is received from a risk-free asset. Any tax that lowers the return below the normal rate will therefore have a distortionary impact.

In contrast, economic rents are over and above the normal rate of return. This might be because of monopoly advantage, a reward for risk-taking, luck or skill in choosing where to invest, or, as we have seen, the returns to work that business owners are disguising as capital income. There are good reasons to tax economic rents and doing so does not necessarily discourage or distort anything, and there are fairly easy ways to arrange tax deductions so that only economic rents are taxed and normal returns, such as cost deductions from investment and/or allowances, are not.

Council tax is another obvious way to increase the contributions of the rich. It's regressive as it stands – that is, it tends to be a lower proportion of a rich person's income than a poor person's. This is partly because the rich tend to spend proportionately less on their accommodation and, importantly, because council tax is still based on property values from 1991, which are very out of date. Of course, raising council tax could also be harsh on those low-income people who have lived in the family home for most of their lives and might be forced to move, but special allowance could quite easily be arranged to allow for this. Freeing up unutilised residential property seems a plus, though the infamous 'bedroom' tax revealed just how harsh taxing unused residential space can be in some cases.

Inheritance tax could also be broadened and deepened. Labour has made a start on this with the loudly protested reintroduction of a partial inheritance tax on farms, but inheritance tax is currently only paid on a very small percentage of estates. Land tax and stamp duty are other candidates. There has also been a rather technical discussion around ending some interest payments by the Bank of England to commercial banks, and perhaps a levy. This is well worth exploring.

NON-DOMS

It was hoped that abolishing generous tax exemptions for non-doms – that is, those who reside in the UK but have their permanent home (domicile) outside the UK – would bring in considerable tax revenue. The OBR estimated it would yield extra tax receipts of £10.3 billion this year. Rachel Reeves was strident: 'I have always said that if you make Britain your home, you should pay your tax here. So today, I can confirm we will abolish the non-dom tax regime and remove the outdated concept of domicile from the tax system from April 2025.' It was always understood that the changes would drive some rich people away, thereby losing the tax they do pay – including VAT paid by big spenders – and those that leave could include much-needed wealth-creating talent. There was some uncertainty over how many would leave and hence whether tax revenue would actually be gained or lost.

Following Rachel Reeves's announcement, there were, unsurprisingly, lots of stories plastered across our billionaire press – and even echoed by Labour Cabinet members – about the flight of non-dom millionaires and billionaires from the UK. It turned out, thanks to the dedicated investigations of financial analysts and the excellent BBC Radio 4 *More or Less* programme, that these stories were based on shaky evidence and rather wild extrapolations. A University of Warwick study, which is rumoured to have influenced Rachel Reeves, had argued that there was good reason to doubt that there would be a mass exodus of very wealthy people fleeing the UK. Primarily because billionaires *like* to live in the UK, with its cultural and entertainment attractions and stable political regime; plus, for the majority of non-doms (the study reported up to 80 per cent) their main taxable source of income was from employment, which is not easily transferred overseas. Add to this their family ties and the fact that UK taxes remain lower than the G7 average, and it seems very unlikely indeed that anything like the feared exodus would transpire.

However, to further complicate matters, there has been a recent challenge to both the Warwick study and the OBR estimates. The Centre for Economics and Business Research (CEBR) has suggested that even if no individuals who held non-dom status left the UK as a result of the changes, the Treasury would only see gains of £2.5 billion in the first year, and that if more than a quarter of the UK's non-doms leave the country then the Treasury would begin to incur a hefty loss. Building on the CEBR critique, former Treasury economist Chris Walker argued that the decision to abolish non-dom status was built on 'overly optimistic and incomplete' data. Walker challenged the Warwick paper that claimed only 0.36 per cent of non-doms would leave the UK. He argues that the study excluded those most likely to leave, including new arrivals, globally mobile entrepreneurs and foreign nationals with minimal family or business ties to the UK. Others have estimated that around one in ten high value non-doms had already left, with many more planning their exit.

To throw yet another conflicting voice into the mix, the Tax Justice Network has also challenged the claim that lots of millionaires will leave the UK. They point out that in the past the reporting headlines of an 'exodus' of the rich have been gross exaggerations and that academic studies consistently show that the tax responses of the wealthy involve minimal levels of migration. They also prompt an additional question: perhaps more important than how many millionaires are leaving is how many are still coming?

It is too early, at the time of writing, for us to accurately predict the net tax revenue to be had from the changes to the non-dom rules.

These considerations do highlight, however, that voters cannot be so certain that it is possible to avoid taxing ordinary people more by greatly increasing the tax take from the rich. As we saw above, the truth that many politicians don't want to tell us is that if our public services are not to deteriorate further, then those on more modest incomes are going to have to bear a large part of the increased tax burden.

WHAT ABOUT A WEALTH TAX?

For many observers, a wealth tax is something of a no-brainer. Influential economists, particularly Thomas Piketty, have advocated a global wealth tax in response to rising wealth concentration in many countries. In the UK, the Green Party placed much hope on the benefits of a wealth tax in their 2024 election manifesto. Unfortunately, it is not as simple as this. For one thing, repeatedly taxing a person's holding of wealth could lower the post-tax return on it well below normal returns, and hence damage investment and precipitate the ever-feared migration of the wealthy. Wealth taxes are also notoriously difficult to administer and the revenue often falls far short of expectations. One reason is that there is invariably pressure to exclude certain categories of wealth, such as business assets, which leaves a bolthole for tax avoidance: we saw how inheritance tax exemptions on farms created the anomaly of 'impoverished millionaire farmers'.

So, failing the unlikely event of an international agreement on taxing wealth, reforming business and capital income taxes in the ways suggested above would seem to be a better approach. That said, to capture revenue from past 'under-taxed' capital gains, a one-off wealth tax would have very few distortionary effects if the valuation date – the day on which wealth is counted – is set before the date of the tax announcement, as it would be too late for the owners of the wealth to change behaviour. In effect, the gains have already been made and so won't produce negative incentives so long as the government can credibly commit to it truly being a one-off tax (this is rather like the 'windfall' tax on oil producers). A justification could be given that would emphasise its exceptionality, such as to offset the enormous costs of the Covid pandemic.

Rather than taxing rich individuals directly, there has been interest in introducing a new corporation tax; more specifically, a tax on corporations' stock shares for all publicly listed companies. Even though it would be a flat rate tax, the pattern of share ownership would effectively make it a progressive tax. An immediate problem would again be the international mobility of finance, and so it would require international coordination – across the G20, say. Generally, these countries do need the tax revenue, but it is doubtful that there would now be the international political consensus, especially with pressure from the US on trade deals.

CAN WE TAX MULTINATIONALS MORE?

It is certainly possible for the government to increase taxes on multinational companies – if they can find them. There have been moves to clamp down on tax avoidance and evasion by multinationals and the work is ongoing across the OECD. Tax experts have reported that these efforts have made it harder for multinationals to dodge tax, but the complexities of companies working across several countries make it trickier than taxing purely domestic firms. Where and what should be taxed? What is the real loss or profit? Such matters are difficult to keep track of as a company's assets can be switched between the countries they operate in, as well as their operations being switched to take advantage of lower tax regimes.

Many people would reasonably think that US tech giants, say, should pay a lot more on the sales they make in the UK. Others argue that the companies are American, and the development and intellectual property is American, so that's where the tax should rightly be paid. There is an inherent irony, therefore, in any efforts to increase tax on multinationals: governments agree in principle on taxing them more while competing with tax cuts to attract more multinationals. Not surprisingly – the clue is very much in the name 'multinational' – to significantly reduce the opportunities for these companies to dodge taxes we would need international agreements. In the current international climate, we are not holding our breath.

WHAT ABOUT UBI?

Universal Basic Income (UBI) would be a guaranteed cash benefit that the government provides to all citizens. It would be non-conditional, so everyone gets it, poor or rich, regardless of their circumstances. 'Free cash' is an attractive idea for many, both from the left and right in politics. Those supporters on the right like its administrative simplicity and the avoidance of very high marginal tax rates, as conditional means-tested welfare benefits are withdrawn, though those on the right usually say a UBI should also be accompanied by a flat rate tax thereafter. Those on the left like the idea that no one falls through gaps in our welfare support system and the protection it offers against desperation, and hence also workplace exploitation of the low paid. Many also like the idea of a civilised social contract of dignity for all citizens.

As we have seen, there are many strong reasons to worry about inequality. As a bare minimum, any decent social welfare scheme should aim to protect people from destitution, control the bill for taxpayers, incentivise people to achieve financial independence and simplify administrative and operational logistics. Unfortunately, of this list, UBI is only really effective at simplifying administrative and operational logistics, and then only if it doesn't require extensive supplementation to address many other personal circumstances, such as health, age and family size. By design, UBI doesn't target redistribution towards those most in need: giving cash handouts to those who don't need them inevitably leaves less for those who do. Unless the welfare bill were to increase dramatically, and efforts are currently focused on containing its growth, UBI would entail giving less to those we already regard as in need of financial support. And, as pointed out by the IFS and many others, with a feasible level of funding UBI would either be an insignificant amount or entirely unaffordable. Of course, if AI changes the very nature of our economy as some predict, then UBI might well be a way of ensuring that everybody gets a slice of the national cake in the future.

THE UBS ALTERNATIVE

A more affordable alternative to a UBI might be a Universal Basic Services (UBS) scheme. This would identify a fundamental set of resources that every citizen should have: housing, a basic healthy diet, day-to-day transport, healthcare, education and information. The aim of UBS would still be to provide a welfare floor in our society by guaranteeing a minimum standard of life as a practical and observable manifestation of our common purpose. It would also entail a massive expansion of social housing, free bus travel, meal provision for those most at risk of food insecurity and basic phone and internet access. Such services need not be provided by the public sector but could be provided by the private sector. In

2017, Professors Jonathan Portes, Howard Reed and Andrew Percy estimated a total cost for this of 'just' £42 billion per annum, or about 2.3 per cent of UK GDP. They wrote:

> As a society, we already accept that certain services like health and education should be provided free at the point of use to the whole population, because we understand that all of society benefits as a result. The concept of UBS is a logical extension of this principle.
>
> A UBI paid to all UK citizens at the current modest Jobseekers Allowance level of £73.10 per week would cost just under £250 billion per year – around 13 per cent of total GDP, or 31 per cent of all current UK public spending. By contrast, the transformative effects of UBS are accessible with relatively minor changes to the fiscal structure of the UK economy: additional UBS spending represents only 5 per cent of existing budgets.

UBS could achieve the main advantages of UBI for much less and would still leave a strong incentive to work to get more of life's luxuries. With the political pressure still to reduce rather than increase public spending on social welfare, UBS seems an attractive alternative to UBI, though it remains unlikely in the current fiscal climate.

A NATION OF SCROUNGERS?

Our popular newspapers, mostly owned by billionaires, get very excited when they find a lazy scrounger. Apparently, it's even more newsworthy if that scrounger happens to be an immigrant. If the scrounger has dared to breed, then the outrage soars even higher with each innocent child. Of course, these same newspapers expend far less energy seeking out the tax-avoiding habits and other antics of billionaires. The often-fallacious rationale they use is that we all aspire to be rich, and their wealth will create wealth for everybody, while over-generous benefits kill the incentive to work and are an unjustified drain on those who actually pay their fair share of tax. In fact, we spend less on welfare as a share of GDP than the average for developed nations, and when it comes to the so-called 'replacement rate' – that is, what an unemployed person receives as a proportion of earnings from employment – we are very near the bottom for comparable countries.[4] There are, of course, 'scroungers'. It would be impossible to design a welfare system that only the 'deserving poor' could access, one beyond the reach of all fraudsters and slackers. It is also true that the growth in the numbers of people off work as a result of long-term sickness is alarming, but as with so many matters, our popular press does not provide a balanced picture of worklessness.

Incentives to engage in productive activities are not only good for the economy but also for individuals. The evidence is strong that being in some form of productive employment is good for one's welfare and mental health. It's not just a matter of carrot or stick, as there are many who would like to work, if only they could get a little more support to get into the labour market in the first place.

* * *

We have increasingly come to rely on the rich to pay our direct taxes. This is OK, as the rich have been busy getting considerably richer. We could tax them more, but increasing the top income tax rate is unlikely to do much good. There are better ways to get more from the rich to protect the poor, though a permanent wealth tax is probably not a good idea. We can raise taxes, but taxing the rich won't be able to raise sufficient revenue, plus putting all the weight of increases on taxes with a narrower tax base than income – such as employer NICs – causes anti-growth distortions. After so many years of underfunding, it is unlikely that we could find many savings from cuts to already depleted public services. The untold truth is that even with other available taxes, such as on gambling, we need to carry on with the freeze on income tax thresholds and, reluctantly, raise the basic rate of tax and some employee National Insurance, which has a lower political downside as people seem less aware of NIC than income tax. Ultimately, all but the poorest will need to pay more tax.

However, redistribution through progressive taxation isn't a panacea for the harmful impacts of inequality. Indeed, towards the end of the extensive IFS Deaton Review of taxation, launched in 2019, it became increasingly apparent that 'pre-distribution' (policies that initially dictate the distribution of income) is as important as the post-tax redistribution of income.[5] In short, living on handouts is not good for one's health, prompting the need for a thorough review of the welfare system and a broader consideration of how we better help people into work, the role of civil society and our overall industrial strategy.

CHAPTER 11

INVESTMENT IS VITAL

The UK economy suffers from chronic underinvestment, contributing to lower productivity compared to other G7 countries. An uncomfortable truth that no politician wants to admit is that we won't be able to increase our investment-to-GDP ratio significantly without also reducing our consumption-to-GDP ratio. According to the IMF, the UK's average national savings rate between 2021 and 2024 was only 15.6 per cent of GDP, placing us thirty-fifth out of thirty-seven high-income countries, only beating Cyprus and Greece. This must rise, through saving and/or tax, if the UK's low investment is to rise too. Nations and businesses alike must invest if they are to keep up with their competitors.

Karl Marx, an astute observer of capitalism though often poor on politics, observed, 'Competition subordinates every individual capitalist to the immanent laws of capitalist production, as external and coercive laws. It compels him to keep extending his capital, so as to preserve it, and he can only extend it by means of progressive accumulation [investment].' This 'accumulate or die' imperative is exactly the same for countries in a competitive international economy: investment in infrastructure, buildings and machines, human capital (education and skills) and research and development does more than just produce more of the same: it also harnesses innovations and spurs technological progress. A major reason for the UK's relativity poor productivity record is that the economy has long suffered from chronic levels of underinvestment, which in the longer run is the main driver of productivity differences between nations.

Investment in infrastructure provides utilities, such as power, water, communications and sewage, to allow new commercial developments. Investment in transport infrastructure does more than increase the capacity of supply chains: it increases people's connectivity allowing them to meet, share ideas and make mutually advantageous business deals. Investment in science and R&D brings the transformations that have shaped the modern world, sustaining a global population way beyond what would have been possible in ages past. When undertaken efficiently, investment, both physical and intangible, including human capital, is a root driver of productivity, and in the long run, productivity is almost all that matters for material living standards, economic growth and international competitiveness. Economic growth also provides the tax revenues that can fund public services without increasing the tax rate. This would undoubtedly make our politicians popular, if only they knew how to do it.

THE UK'S POOR INVESTMENT RECORD

In recent history, the UK's overall investment – public, private, household and not for profit – fell from around 23 per cent of GDP in the late 1980s to around 17 per cent from 2000 onwards. By contrast, investment rates in typical G7 countries remained largely in the range of 20–25 per cent. UK public investment dropped from an average of 4.5 per cent of GDP between 1949 and 1978 to just 1.5 per cent from 1979 to 2019. This is partly explained by the privatisation programme of the Thatcher administration in the 1980s and the subsequent reliance on regulators who were typically outsmarted by the now privately owned utilities and transport operators, though investment in the public sector has also been low, not to mention plagued by short-termism and stop-start policies. Not only has the UK been bottom of the G7 league table for total investment, in twenty-four of the last thirty years, we ranked a pathetic twenty-eighth out of thirty-one OECD countries for business investment. The UK's productivity gap with France, Germany and the US doubled in the twelve years after the financial crisis, to 18 per cent, costing £3,400 in lost output per person.[1] Our economy has also been held back by chronic levels of underinvestment compared with economies that have delivered larger increases in living standards. In July 2024, the Institute for Public Policy Research (IPPR) noted that the last time the UK achieved the 'average' for total investment in the G7 was 1990. It also estimated that, had the UK maintained an average position over the last three decades, there would have been a staggering additional £1.9 trillion worth of investment in real terms.

The ONS has become better at measuring intangible investment, but even here we seem to lag behind, though there seems to have been a steadier flow of spending on intangibles such as knowledge, patents and brand values. A large component of this is intellectual property, investment in which is broadly constant at around 4 per cent of GDP, thereby slightly increasing its share in investment as a whole. Unfortunately, over the past thirty years or so, the share of R&D expenditure has fallen to below 2 per cent of GDP. Again, precise measurement can be problematic, but the data suggest that UK R&D spending is low compared to other G7 countries, despite our strong science base. Germany and the US, for example, spend approximately 2.8 per cent of GDP on R&D, while Japan spends 3.5 per cent.

PLANNING AHEAD

Unless there is spare capacity that can be 'crowded in' – the stimulation of private investment through public sector spending – by more public investment, there will need to be a difficult trade-off, with some short-term pain for longer-term gain through increased investment. Our low investment has been reflected in a rising share of GDP by consumption and the trade deficit. Consumption in UK GDP rose by some eight percentage points between 1970 and 2023, likely at the cost of investment falling by six percentage points, while the trade deficit increased by about two percentage points of GDP. Such a trade-off is not a one-to-one; it can rejuvenate some sectors too, and, even if there is some 'crowding out' of consumption, the fact is that more investment is needed to escape the low growth-higher tax 'doom loop' in the longer term.

What is needed is a more investment-friendly environment for business and more spending on public investment. Sadly, there won't be spare tax revenues for the latter and so extra borrowing will be needed. This does entail a risk, for if growth doesn't follow then we end up deeper in debt. And in the meantime, the monies raised will be tied up in investments that will take at least several years, even a decade for some, to bear fruit. The truth is that there are no easy choices. The 'do nothing' option simply looks like more of the same: yet more mismanaged decline. However, if the investments are chosen well and have the potential to be growth-enhancing, then they can be presented as a convincing strategy for growth and the markets will not react adversely. Just as with any business plan, if it is a well-evidenced plan for growth and hence has the ability to pay back the loans, then financers will invest in it. Conversely, economic plans like Liz Truss's – which essentially said, 'I'm making unfunded tax cuts to benefit my type of people in the vague hope that they will respond by doing more' – will no doubt be punished by the bond markets.

WHY IS THE PRIVATE INVESTMENT RECORD SO POOR?

Private sector investment depends on the expectations for future profits from the investment. As Keynes pointed out, this is typically far more important than the direct costs of changes in interest rates, though such changes in interest rates can and do affect expectations of future profits. Keynes's point was that even if the interest rate were zero, a capitalist is not going to invest in building a factory that won't be able to sell anything. The capitalist would simply have lost the cost of the building for whatever second-hand value the redundant factory might have in an alternative use. The economic prospects of particular countries are highly important for multi-national firms and investors, as they can pick and choose where to invest their funds in the world. There are, of course, a number of important factors to consider when investing.

Uncertainty

Not surprisingly, as investment is determined by expectations of the future, investors hate uncertainty. So, for projects with similar expected returns, the value will be largely determined by the risk factor: a bet with a 99 per cent chance of winning a million pounds is worth more than a bet with a 50 per cent chance of a million pounds. Unfortunately, the UK has had more than its share of uncertainty. This came with Brexit, of course, but also frequent and large changes in government policy, along with austerity, changes to industrial policies, regulations and the tax treatment of investment spending. Unfortunately, whatever its wider merits, democracy does not lend itself to policy consistency beyond the electoral cycle, or even within it sometimes in the face of powerful lobbyists. This is not the first time we have noted the likelihood of a trade-off between democracy and good economics, and policymakers should be working on how to minimise such a tussle.

Short-termism

Looking for quick payoffs rather than building and embedding long-term increased returns has dogged UK investment. This short-termism may stem from the mentality of and pressure from our large financial sector. A CEO whose company falls too far behind the current stock market valuations of competitor companies may face the ire of shareholders and will likely lose their post, even though maximising short-term share prices can be at odds with building longer-term productivity and resilience. Added to this, we have seen how the frequent chopping and changing of government policies has made planning difficult and hence encouraged short-termism. Allied to short-termism, the UK has also had a long history of small- and medium-sized enterprises struggling to secure the funds they need to grow.

Lack of complementary public sector investment

Lack of public investment can significantly raise the costs of private firms. Poor transport links, high energy and utility costs, slow regulatory processes, high accommodation costs for staff and businesses, a high cost for filling gaps in education and for upskilling the workforce, all make the UK a less attractive place for internationally mobile investment.

Lack of joined-up industrial strategy

The government's industrial strategy is normally overseen by whatever the Department of Trade and Industry happens to be called at that moment in time; currently it's called the Department for Business and Trade (DBT). A problem with this arrangement is that this department lacks powers over most of the other parts of government involved in the strategy. In other words, it doesn't have the authority to put all the ducks involved in the industrial strategy in a row. For this reason, in March 2025 the government found itself struggling to achieve the necessary coordination to drive its growth agenda; the National Audit Office (NAO), a powerful public spending watchdog, reported that the 'DBT faces challenges in its relationships with departments who view growth as integral to their own work and therefore have a different approach to growth and prioritisation in those sectors'. Tellingly, the NAO reported that the DBT is struggling to achieve coordination with other departments covering key areas of the strategy, such as 'education, immigration, infrastructure, skills and taxation'.

Brexit

The self-harming economic folly of erecting trade barriers against one's own country is discussed in Chapter 5. Here we note that a considerable amount of foreign direct investment (FDI) into the UK was by virtue of our membership of the EU, and it is generally agreed that FDI increases productivity by adding capital stock, while bringing know-how and better management than exists in the average UK firm (there is evidence that the quality of UK management is low by international standards). Before Brexit, foreign multinationals could use the UK as a base for accessing the EU single market, a pull factor that no longer exists as Brexit ended

Britain's status as the English-speaking bridge between the EU and the rest of the world. It's true that under the Trade and Cooperation Agreement (TCA) between the UK and the EU, effective from 1 May 2021, goods trade between the EU and the UK is tariff free (subject to rules of origin). Unfortunately, that still leaves the often more significant non-tariff barrier obstacles and frictions, as we discussed above. The bureaucracy in checking the origins of all the component parts of a product and conforming to the checks needed can be a nightmare of stifling red tape and requires the UK to pay for a duplicate bureaucratic army of customs officials. And the TCA doesn't apply to most services, so some service sectors, like financial services, have faced more significant challenges due to the loss of 'single passport' privileges, affecting their ability to operate seamlessly across the EU. The data on FDI is woefully incomplete, but it does appear that although the accumulated FDI stock remains strong due to continuing value added, the value of FDI flows has generally fallen since 2025.

Brexit also affects investment in other ways. In particular, the frictionless single market meant that UK firms had to compete with firms right across the EU, requiring investment, innovation and efficiency to guarantee the leading edge. It was therefore a major spur to increased investment and productivity. Conversely, faced with too little competition, firms might just restrict output to raise prices, rather than invest in cost reductions and improved quality to grow market share.

WHAT SHOULD BE DONE?

Despite our woeful record, the Conservative Party went into the 2024 election promising cuts to public investment. This shows very poor judgement, but for all her talk of 'growth, growth, growth',

Rachel Reeves only removed these cuts in her first budget, rather than significantly increasing investment. She did, however, wisely rearrange the fiscal rules to allow for more 'fiscal room' to increase investment, and switching to 'persnuffle' allows the government to present a more comprehensive picture of its financial position, increasing headroom within its fiscal rules to increase public sector investment. This switch also promises to address what had been an unintended consequence of establishing the OBR and fiscal rules: creating incentives to trim public investment in the face of forecasts to meet deficit targets. As Jagjit Chadha, Director of the National Institute of Economic and Social Research, has pointed out, having the OBR focused on short-term output and debt projections did not allow for the effect of public investment on the supply side of the economy and subsequent growth, which increases the denominator of the debt-to-GDP ratio and hence acts to reduce the percentage of debt to GDP. Labour's rejuvenated National Wealth Fund (see Chapter 11) is also a step in the right direction.

In fact, most governments do end up having some form of industrial strategy, whether explicit or not. There are always risks involved, but if we are to break through the current economic stagnation, it is a time to take risks. And a well-thought-out strategy is better than a reactive and incoherent one.

PICKING WINNERS

You may have noticed the throwaway remark above about investments being 'chosen well'. Unfortunately, such a thing is easier said than done, of course. The future is unknown and what looks promising now may turn out to be a disappointment. Nick Crafts, the much-loved and recently departed economic historian, used to tell of the invention of polyester, once a source of great hope for the UK.

Polyester is a British innovation, developed by chemists at Imperial Chemical Industries in the 1940s. It was a revolution in textiles, making them cheap to produce, durable, wrinkle-resistant and easy to care for. Many thought that it would rejuvenate the declining UK textile industry, but like other British inventions, production of polyester shifted abroad, attracted by lower labour costs. Sadly, the UK has a record of failing to benefit economically from its own often remarkable scientific progress. The difficulty in successfully spotting winners isn't the only problem: the politics is as big a problem in ensuring that funds go to where they are most likely to cause growth. Sadly, politicians are notorious for putting vanity and votes above sound economics (just think of Boris Johnson's outlandish ideas for a Garden Bridge and an airport in the Thames Estuary, or Tony Benn's futile attempts to shore-up industrial lame ducks, such as the hopelessly inefficient British Leyland, or the Conservatives pouring public money into Upper Clyde Shipbuilders – the list is endless). Anglo-French Concorde was a technological triumph but a commercial failure. Regional aid and 'levelling up' have also had only moderate success, as it is difficult and very expensive for specific industries to overcome structural changes due to market forces.

Over the past two decades alone there have been at least ten major government growth plans. Each has had a limited impact beyond leaving behind a hodgepodge of public bodies and funding pots. Does that mean that picking winners must always fail? Of course not. Margaret Thatcher cleverly promoted the European Single Market and then went off to Japan offering subsidies and tax relief to their car companies if they agreed to set up plants in the UK to access the European market. It was a successful strategy that revitalised the British car industry. A severe critic of many of Thatcher's positions and subsequently a failed rival for the leadership of the

Conservatives, Michael Hesletine had considerable success when Secretary of State for the Environment in the early 1980s in revitalising the dockland areas of London and Liverpool. David Willetts as Minister of State for Universities and Science picked technologies for state sponsorship that mostly stood the test of time. It is also difficult to dismiss the success of China with much of its strategic sectorial investment.

Governments occasionally come to power with a strong belief that only free and unregulated markets are the panacea for poor growth. Though they may start with measures to 'free up' markets, they inevitably get drawn into more interventionist policies. It may start with generic strategies which apply across the whole economy, such as infrastructure, and then more specific cases of interest or concern will arise: often, at first, large firms and/or particular sectors 'ripe' for deregulation, subsidies and tax breaks. It makes sense to have a more coherent framework in the first place for taking these sorts of decisions. Indeed, we have already seen a useful set of sector growth partnerships that have continued through successive political regimes, including aerospace, AI, automotive, construction, life sciences, creative industries and offshore wind. They all have some form of leadership council involving business leaders, experts and Whitehall departments. The bottom line is that whatever the government does, no industrial strategy can succeed unless it provides a clear direction that gives businesses and investors the confidence to make long-term decisions. Industrial strategies have relied too heavily on driving growth by dishing out public funds to industries and regions while failing to improve the underlying business conditions by removing obstacles and addressing investment in skills. Labour's new industrial strategy, it seems, is a step in the right direction.

INDUSTRIAL STRATEGY

Although picking winners can often be a mug's game, providing the generics for a business environment in which firms old and new can flourish is simply a necessity for growth. Here, Labour's proposals for a National Wealth Fund (NWF), announced in October 2024, to invest mostly in generic infrastructure – including some no-brainers like better insulation for homes – together with its new industrial strategy, offers some hope. Although the NWF was launched with some over-egged claims about its potential impacts, given the short-termism in UK financing, it is, at least in principle, a sensible rejuvenation of existing policy. It is helped along by 'persnuffle' and is needed more now we have lost long-term, low-cost investment funding from the European Central Bank. It is not, however, really that new, evolving from and absorbing the UK Infrastructure Bank (UKIB) and the now sold-off 'Green Investment Bank'. The NWF will partner with the private sector and local authorities to finance infrastructure and some other projects, with the hope that it will 'crowd in' private sector investment by taking some of the risk and providing a long-term return on funding. More controversially, it may also consider using pension funds for a better return, something other countries have successfully managed to do but where the UK again lags behind (one can imagine how the populist press would present any such direction of pension funds).

By the end of this parliament, it was originally proposed that the NWF would have been capitalised by the government with a total of £27.8 billion. Unfortunately, this is very likely to be cut back now given the disappointing emerging fiscal balances. Cutting this would be a mistake, however, as lots of countries have successful equivalents of the NWF; in fact, there are 179 of them holding some $12.4 trillion in assets. The NWF would still be smaller than similar European policy banks, such as the German KfW and French Bpifrance, each of which invest about 1 per cent of their nation's GDP annually. Under current proposals, the NWF will only reach 1 per cent of UK GDP by 2028. Importantly, although the NWF is wholly owned by the Treasury, it operates at arm's length from the government and has an independent board who monitor the objectives of tackling climate change and driving growth, generating a positive financial return and mobilising private finance. It may be tricky to always marry a green agenda with maximising short-term growth, but the main danger is that politicians cannot resist overriding experts and long-term investments are simply ditched when another party comes to power. Long-term investment over, say, twenty years, doesn't well match a five-year electoral cycle.

WHY PROCUREMENT OFTEN FAILS

Once, while engaging in a procurement process to commission training in economics for the civil service, one of your authors was admonished for saying, 'I know this teacher, he has won teaching awards and is considered one of the best teachers of economics in the country.' The problem was that said teacher had not mentioned this in his submission, which was indeed quite sparse, and so the evidence of their world-leading teaching was deemed inadmissible. Instead, the procurement lead held up a glossy, expensive-looking submission from a large supplier, well used to bidding for government contracts, as a good submission. Needless to say, as the contract was a minor one, the supplier simply advertised for and employed the first economist they could find who would do it for a small fee, despite all the promises cut and pasted into the brochure from their many other submissions. The lessons are that overly rigid rules and box-ticking for procurement are no substitute for expert knowledge of the actual record of the providers. As with so many other things, experts in the field should be listened to and any expert who fails to declare all conflicts of interest should be banned from participating. The important consideration here for industrial strategy is that public procurement can be used to provide opportunities and indicate future levels of procurement spend in key areas, to give confidence both to business and private investors.

* * *

We need a more stable policy environment for public investment and a consistent long-term industrial strategy for private business. There are risks, but to break the cycle of stagnation these are risks worth taking. We will need to borrow a lot more for growth-enhancing public sector investment and for supporting private investment, while distancing politicians from pursuing pet projects or making decisions simply to please their favourite stakeholders. Projected cost-benefit ratios are very important and the Green Book – a government manual offering core professional guidance (see Chapter 12) – must not be made subservient to the wishes of ministers. We also need to find ways of preventing Chancellors of the Exchequer from gaming their fiscal rules to bolster short-term current spend by leeching from their capital spend commitments.

PART III

FACING THE FUTURE

CHAPTER 12

THE ECONOMY IN A CHANGING WORLD

Overall, the world has benefitted from globalisation, though, as with the Industrial Revolution, there have been losers. Indeed, by accelerating economic growth, globalisation has been a major contributor to lifting over a billion people from poverty. India and China have prospered in large part due to policy reforms that embraced globalisation, enabling them to supply products that were cheaper for Western nations to import than to make domestically. This helped growth in the West too, though at a slower pace than the emerging giants. Throughout the 1990s and 2000s, the world enjoyed a dramatic fall in policy barriers to international trade as well as rising international integration of national markets. This progress has stalled since 2010, with the global trade-to-GDP ratio hovering around 30 per cent. In this time, we have seen Britain's exit from the EU, the 2018 US–China trade war, major trade sanctions against Russia and, most recently, the threat of broader American trade restrictions. This is about more than just events, though: the post-war order could be changing, and no one can know for sure what will take its place.

That said, we find it most unlikely that globalisation will be reversed. President Trump cannot turn back the clock on technology and the extensive global supply chains that are now so integral to profit margins. Tariffs will not resurrect jobs in the US rust belt, even if they do prompt some high-tech new plants to set up there. Trump has undoubtedly damaged the US and others, but he can't control global economics from the White House. The Smoot-Hawley tariffs that prolonged the Great Depression lasted four years, Nixon's tariff war four months and Trump began buckling on many of his own tariffs in days, leaving more rhetoric than action. We predict that Trump's stakeholders will not tolerate the cost of his attempts to force multinationals to relocate to his voters' heartlands and to stave off the economic advance of China and India. Indeed, he may well have hastened the inevitable. It now seems clear that there will be a new political world order rather than a new economic order. Just as global economics drove the relative decline of the UK, the US is now experiencing the discomfort of its relative decline. This does not mean its *absolute* decline, as the US can continue to grow, and it is that potential for profit that Trump's stakeholders will be unwilling to see sacrificed.

We saw in the first chapter how global economics eroded British supremacy. No matter how savvy our governments could have been, that type of relative decline was inevitable. Longer term, as the age of empires passed, the economics was simply against our continued dominance as the world power. The US, on the other hand, didn't need an empire to shape so much of the modern world; it could use its enormous political and military power, which, as with the British, stemmed directly from having the world's leading economy. That dominance has been severely eroded since the 1980s, as other nations have advanced economically, especially China following the reforms of Deng Xiaoping. By some measures, such as the cost of the same basket of goods and services in both countries, China is already the bigger economy in real terms, even though the US's nominal GDP in 2024 was approximately $29.17 trillion and China's around $18.27 trillion. In any case, events have shown that Francis Fukuyama's phrase about 'the end of history' was clever rhetoric, but, as with Gordon Brown's more parochial, 'We've ended boom and bust', it was never remotely true.

TRUMP'S FOLLY

The US was never going to take its relative decline in the world's economy lying down. Having benefitted so much from the economic boost and cheap commodities coming from China, fears of being overtaken by the 'awakened giant' in this century led to growing concerns in the US about being replaced as the world's top dog. Despite much talk of China's growth rate having peaked and being set to fall, in recent years China's economy has continued to grow at more than twice the rate of the US. Unfortunately, Trump set out to reverse this inevitable relative decline in his own ham-fisted way: by denying the enormous wealth-creating power of globalisation, and by incidentally taking everyone else down with him. His AI-authored clipboard of concocted tariff 'retaliations', which bore little to no relation to actual tariffs, sent shockwaves through financial markets and threatened a global recession. Some economists saw it as the biggest disruption to the global trading system since the Bretton Woods collapse in 1971. The almost comical element is that Trump's advisers provided him with a nonsensical 'formula' for setting these ludicrous tariffs: they simply divided the US trade deficit with a country by that country's imports of US exports and then – as Trump is 'kind, so kind, probably the kindest person in history' – halved the ratio. Of course, trade deficits can reflect many things other than tariffs, and so even countries with very low tariffs against the US were hammered by high tariffs simply for providing the US with things America likes to buy.

Worse, the Trump administration tried to dignify their calculations by issuing an impressive formula made to look even more impressive by using Greek letters to depict the responsiveness of trade to changes in prices caused by tariffs. These were irrelevant to the tariffs set, as it turned out they chose numbers that meant the Greek letters merely cancelled out to equal one. If they had used more reasonable numbers for these price responsiveness coefficients then, by their own flawed logic, the actual tariffs would have been some 75 to 80 per cent lower. So, a huge negative impact on the US and the rest of the world was caused by both incorrect economic theory and bogus calculations – not quite so funny when you consider the gravity of what *The Economist* described as 'the most disruptive policy in the history of trade'.

Now, there is a case for lowering tariffs against the US, if that is Trump's longer-term target. In fact, there is almost always a strong case for lowering tariffs. That said, Trump ignores that the US deficit is largely the result of the 'dollar premium', which for many decades has allowed the US to spend more than it earns, both domestically and internationally, and to keep taxes below what would otherwise be necessary to fund even its relatively small public sector. The dollar premium comes from the perceived strength of the US economy and, in particular, the dollar's status as the world's primary reserve currency. Governments and speculators around the globe have been willing to take dollars as payment and to buy the US bonds that finance US debt without an ever-lower dollar exchange rate. The last time the US had a trade surplus was briefly in 1975.

By 2024, foreign countries owned approximately $7.9 trillion in US Treasury securities, close to a quarter of the total US debt.

It has been a privileged position that Trump might well weaken with his 'bull in a china shop' approach. Indeed, in May 2025 the ratings agency Moody's lowered the US credit score to 'Aa1' from 'Aaa', joining Fitch Ratings and S&P Global Ratings in grading the world's biggest economy below the top, triple-A position. Although a gentler approach might allow the dollar to fall more slowly and do much of the work Trump hoped his tariffs would do, his reckless behaviour, resembling a super-charged Truss cobbling together a mini-budget, could bring the US much pain and considerable loss of influence, especially if the dollar rapidly loses its privileged position and US Treasury bonds become less attractive to investors. If that happens, then the US cost of borrowing will soar and outpace the revenues from tariffs, the latter being offset by slower GDP growth and reduced imports. The Federal Reserve would then no doubt step in by buying up US debt, but that will further add to speculation that the dollar is an unreliable currency to hold. In the event, his bluster was checked by bond markets and he was forced by his stakeholders – who didn't invest billions in him just to lose billions more – to announce a ninety-day stay on his higher set tariffs above ten per cent, except on his real target, China.

Trump also seems not to notice that the US economy has been doing pretty well from the international order it did so much to create. He failed to understand the basics of modern economics as revealed as long ago as 1776 by Adam Smith. In *The Wealth of Nations*, Smith debunked mercantilism, the doctrine that surpluses from trade are always an increase in a nation's wealth and deficits a drain on a nation's wealth. Adam Smith understood that a prime purpose of exports is to buy the imports that are needed and desired, and that there can be more for everyone from specialisation. Several decades later, David Ricardo formalised how specialisation by countries in goods where they have a comparative advantage raises overall output, so that we can benefit from trade even with countries that are less efficient than ourselves. Think about it this way: you no doubt have a trade deficit with your grocer. You could set up as a grocer yourself, but you would both be better off if you get on with what you are best at and use that surplus to pay for your groceries, making you both better off materially. In short, it is trade – not surpluses – that creates wealth.

Overall, blocking imports lowers a nation's living standards. If people are displaced by imports as the comparative advantages of trade shift between nations, then the rich nations that gain from those cheaper imports should use their increased living standards to retrain and support, to provide the infrastructures that foster new developments, or failing all else, use the state to usefully employ the otherwise 'left behinds' of economic forces. Trump may, hopefully, be bluffing on tariffs to get easier access to world markets. As he puts it in his characteristically crass and undiplomatic style, 'These countries are calling me up, kissing my ass ... They are dying to make a deal.' But it is his volatile character, surrounded by 'yes men', that presents the very unpredictability and uncertainty so hated by business.

* * *

Globally, it is of course daft to think that the US's comparative advantage lies in labour intensive industries, and manufacturing is far less labour intensive than it used to be anyway. This means Trump's tariff war is unlikely to rejuvenate the rust belt and assist the voters in the US's 'left behind' regions. It isn't even clear that the US now has sufficient infrastructure to rapidly expand energy-intensive production. And given that the trade deficit comes mainly from the US's own domestic policies and imbalances, it is also unlikely that his policies will eradicate it, even without the tariff retaliation from other countries. Trump's bizarre view of 'unfair' was summed up by the columnist and blogger S. L. Kanthan:

'Look at this girl in Bangladesh ripping off America!'

'Calvin Klein generously pays her $1 an hour, but she never buys any luxury American clothes.'

'This lopsided trade is so UNFAIR!'

Trump has also underestimated China. Unlike the popularity contests that can determine who gets to rule in democracies, it takes guile and savvy to get to the top of China's political system. That makes for smart strategic thinking and consistency of approach. So, China has been spreading its wings, or tentacles, since the previous spate of tariff wars with the US in 2018. China has very clever people who do not have to worry about being voted out, and they learned quickly from previous US attempts to make them kowtow to American economic might. This time around, China was more prepared. Trump was no doubt expecting China to seek a humiliating tariff-reducing truce after his imposition, in April 2025, of tariffs against China of up to 54 per cent. Indeed, he had been bragging to his supporters that it would be easy to force China into submission. But this is not how things transpired. China immediately hit back hard with an 84 per cent tariff on US goods, aimed at where it hurts Trump most.

For example, China strategically targeted $15 billion in US agricultural exports (during peak planting season, no less), aiming at the Republican Party's voter strongholds among farming communities who had looked to Trump for relief. Since the previous tariff spate, China had turned to Russia and Brazil to halve its reliance on US agricultural products, from 40 per cent down to 20 per cent. Moreover, China has deliberately diversified and secured its supply chains, reaching out through its Belt and Road Initiative and 'Silk Road' programmes of overseas investments, loans and alliances to central, south-east and south Asia, as well as the Middle East and Africa. Although China still has a massive absolute volume of sales to the US, it only amounts to 2 per cent of its GDP. For China, the tariffs are a demand shock; for the US, they are also a major supply shock, and it is far easier to replace lost demand than missing supply. The US can hurt China, but it cannot halt its rise.

Not only does Trump lack the leverage he anticipated, but he also risks alienating allies like the UK and the EU, who, alarmed by his isolationist military stance, are looking for more opportunities to forge new trading links with the huge economy of China and the giant trading blocks of the east. In response to Trump's tariffs, rather than giving in by removing its new tariffs on US exports, China's leaders embarked on a courtship tour of countries hit by the tariffs. President Xi visited Malaysia, Vietnam and Cambodia, and his ministers met their counterparts from South Africa, Saudi Arabia and India, to talk about greater trade cooperation. Trump's tariffs also look like bringing the EU and China closer together in resistance to the US with mutually beneficial trade agreements. The President's deranged threats dramatically reversed the political fortunes of Mark Carney in Canada, a highly intelligent, well-respected ex-governor of the Bank of England well placed to help rally international opposition to Trump's belligerent transactional approach. In many ways, it is not unreasonable to suppose that Trump has hastened the US's relative decline by increasing China's influence.

IS THERE A WOKE 'BLOB'?

Trump claims that he has had to fight a 'deep state establishment', just as in the UK we have seen those to the right of traditional Conservatives vigorously blaming an establishment 'blob' for resisting change. The change they hope to see, of course, is a move to the right with much lower taxes and the extirpation of the 'woke' from major institutions. Increasingly, towards the end of the Conservative Party's fourteen years in power, we heard complaints that this entrenched 'blob' was preventing the changes that would ultimately save our country. It isn't just Liz Truss who has blamed the 'blob': Jacob Rees-Mogg scolded civil servants for working from home; in earlier times, Labour's John Reid referred to the Home Office as 'not fit for purpose' as if the then government had nothing to do with it; even Keir Starmer seemed to side with Dominic Cummings's negative view of the civil service by suggesting that too many civil servants were, as he put it, 'comfortable in the tepid bath of managed decline'. Not surprisingly, civil servants, whose pay had fallen behind those working in other public services since 2010, pushed back, the general secretary of the Public and Commercial Services Union saying, 'One of the reasons trust in politics is so low is because of politicians' refusal to be accountable for anything. It's always someone else's fault.'

In truth, the UK civil service is one of the best in the world. League tables have placed it joint sixth out of 120 surveyed.[1] Its specialist fields, such as the Government Economic Service (GES) and the Government Statistical Service (GSS), as well as its social scientists and operational researchers, are the envy of the world, with strict professional entrance and promotion requirements. These specialists analyse and assist in assessing options for policy to ensure value for money and avoid unintended consequences that will have to be dealt with later. These wholly legitimate roles of providing reality checks can irk politicians who are intolerant of facts getting in the way of their preferred policies. A quote, often attributed to Keynes though perhaps apocryphal, sums this up: 'There is nothing a government hates more than to be well-informed; for it makes the process of arriving at decisions much more complicated and difficult.'

The real problem is that the advice of such professional civil servants is too often ignored in favour of external partisan lobbyist think tanks, although, admittedly, the machinery of government makes cross-working so difficult. In general, poor outcomes and a good deal of waste are very much down to the politicians rather than whoever happens to be Cabinet Secretary. The real-world results are plain to see. The Rwanda asylum policy's value for money was always atrociously poor, but it still went ahead with hundreds of millions of pounds wasted before the Labour government put a stop to it; likewise, internal government workings estimated that cuts in the winter fuel payments which were announced by Labour would potentially plunge tens of thousands of pensioners into poverty.

Ignoring civil servants in favour of partisan external think tanks is not the answer. If we lived in an evidence-based regime, then the list of favoured think tanks would not change with the political party in power. Unfortunately, when the government tries to bypass the civil service by bringing in external independent advisers, they are often ignored. Jeremy Hunt assembled an impressive group of academics and others in his council of economic advisers, but we understand that they only met once and were then routinely ignored. Rachel Reeves also seems to have chosen a dedicated group of externals at the Treasury on secondment from their organisations who are tasked with providing advice on various areas including developing an industrial strategy. We wish them the very best of luck. Sadly, when it comes to many high-profile issues so far, it doesn't look like much advice was taken, leading to a dramatic fall in the polls. We all hope that the economy regains at least its pre-financial crash momentum, but if it doesn't, it won't be because civil servants have refused to rise to what Starmer in his December 2024 milestones speech referred to as 'the gauntlet landing with a thump on their desks'.

REGULATIONS AND REGULATORS

Although allegations that we are being held back by a 'blob' are pretty silly, there is a real debate about the burden of regulations on business and our regulators. Quite rightly, there is public dissatisfaction with some of our utilities regulators, particularly OFGEM and OFWAT. The public disquiet over the well-publicised discharges of raw sewage and lack of investment has led to the Independent Water Commission, chaired by Sir Jon Cunliffe, which at the time of writing is reviewing the water sector regulatory system in England and Wales. As we have seen above, the overall picture for UK regulation is certainly not one of excessive regulation, although in certain areas, such as planning, there is clearly overreach. Importantly, some types of regulation matter more than others. For example, it can be argued that the perennial urge to deregulate the financial sector may have less impact for overall productivity and growth than other types of measures.

On other aspects of regulation, the UK is tougher than the US on environmental issues, on food and other areas where it has stayed in harmony with the EU so as to ensure that tariff-free trade continues to flow, albeit with much more bureaucracy since Brexit. During the last Conservative government, environmental obligations linked to climate change targets were increasing. In addition, the long-debated Digital Markets Competition and Consumers Act became law in May 2024 and gave powers to the competition regulator to stop major players from abusing their monopoly positions and to penalise firms that break consumer protection laws. The EU is also pushing hard in this field and already imposing major fines on digital firms for anti-competitive practices. On the labour front, the government is moving ahead with reforming workers' rights and so adding costs to anyone operating in the UK. The costs are significant. The government's own impact assessment puts them at up to £4.5 billion per annum once fully implemented.[2]

So why is the financial sector such an exception, at least in the government rhetoric? It may be true that a reform of local authority pension funds, which was part of the previous government's plans and which Rachel Reeves has also majored on, makes sense. Also, encouraging pension funds and insurance companies to buy more UK companies' shares as a percentage of their overall portfolio is part of this. However, these policies take time to have an impact and in most areas we have pretty much followed international norms, such as the Basel rules on capital requirements for the financial sector, all of which have been progressively strengthened in response to the financial crisis in 2008/9. Trump, during his first presidency, lowered capital requirements and reporting requirements for smaller institutions, which came back to haunt the US banking sector during the Biden administration with the collapse of Silicon Valley Bank. It prompted the need to intervene and prevent others from collapsing too.

Even so, listing requirements in the UK have been too severe. The Financial Conduct Authority (FCA) permitted some relaxation of the rules to ensure the UK was more in line with the US and to hopefully attract more IPOs, as well as to potentially increase the valuation of companies here. New categories of shares are allowed to give more voting control to original owners even if share ownership is diluted as a result of an IPO or further fundraising. The regulator admitted that the changes add to the risks but argued that the changes 'will better reflect the risk appetite the economy needs to achieve growth'. It is true that the risk appetite in the UK is below that in the US, though it has tended to be higher than that seen in Continental Europe. To sweeten the cake more, the requirements of briefings and consultations by the board for some company activities and plans have been reduced, admittedly causing some consternation among activist shareholders worried about the diminution in the quality of company governance.

So, why should the City be given sweeteners? Given the bad reaction by businesses to her October 2024 budget measures, Rachel Reeves likely added the requirement for financial regulators to have economic growth as a part of their remit to reassure the City. She was also flagging that she did not intend to reverse earlier regulatory relaxations by the previous Conservative government. It is, of course, still too early to know if it will make a difference.

WHAT REGULATORY CHANGES HAS LABOUR MADE?
Labour says its regulatory action plan will support growth. That has yet to be seen, but it seems a good start and, although the government has a target to reduce the regulatory burden on businesses by 25 per cent, it is not only the usual naive and indiscriminate 'slash red tape' approach. It is intended to combine with Labour's industrial strategy, which is also designed to prioritise growth. It would be useful if these initiatives can clarify and facilitate how the roles and remits of regulators can work together. Currently, regulators are not joined up: they need to be better at data sharing; achieving cost

savings through standardised operations, which would also allow for a more uniform experience for businesses across various regulators; they also require clearer governance and objectives, which would again help businesses understand what is required of them. Of course, simplifying processes would help everyone involved and anyone who is affected by regulators and regulations.

Unfortunately, the pattern of authority and responsibility in government for all this change is confused. The Cabinet Office seeks to lead on public bodies and the Treasury has teams working on regulation policy, but most of the civil servants working in this field sit in the Department for Business and Trade (DBT); this is where accounting officer responsibility formally sits. This split approach should be unified, perhaps by moving all decision-making to the DBT – though the Chancellor, sitting in the Treasury, might object to such a move – or by moving policy civil servants working on regulation to the Treasury, which may not grasp the overall picture for businesses. As the government is trying to reduce the size of the Cabinet Office, this doesn't seem to be a likely route to channel regulatory responsibility.

And so, it's currently undecided who will oversee and coordinate cross-cutting priorities at the centre. Whatever happens, the history of regulation tells us that it will take strong ministerial leadership to get all public sector ducks in a row, necessary if we are to achieve the required streamlining and a clear direction of policy for business and industry in a rapidly changing world.

REGULATION, COMPETITION AND GROWTH

In her blog for the Birmingham City University Centre for Brexit Studies, Vicky Pryce notes that a properly competitive environment, one which avoids excessive monopoly or oligopoly profits, is good for growth.³ This is because competition is one of the main drivers of productivity, as it requires a continuous programme of investment and innovation to preserve a competitive position. Despite this, the UK has increasingly seen damaging infringements of competition law. The banking sector, for example, had to have its arm twisted by the previous government so it would offer better savings rates to customers when lending rates were soaring, while the gap between what was charged and what was paid on accounts was widening to the banks' benefit in terms of profits. Similarly, in another supposedly competitive market, the Competition and Markets Authority (CMA) found that all motor fuel retailers, including independents, had practically doubled their margins recently for no obvious reason, costing drivers an estimated £1.6 billion extra that could have been spent elsewhere, and one assumes more productively. The CMA's recent report on the housebuilding market, which is a vital priority for the Labour government's economic plan, also included the launch of an investigation (under the Competition Act 1988) against eight developers, to see whether competition law had been infringed. And, earlier, the CMA had felt it necessary to intervene and order a ban from next year on mobile phone, pay TV and broadband companies' practice of surprise price rises during the duration of contracts, encouraging advance warning and greater transparency.

In short, despite long-standing and generally internationally praised competition and regulatory regimes, such practices have become commonplace in so many sectors. A closer look is needed at our competition and regulation regime. Both areas are vital for productivity and growth, as Pryce notes in her blog:

Do we need all the different regulators we have, including those dealing with the financial sector, all running different regimes of supervision and control? Are worries of 'regulatory capture' legitimate? Is this constraining growth and keeping prices higher than they otherwise should be. Is it discouraging smaller firms from entering markets? Is the consumer best served by the current system in operation? Certainty for smaller businesses and the consumer at large, an 'audit' of their functions in serving the economy and encouraging growth is arguably also an urgent must.

THE JUNE 2025 SPENDING REVIEW

As we write, the next phase of the government's spending review, which is a comprehensive examination of all department spending, is taking place. Rachel Reeves is insisting that it will continue to be a 'zero-based review', one where, apparently, 'every single pound the government spends is subjected to a line-by-line review' to make sure it's being spent to deliver Labour's 'Plan for Change' while offering value for the public's money. The review is the first multi-year review since 2021, and so is the first not to be dominated by the 2020 pandemic since 2015. It still occurs amid overall mediocre growth forecasts, necessitating difficult trade-offs as Labour's plans are prioritised. The equal allocation percentage cut of ten per cent across the board for many departments suggests that the level of analysis may not have been consistently thorough. Again, given the significant changes in the global economy since the election manifestos were written, there should be room to credibly excuse some tax promise retractions and allow flexibility on fiscal rules. As such, the balanced current account deadline of 2030 is likely to slip somewhat.

The more the Chancellor prioritises Labour's flagship areas and those most salient for the public – such as the NHS and education – the harsher the trade-offs with the less salient areas will be, particularly with the obligation now to raise defence spending. In fact, despite the Chancellor announcing that 'total departmental budgets will grow by 2.3 per cent a year in real terms', this headline figure doesn't tell the full story. The 2.3 per cent is only the average annual real terms growth in total departmental budgets if measured from 2023/24 to 2028/29. That includes spending changes that have already been implemented for both the current (2025/26) and previous (2024/25) financial years. The average annual increase between this year and 2028/29, in fact, is only 1.5 per cent. Hence, the IFS points out, that to understand the spending review:

> You need to understand what the government is calling Phase One and Phase Two. Phase One is last year and this year, 2024/25 and 2025/26. Phase Two starts next year, 2026/27, and covers the rest of the parliament … Take Phase One and Phase Two together, as the government does, and growth in government spending looks rather strong. Take Phase Two only and things look tighter. The crux is that most departments will have larger real-terms budgets at the end of the parliament than the beginning, but in many cases much of that extra cash will have arrived by April.

The announced 2.3 per cent per year increase also mixes both day-to-day spending and investment spending. Capital spending is set to be increased by 3.6 per cent a year on average in real terms between 2023/24 and 2029/30, but only by 1.8 per cent between 2025/26 and 2029/30. In short, the overall planned growth in government spending was set by the previous fiscal event: day-to-day current spending was set to grow by an average of 1.2 per cent each year in real terms over the next three years and total investment (capital) spending growth was set at 1.3 per cent each year in real terms over the next four years. Despite the 'splurge' headlines, these sums seem modest in relation to the needs. It will be no surprise, then, if the Chancellor prioritises the most electorally popular areas, as many of her predecessors did. In fact, over half of the increase will go to the Department of Health and Social Care, with education and now defence accounting for much of the rest. The first will get the lion's share, with 44 per cent of the increase in department spending from 2023/24 to 2028/29. Providing free school meals will in effect mean a real spend freeze for the rest of the education spend. Falling pupil numbers might seem to offer scope for some savings, but this will most likely be swallowed up by the worrying increase in demand for special needs.

The problem is, as we have seen with our justice system and asylum processing, it can lead to even bigger problems further down the line as other areas are starved of spending. And even for the most favoured areas of Labour's spending, namely health and defence, there is likely to be renewed pressure for increases later in this parliament. The impressive 3 per cent a year increase for health is in fact below the historic average. It will help, but it is un-likely to meet demand, especially given the significant backlog and wage demands in the sector. Defence is planned to rise to 2.5 per cent of GDP by 2027, but with no scheduled spending to increase that percentage thereafter. The commitment to increase defence spending to 3 per cent at an unspecifed future date, along with con-siderable pressure from NATO, mean it's very likely that we will see that percentage revisited, too, in the near future. Of course, this all then leaves much less for the less-favoured areas. In short, the spending review plans are likely to be significantly updated before the end of the parliament, most likely in the next scheduled review in 2027.

The change to the accounting of the fiscal rules allowed more capital spending, and it is also likely that the hard-pressed Chancellor will do more to exploit the asymmetry of her rules for the capital and current account. The former is restricted to meet a balance by 2030 and the latter is not. That is, by reclassifying current spending as capital investment, Reeves could continue borrowing without apparently breaching her fiscal rules. For example, the routine maintenance of existing infrastructure could be labelled as capital investment spend, education could be labelled investment in 'human capital' and part of NHS spending could be investment in the health of the workforce. Another now well-established wheeze is the moving of public spending off the government's books through privatisation and private finance initiatives (PFIs), where previously state-owned and state-run infrastructure is moved off the public sector accounts. This reduces the debt-to-GDP ratio in the accounts, but as the debt for maintenance and genuinely new investment is then paid through utility bills, rather than just taxes, the cost to the public remains real, especially with rising interest rates pushing up the burden. This won't necessarily happen soon but is a likely route to pursue at some stage, particularly if growth remains sluggish.

As Liz Truss discovered, bypassing the OBR does not go down well with the bond markets. Abolishing the watchdog would no doubt be even worse, but the Chancellor being charged with fiddling the books by the OBR would be the gravest of all scenarios. Fortunately, although the OBR strives to remain an independent agent and has always had impeccably honest chairs, it would be naive to think there isn't a lot of toing and froing between the Treasury and the OBR before any major fiscal event. That said, it is assumed that the Chancellor's U-turn on pensioners' winter fuel payments won't have pleased the bond markets. It will not be helpful if the market asks, 'What sort of self-styled "Iron Chancellor" backs down on ending the giving of free money to millions who don't need it because they protest loudly?', or 'If they give in so early in this parliament, then how weak will they be closer to the next election?' This is all especially worrying at a time of great increases in global bond yields and hence increased borrowing costs for government in general, costs which are higher for the UK in the bond markets than many competitors.

THE GREEN BOOK

The Green Book is the UK government's core professional guidance for appraising policies, programmes and projects, and its existence and influence have been cited as an obstacle by some politicians. The Green Book originated from an intention to provide decision-makers with objective advice on the costs, benefits and risks of different options. Indeed, it is often not understood that the Green Book framework was built on microeconomic theory to, in effect, maximise the 'national cake', which could then be shared out if that was wanted. It came from the distinction between 'positive' and 'normative' economics, which was emphasised so much by economists in the mid-twentieth century. Positive economics was meant to be about 'what is' and normative was about 'what ought to be', in line with the philosopher David Hume's assertion that you can't get an 'ought' from an 'is'. The Green Book's intention was to reveal when decision-makers were overriding the 'facts' of the expected benefits of a policy, project or programme. Considerations of equity and regional balance, or other considerations like ministerial vanity, came after the essential cost-benefit test of whether, in principle, the gainers from any public investment could compensate the losers.

Despite claims to the contrary, the Green Book has never been a binding restraint on ministerial decisions. As elected representatives, ministers are free to ignore any expert advice, including economic benefit-cost ratios (BCRs). That said, they might be rather miffed or embarrassed if the analysis of the Green Book didn't give them the BCRs that they would like to claim for any particular project that they backed. Both David Cameron and Rachel Reeves ordered reviews of the Green Book, though it is doubtful whether either of them really understood its deep theoretical underpinnings. In fact, the most recent review confirmed that there is no conclusive evidence that the Green Book's methodology is biased towards certain regions; rather, poor transparency around government business cases makes it difficult to demonstrate that BCRs are not biased towards London and the south-east of England.

The danger of ignoring BCRs or modifying them according to wider policy objectives is that ministerial decisions using a modified Green Book could become circular – that is, policy objectives could be used to weight the elements of Green Book analysis, so that the resulting output is then used to justify the policy. If a Green Book analysis sometimes embarrasses a minister over a pet project, then that is a good thing, and ministers are always free to voice their misgivings over the Green Book or to ignore it entirely if they so wish. Government analyst professions will take their misgivings on board and reconsider the rationales behind the Green Book, but the integrity of the Green Book comes from the expertise of civil service analysts, particularly those in the Government Economic Service working with external experts.

LABOUR'S INDUSTRIAL STRATEGY

The Labour government introduced its ten-year industrial strategy in June 2025, stating that it is central to its primary goal of growth. The rhetoric for green energy remains, with plans for less regulation on business, fewer planning delays, more competition and higher private sector investment to boost productivity. The strategy favours advanced manufacturing, high tech and life sciences, targeting eight broad areas for higher growth potential. These are advanced manufacturing, creative industries, clean energy, digital technologies, professional and business services, life sciences, financial services and defence. Within these sectors, five critical technologies are being prioritised for strategic advantage and growth: AI, engineering biology, future telecommunications, semiconductors and quantum technologies, together with supporting technological frontiers in advanced connectivity, cybersecurity and robotics. Importantly, there will also be more funding for R&D and apprenticeships and skills for these areas. Funding will come from the National Wealth Fund (discussed in Chapter 11), UK Export Finance and UK Research and Innovation.

The eight target areas cover about one-third of the economy, in areas that rely heavily on higher education and immigration, and yet despite this there is little said about universities, which have been seriously affected by curtailing the numbers of overseas students. Also, to a considerable extent, the strategy shifts existing cash allocations towards the eight areas while diverting it from other industries deemed to be insufficiently cutting-edge for growth. And although it ring-fences £4 billion of capital from the state-owned British Business Bank for industrial strategy sectors, this will come out of a previously announced £25.6 billion increase in financial capacity. State funding for research and development will increase to £22.6 billion per annum by the end of the decade, up from £20.4 billion now, with more than £2 billion for AI and £2.8 billion for advanced manufacturing over the next five years. Importantly, as we have argued above, it also includes a much-needed focus on reducing energy prices for industry. Unfortunately, energy-intensive businesses will be obliged to undergo a two-year consultation period to determine whether they are eligible for the new pricing, and even then, their prices will still probably be higher than for their overseas competitors.

WILL THERE BE A DEFENCE PREMIUM?

For decades, Europe has enjoyed a peace dividend by in effect free-riding under the US-funded security umbrella. As the IFS has often shown, the percentage spend on the NHS and on defence plotted on a graph look like mirror images of each other. New geopolitical developments, and particularly President Trump's threat to abandon Europe, have compelled governments across Europe to commit to large increases in defence spending. An important question is whether this spend will provide a boost to GDP growth. Obviously, on a global level, defence is not a boost in living standards per se but rather is seen as a 'regrettable necessity'. Clearly, for the sake of humanity, it would be much better if the money could be spent on poverty relief and health. However, that does not mean it can't be a boost to the UK economy and hence indirectly raise our GDP and living standards. A lot depends on whether our increased spend goes abroad, if foreign governments buy our defence systems and if there are technological spin-offs for the rest of the economy. For it to be a boost overall it must create growth and disposable income over and above what could come from spending on the best alternatives in the economy, for any individual sector can be made to grow by essentially throwing money at it.

Unfortunately, research on the economic 'additionality' of defence spending is sparse. Another problem is that, for obvious reasons, defence spin-offs may be kept secret. For example, the RSA (Rivest–Shamir–Adleman) public key cryptosystem is widely used now commercially. It was discovered by Clifford Cocks at GCHQ in 1973 but, as it was classified, it was then independently discovered in MIT in 1977 by those it is now named after. There is some evidence though, mostly from the US, that defence spending increases the percentage of GDP that goes to R&D, and that can have beneficial spin-offs for the broader economy.[4] The internet is one obvious example, along with the Manhattan Project during the Second World War that led to the civilian use of nuclear power or the moon landings which spurred the development of GPS. But these are anecdotal rather than a well-researched area of macroeconomics. Besides, in the UK it doesn't seem that R&D is more than a tiny percentage of the proposed increase in defence spending; as the eminent defence economist Professor Ron Smith has pointed out, peacetime defence is not currently a major source of general-purpose innovation. Rather, the inverse is true: commercial technology and innovations are being put to military use. Of course, being at war can change that, but that's certainly a cure worse than the disease.

Oxford Economics have made a baseline forecast of a rise in defence spending to 3 per cent of GDP by the end of the decade.[5] They predict that equipment procurement will be the main beneficiary, going towards replenishing ammunition stocks, upgrading heavy ground forces and procuring new tech such as drones. The Oxford Economics Briefing estimates that the boost from defence spending may be sizeable but that US producers will be the major beneficiaries, at least at first, as domestic industry may struggle to ramp up production quickly.

* * *

Notwithstanding persnuffle, whereby the Chancellor can in effect bank future growth to invest on investment spending now without breaking fiscal rules on day-to-day spending, the strategy has been set with one eye kept firmly on the Chancellor's overall fiscal plans. And so, by international standards, spending plans are modest. It will also worry some that the focus is not on left-behind ex-industrial towns, but rather on city-regions and clusters that are seen to have potential benefit from 'agglomeration', agglomeration being that poorly understood but well-evidenced improvement to innovation and productivity that comes from concentrations of businesses and people. However, it is doubtful whether the target of doubling business investment in advanced manufacturing to £39 billion by 2035 will be reached, and its success or failure will ultimately depend on private sector investment. All that said, it is undoubtedly a welcome step in the right direction.

Unfortunately, no matter what any government is able to do now, there will be no quick turnaround in the performance of the UK economy. That means that action to improve the performance of the economy is more, not less, urgent. It will inevitably involve taking risks by borrowing more for investment, when the national debt is already as big as the nation's income. Labour's problem is that over the years until the next general election, the costs of borrowing will almost certainly be more apparent than any improvement in the economy.

CHAPTER 13

CREATING A BETTER ECONOMY

Over the course of this book, we have looked closely at myriad issues facing governments as they chart a course through our increasingly uncertain world. Economics, as we have seen, is of vital importance for national wellbeing. We have also noted that there are many things that we can do little about. In this chapter, however, we pull together the things that the government *can* do to create a fairer and more robust economy.

KICKING OUT IDEOLOGIES

Whether left, right or middle, ideology is simply not a good guide for policy. Pragmatism based on reliable evidence is our best hope for improved economic welfare. Unfortunately, human thought is intrinsically metaphorical: we organise our perception and thoughts, even our identity, through deeply embedded and abstract frameworks of beliefs and assumptions, influenced by biology and, particularly, our socialisations into the cultures we live in. It is easier and more emotionally satisfying to shape our perceptions of the world through these internal constructs than to alter them in the light of new evidence. It's known as 'confirmation bias'. Although a good analyst will always resist it, we are all prone to it. It's why the spin of skilful politicians and media so often gets in the way of evidence-based, or at least evidence-informed, policies. Ideology is rather like a religion's spiritual conception of the perfect human; this vision may or may not have merit, it may be a powerful aspiration that shapes our outlook, but it is not a manual for effective surgery.

In a democracy, and in other regimes too, an unscrupulous politician may court populist favour by, say, campaigning for a drug to be available on the NHS against the considered advice of the experts at the National Institute for Health and Care Excellence (NICE). They know that the populist tabloids would spawn headlines along the lines of, 'They left little Johnny to rot', rather than 'Analysis by NICE leads to a net saving of lives.' Hopefully, Michael Gove now regrets his populist nonsense during the Brexit referendum when he proclaimed, 'I think the people in this country have had enough of experts from organisations with acronyms saying that they know what is best and getting it consistently wrong.' For effective policies, we need good evidence, and to analyse the evidence and draw useful conclusions from it, we need experts.

That said, a vital concern is that evidence-based policies do ultimately have to carry the overall consent of the populace. Our current Punch and Judy democracy, with a strong dose of oligarchy, does not work well for establishing a consensus on the evidence. A successful politician must have the leadership and communication skills to convince others and so succeed. Sadly, that does not make them a worthy politician, as an unscrupulous one will use these same attributes to exploit emotions and use misinformation for their own vested agendas, or simply for short-term electoral popularity. A worthy politician is one who possesses all these attributes and can eschew reinforcing populist misinformation and base instincts to promote humane policies that have a real chance of working. Many would laugh at the naivety of that, but it is perhaps their naivety that is the problem; far from preventing the rise of populism, we have seen our politicians reinforce it by aping populist memes.

Another problem is the lack of trust, which has been reinforced by the development of the digital age. That lack of trust, according to Thales Survey of 14,000 people in fourteen countries, showed that it is widespread. The percentage of people found to be trusting different organisations in terms of their message and in relation to data protection and privacy is astonishingly low, as we saw in Chapter 8. Overprotective passwords and other security requirements are a key issue in maintaining trust in a digital context but cyberattacks have increased worldwide, despite advances in security. Demonstrating that data is safe, and being transparent about how data is protected from these attacks, is key. Though attacks have become more prevalent, cybersecurity does not top lists of priorities; indeed, the percentage of boards having a cybersecurity expert on them seems to be down.

Policy practitioners who care about outcomes rapidly learn that there is no 'OBE', or One Big Explanation, such as 'private sector good public sector bad', or vice versa. For example, the private sector might be good at responding to the nuances of consumer wants, but as Professor Mariana Mazzucato has pointed out, the public sector is better at fostering the deep science that provides the private sector with the opportunities for its transformative products. Although it made it rather a pleasant place to work, having the state run the General Post Office as a monopoly to provide the UK's telecommunications was clearly not efficient or dynamic. Conversely, privatising the natural monopolies that provide our water and sewage was simply an invitation for capitalists to milk them for profit rather than delivering and embedding good public services. As Sir John Vickers highlighted a couple of decades ago, competition matters more than ownership. The truth is that the private sector is good at some things and the public sector is better at other things, and civil society can reach some parts that neither of those can reach effectively. The rigorous compiling, collection and scrutiny of the best evidence available may be less exciting than emotionally charged speeches, but this is how real progress is made.

BREAKING THE 'DOOM LOOP'

We saw that even the intrinsically pro-capitalist markets didn't like Liz Truss's ideologically based mini-budget, let alone Trump's own ideologically deranged and capricious tariff onslaught. The notion that low taxes or protectionism can dramatically drive prosperity goes against both economic theory and real-world evidence. Liz Truss spoke of a 'doom loop' of ever higher taxes causing low growth and hence a reduced tax base that then requires higher tax rates to fund an ever-increasing level of state spending. She learned the hard way that the bond markets simply don't believe that unfunded tax cuts will quickly awaken a 'magic growth fairy'. A different route is supported by many economists, one of investing rather than cutting for growth. As noted, Rachel Reeves's first budget merely cancelled the Conservatives' planned investment cuts, cuts that would have simply caused, in time, greater fiscal stresses, in the same way that Osborne's austerity weakened the capacity of the economy. Rather than matching the level of investment reached in the previous parliament, what is needed is more spending on public investment. Unfortunately, there won't be spare tax revenues for that, and so extra borrowing will be needed. If the investments chosen are strategically growth-enhancing, such as in skills, R&D,

energy and connectivity infrastructure, then the government's investment strategy can be presented as a convincing plan for growth and the markets won't necessarily react adversely, though market turbulence remains a risk.

GOING FOR SHORT-TERM GROWTH CAN REDUCE LONG-TERM GROWTH

Understandably, individuals and organisations are prone to seeing regulations on trade and commercial practices as standing in the way of making extra profits. Such frustrations may also arise in the public sector. For example, 'If only we could relax planning regulations, environmental rules and health and safety, our budgets for housing and transport could go a lot further or we could reduce the burden on taxpayers.' Given the large financial sector of the UK, there is a huge temptation for a government to 'let finance rip' to fuel more rapid growth. And the monied interests who stand to gain from such relaxation will lobby hard for just that, while their cronies in Parliament will be criticising the 'clunking fist of regulation' holding the economy back.

There will be calls for a 'bonfire of red tape'; bureaucrats, particularly the civil service, will be blamed for not understanding commercial needs. Some more unscrupulous politicians may call these bureaucrats names such as 'the blob' and claim that if only these 'establishment' obstructors could be removed then all would be well. All this is despite the fact the regulations were generally proposed and enacted by past politicians through parliament in response to public concerns and/or in response to Minsky-type cycles of tightening and then relaxing regulations.

The problem with letting things rip for maximum growth

short-term is that it often sows the seeds for a painful market correction in the future, or even a crisis, that then severely slows the economy. Not only does an economic downturn lead to economic hardships for many citizens, it also means a loss of GDP that is gone forever, as although there are limits to how much growth can be accelerated for a while, there is no limit to how much an economy can slow down.

WHAT SHOULD BE DONE NOW

Reversing Brexit

The UK is an 'open economy'. That means our economy and living standards are heavily reliant on trade. Trade tends to flourish according to the 'gravity model' of trade – that is, the larger the GDPs of the trading blocs involved and the closer they are together, in both geography and in lack of restrictions to trade, the more trade there is. This is one reason why the harm US tariffs can do to the UK is still a fraction of the damage done by leaving the EU's single market and customs union. When, or if, it becomes possible, the best course of action would be to try and rejoin the EU. That would not only benefit us with being in the single market but also give us access to the whole gamut of EU trade deals with the rest of the world. Staying out of the Eurozone would be beneficial, but even if that's not possible then the balance of advantage would still be in rather than out of the EU. Short of rejoining, which may not be politically possible for a decade or so, it would still be economically advantageous to get as close as possible to the EU even while not being a full voting member. That does mean something of a democratic deficit in that we would be bound by EU decisions that we have not participated in, but then this only highlights the absolute folly of leaving in the first place.

Other trade deals

Short of rejoining the EU, which is likely to be some way off, we need to get a balanced portfolio position with all the countries whose decisions and prospects largely determine our own success and failure. This means no more over-reliance on the US, where trade deals will come with unacceptable conditions and threats; it means reaching a better deal with the EU while moving closer to, and exploring the options for, full membership; it involves exploring new deals with India and others, and doing more to woo China (even if reluctantly).

Taxation

Even before Trump's tariffs onslaught, Paul Johnson of the IFS observed that 'the 2020s will be an historically extraordinary decade in terms of the almost certainly permanent increase in the size of the state. Both tax and spending will be more than 4 percentage points of GDP – well over £100 billion – higher at the end than the start'. Of course, Trump's actions could only make it even harder to sustain the level of public services the public expects. As we saw in Chapter 10, we can and should make the rich pay more tax. A recurring wealth tax is probably just too difficult to pull off and there are better ways to raise more tax from the rich, but the notion that this alone could raise the amounts required is at best a delusion and at worse a deception. That said, we could emulate some other countries with a levy on commercial banks to recoup some of the unintended 'windfall' boost to their profits by the Bank of England's massive quantitative easing, and reduce the interest payments it makes on reserves held there by commercial banks. There are potential downfalls, however, such as capital flight, bond market reactions and damage to the transmission mechanism whereby the

Bank of England influences interest rates. The balance of evidence, though, is that it's worth pursuing, at least to an extent. The Institute of Public Policy Research suggests it could free as much as £100 billion over this parliament. That would help the fiscal balance a lot, but given potential market reactions it's likely to be considerably less.

The truth is that if we want good public services, all of us, except the poorest, will have to pay for them. The Conservatives and Reform pretend that cutting public services to keep tax down is an unalloyed good thing. They ignore the weakness of the evidence base that it would encourage growth, while overlooking the misery it would cause and the inequality that corrodes society and hampers economic growth. On the other hand, Labour persists in denying that the average person will have to pay more tax, hemmed in as they have been by their own reckless election promises. Trump's tariffs and the changing world order give them license to do the inevitable: to renege further on their election pledge not to raise tax on 'working people' – with minimal loss of face – and, reluctantly of course, raise the basic rate of income tax, or at least reverse some of Jeremy Hunt's cuts to employee National Insurance contributions.

Investing for growth

Without investment the economy will not grow. However, selectively 'picking winners', beyond a few no-brainers, is usually tricky and it is often just too tempting for politicians not to bother. Trying to reverse our history of deindustrialisation with Trump-style tariffs is not practicable or efficient and would no longer bring the types of employment of old anyway. It is a time to take risks by investing in specific technologies and sectors where we have comparative advantage and, to mitigate the particular risks, we need to balance this by providing the infrastructure that allows enterprise and commerce to flourish. We will need to borrow more to invest more in the generics of connectivity, both physical and virtual: human capital, education and training; health; knowledge and state-sponsored research; and a sustainable, reliable energy supply. Overall, in the UK, the most immediate problems are poor provision for non-university skills training, poor infrastructure, low business investment, a long tail of unproductive firms and burdensome planning restrictions.

This is not a call for grandiose physical investments. HS2 was not good value for money and much cheaper investments – in broadband connectivity, for example – would have a higher benefit-to-cost ratio. In education, investment in skills-based further education might have a higher rate of economic return than sending a higher percentage of people to universities. In our universities, business schools could receive more incentives to provide graduates who are better suited to those sectors struggling with a short supply of new recruits; this could be by sponsoring and helping with the design of degree programmes that prepare people for jobs rather than arcane academic PhDs, for example. The government's Skills England organisation should help promote this, especially considering graduates are often keen to work on applied research projects involving business. Centres for Doctoral Training (CDTs) are a great way to produce highly skilled workers and low-cost research for business. CDTs are co-funded with business, and so it is a pity that proposals for new CDTs with substantial business funding were turned down on the grounds of lack of public funds.

The fiscal rules can now be adapted to allow for asset values invested in by the state, which should allow more scope for investment. A cautious development of the National Wealth Fund should be explored to emulate the higher returns that just about every comparable country gets from its pension funds – foreigners have invested in UK infrastructure, so perhaps we should too. Again, the emphasis must be on investment, including in housing, and in improving conditions for growth by enhancing private/public partnerships. The establishment of a National Wealth Fund is one step towards this, as is the promised GB Energy company, with veteran industrialist Jürgen Maier as chair. Attracting foreign investment with new relaxed rules for IPOs and shareholding should help build a better environment for attracting foreign investment.

The National Wealth Fund aside, regions might benefit from less centralisation. For example, in Germany, cities like Dortmund and Duisburg benefit from one of the most decentralised fiscal systems in Europe, where about half of government expenditure is managed at the regional or municipal level. This facilitates close coordination between city and regional governments, with spending power held locally. By contrast, UK regional and local governments have relatively little power to make their own investments compared to almost all of Europe. You won't be surprised to read that your authors believe economists and rigorous cost-benefit analysis, along with some informed futurology to factor in transformational developments, are vital to value-for-money capital investments at all levels of government.

Countering short-termism

We have had a chronic preference for short-term private financial instruments and public sector fiscal rules over long-term real investments. The electoral cycle itself is an obstacle to long-term investment and so requires structures that can provide more continuity. The National Wealth Fund is a relatively small step in the right direction for addressing this short-termism. We need to learn from competitors about how to channel and then protect funding for long-term projects that will increase growth, and importantly, our national wellbeing. Allowing the OBR to consider accounting for public sector net financial liabilities (persnuffle) is also very sensible and will hopefully reduce the leeching off capital accounts that Chancellors under pressure are prone to do. Persnuffle also permits a wide scope for 'creative accounting' if left to politicians, and so the independence of bodies like the OBR, IFS and NIESR is vital for transparency.

In addition, hopefully the 'debt falling in five years' fiscal rule, which Rachel Reeves had even suggested could be shortened to just three years, will be amended. Unlike the more reasonable part of the fiscal rule – that taxation should cover current spending – the focus on debt falling is largely meaningless and just encourages short-termism and hasty decisions. As we discussed, the winter fuel payments and disability spending reforms are prime examples of this. When interest rates are low, meaning the Bank of England has limited power to ward off recession, there is also the risk of a fiscal 'doom loop' – that is, a downturn that lowers tax revenues and causes a forecast of a fiscal deficit that prompts spending cuts in response. This then further lowers growth, the fiscal deficit increases, taxes fall more and so on and so on.

Deregulation

We must be alert to short-termism in removing regulations and acknowledge that they are often implemented for very good reason. The Great Financial Crisis of 2007 and the horrific Grenfell Tower fire of 2017 are reminders of that, but NIMBYism and overly bureaucratic processes, which are biased against new housing and expensive for developers, must be reduced. Labour is right to 'back the builders not the blockers', for construction is a reliable, if not always quick, spur to economic growth. We must find ways to reduce the inherent bias towards incumbents who are keen to strengthen deregulation and let the financial sector rip, but the UK simply cannot afford to be outcompeted by overseas financial centres. As with taxes, international agreements are important for avoiding a race to the bottom.

Tackling inequality

There is no guarantee that growth will be spread equally, while incentives do not require the level of inequality that we see in the UK today. Inequality stifles opportunity and corrodes the social contract that underpins a stable political regime; it also brings resentment and fuels populism. As most populist policies, such as Brexit, simply do not work, they damage the economy further, leading to more populism. Inequality must be reduced. Yes, it will require more redistribution, but also pre-distribution, as generally our poorer citizens want to contribute through working. Living on handouts is not conducive to one's self-esteem or good mental health. To create such opportunities, we will need more investment in the infrastructure of regions and support to help those who lack economic access into work, including through reducing health inequality, as health is so adversely affected by one's lack of a meaningful role in society.

Immigration

It is reasonable to be concerned about an increasing population if there is lack of investment to provide for the social services new citizens will use. It is also reasonable to be worried about social cohesion and the critical masses of more extreme aspects of some subcultures, especially those which refuse to accept multiculturalism or to practice tolerance. That said, it is not reasonable to regard immigration as the reason for all our troubles, let alone to speak of an 'invasion'. After all, young men are of working age rather than 'fighting age'. It is reprehensible and dangerous to use fear of immigrants for clandestine political agendas. Like it or not, we will be economically reliant for decades on higher immigration than we saw for most of the last century. Politicians need to stop competing for xenophobic votes with such measures as the cruel cut in visas for care workers. They should show leadership by explaining the benefits of immigration and busting the many negative myths that abound about immigrants.

Women
Quite apart from the obvious morality of equal gender opportunities, we need GDP to pay taxes. As discussed at length in Chapter 10, we must improve and increase opportunities to ensure all women are able to contribute their full value, and not just for GDP.

The environment and energy
The threat of climate change is too big an issue to ignore, while the UK's competitiveness is being hampered by high energy costs. To reconcile this apparent dilemma, we do not need to be setting fanciful targets that may make things worse: the target for net zero by 2030 is such a target. It's important to note that environmental levies are not the main reason why UK energy costs are so high and renewables may well significantly reduce energy costs in the longer run. However, electricity from renewables, once the full costs are factored in, is not cheaper. The main reason for our energy costs being so high is our heavy reliance on a volatile market for

gas, lack of energy storage and an absurd 'marginal cost of the most expensive generator' pricing system. These all need to be addressed urgently, especially for heavy industrial users.

Given the seriousness of the consequences of climate change, the price of energy should not be a deterrent when it comes to moving towards renewables. We should address our pricing of energy while demonstrating that the world's first industrial nation can successfully transform its economy to run on renewable net zero power – this would be a powerful and important message to others. It will take a mix of nuclear (we welcome the £17 billion of state support for a nuclear power station at Sizewell), wind, solar, hydro and tide energies, and perhaps hydrogen too, combined with innovative energy storage. We should continue to participate in COP conferences, but it seems futile to put too much trust in them. Rather, we should join with like-minded countries to use carbon taxes across a coalition of the willing in a way that compels others to join.

The welfare state and health

Not only has life expectancy declined in recent years, especially among the most disadvantaged, but there is something of a mental health pandemic in the UK. Although the overall levels of economic inactivity in the UK are not unusually high by international standards, we are exceptional as a country when it comes to the increase in new sickness and disability claims. Even allowing for the ONS's struggles to accurately monitor the numbers, levels of economic inactivity have significantly increased since the Covid pandemic. That said, Labour's changes to incapacity payments were hasty and driven by a specious imperative; an investment rather than a cuts approach is needed to reduce what would otherwise be a runaway spend.

Housing

Building affordable housing in the right places helps workers to move to where they are most needed. It also improves health as well as reducing the resentment that stems from myths about migrants jumping housing queues. But the £39 billion allocation of spending is heavily backloaded to after 2029/30, leaving only about £9 billion to cover the period until the next election, which is broadly equivalent to the current budget. And despite the bold promises of deregulation, planning permissions for homes at the beginning of 2025 were at a thirteen-year low, compounded by severe shortages of skilled construction workers.

Artificial intelligence

It turns out that AI can be cheaper than expected, so the US AI giants are not going to have things all their own way. At the time of writing, we are well behind in investing in resources for AI applications and R&D, which is a pity as Britain is well placed to do well from the AI race. According to *The Economist*, we are sixth out of a hundred nations in the ranking of the critical technologies index.[1] There is clearly a long way to go, but on average we still rank higher than Germany, Taiwan, France and India. We are still badly lacking in areas such as semiconductors where the US and China are way above the rest. Our immigration system should be designed to entice AI talent from other countries, and we should work with these nations to pool resources for AI development.

Experts v. populism

A democracy can only work well when voters are informed enough to understand the issues and their priorities, and so can effectively judge the efficacy of policies. For that to be the case, populism must be fought, not reinforced and pandered to. Leadership must make democratic space for policies that have the best chance of working, and that means heeding the advice of experts. Poor policies lead to poor outcomes and poor outcomes tend to strengthen populism, at least until it's too late and the dire reality dawns. Although attacking sources of reliable information is not a solely right-wing agenda, it is now from the populist right that we are seeing sustained attacks on our universities, judges, civil service and national broadcasting services. Evidence is the enemy of populism, and we need independent experts, away from politics, to rigorously collect, compile and analyse evidence. We do not mean a technocracy (anyone familiar with academia would be wary of a call for 'more power to the professors'), but our elected decision-makers need quality advisors.

In the immediate future, we must accommodate living with a US run by a volatile narcissist with no respect for the truth. In the UK, we are still suffering from the impacts of a Brexit largely brought about by our own home-bred narcissist, Boris Johnson. He knows more about economics than Trump, but again put his ambition to become Prime Minister above all else. The danger from populists goes beyond economic damage when they set about dismantling the checks and balances that sustain a pluralist democracy, all supposedly 'in the name of the people'. To think that it's OK to endorse populist themes and appease discontent by doing what they would do – all while claiming, 'We are the good guys, and we deserve to be in power' – is simply to abandon the field. Populist leaders work hard on behalf of their sponsors to extirpate all opposition. Leaders, including the media, who deserve our trust need to work much harder to promote a liberal constitution over arbitrary executive power and to use the sunlight of reason and evidence to expose and counter the sophistry and hidden agendas of populism.

Back to growth

Lastly, and most importantly, without growth, including in GDP and the many wider contributions to purposeful activity currently undervalued, we are heading for a more unequal, more unjust, more divisive and less sustainable future. Cutting taxes won't deliver the growth that we so badly need; bond markets know that, and whatever immediate popularity tax cuts might bring, they would soon be overtaken by the further deterioration in our public services and infrastructure.

Meanwhile, in the short to medium term, if reducing the fiscal deficit and national debt is required, and the IMF says it is, then monetary policy will have to counter the fiscal impact on growth. Right now, we are witnessing the way the post-Covid interest rate-raising cycle unravels. Being on top of this balancing act between fiscal and monetary policy will be crucial. Some investment can be financed by creating new money when macroeconomic conditions allow, but mostly the funds will have to come from yet more borrowing. As with any business venture, borrowing and investment come with risks, and it is no longer 2007: bond markets are more jittery and the national debt is much bigger now. The size of the interest payments, and so the potential impact of changes in interest rates, is much greater.

* * *

Any Chancellor of the Exchequer has a tricky tightrope to walk; for this parliament and the next things will be exceptionally tricky. The demand for public services is ever-increasing and GDP per capita since the Great Financial Crisis has been flatlining. Because of this and the increasing demands made upon it, the size of the state has grown sharply over the decade as a percentage of GDP. Unfortunately, that does not mean there is lots of fat in the public sector left to cut back on. To help their party get re-elected, the Chancellor must spend on the services that the public care most about, particularly health, plus spend more on defence to meet international obligations. That means relatively little is left over for other things, necessitating severe cuts for some unlucky areas, such as for foreign aid which is now, distressingly, at its lowest for decades, but also for DEFRA and the Department for Culture, Media and Sport. Even the Treasury's own reserve fund is now the lowest it has been for decades. And yet it is still imperative to end the UK's chronic lack of investment, in both the private and public sectors, to get the growth that would ease these problems in the longer term.

Spending on health is understandably popular, as health matters more than riches, and defence may be a necessity, but neither has the same potential for growth as investment in other infrastructure. The Chancellor may well feel compelled to compensate for Labour's earlier loss of popularity due to the winter fuel payments. Despite the headlines, Labour's seemingly overwhelming general election victory was merely a 'loveless landslide', as British political scientist John Curtice has described it. Together with the threat of losing votes to Reform, or to the left to the Greens, or to the centre to the Lib Dems, this may explain why, so far, Labour's fiscal policy has not yet actually prioritised spending for growth, for all their rhetoric of 'growth, growth, growth'. Despite the extra £113 billion planned to go towards capital spending, and even with the increases in energy security, science and R&D – and the spin-off growth benefits from health and defence – the increase in capital spend overall is not directed at those capital investments most associated with rapid growth. That said, the literature on defence as a boost to GDP and growth continues to grow. The programme does allow for big increases in priority areas like green energy, transport infrastructure outside of London and the south-east, new prisons and housing, but it also comes with a forecast extra borrowing of £140 billion over the same period, even before the inevitable project overruns such as we saw with HS2.

Given the size of the investment backlog, it cannot be said that Labour's industrial strategy is particularly bold, but it is constrained by the straitjacket of fiscal reality and the Chancellor's own fiscal rules. The attractiveness of the UK as a place for inward investment has been reduced since Brexit, and it can no longer be seen as a gateway to Europe. Partly because of the attractions of the large capital markets in the US and investment inducements offered by President Trump, big pharma companies are refocusing planned investments away from the UK. The reliance on US AI and tech investment following Trump's UK visit in September 2025 not only produces little in terms of extra jobs but brings with it its own difficulties. This is partly through extra energy demands and also by entrenching over-reliance on large oligopolistic organisations which will, inevitably, reduce the ability to develop policies that limit impact on competition and data privacy. It remains to be seen what concessions will be asked for by those firms in return for their investments in data centres, supercomputers and suchlike.

As a wider point, the government must also learn to abandon projects that go nowhere. Yes, the second leg of HS2 from Birmingham to Manchester and Leeds has been scrapped, but without this second leg even the first part to Birmingham now makes no economic sense. What the government needs is the ability and courage to say enough is enough. The HS2 project, which is now delayed even further from the original 2026 deadline – to 2033 and beyond

– has also seen costs rise due to over-engineering, over-designing and too ambitious a speed target that has required huge extra expense to accommodate the track and platforms needed. Costs increased by £37 billion between 2012 and 2024 and the overall cost is now budgeted at over £46 billion compared to initial estimates of £17 billion. Many estimates now put the figure to nearer £100 billion on completion. In any case, the original justification of needing to speed up connections to Birmingham has now been abandoned to one of releasing capacity and helping the regions. But even that is being contested. And at what cost? Anti-HS2 campaigners, and most economists we know, put the thumbs down even to those supposed benefits, pointing out that a faster/better route and increased capacity will just as likely allow for more people to come down to London rather than the other way round, along with more spurious benefits. What was always needed was more connectivity between cities in the north and from east to west and vice versa, where the cost-benefit ratio is much better.

As we have seen, although affordable housing can help workers move to where they are most needed, the proposed spending is heavily backloaded and there are severe shortages of skilled construction workers anyway, with planning permissions for housing down to a thirteen-year low. Of course, as with elsewhere in policy, saying that 'growth matters most' while also promising to crack down on immigration is an economic oxymoron, whatever the politics and social concerns.

To a greater extent even than after the Great Financial Crisis of 2007, the Chancellor is being forced to choose between discontented taxpaying voters demanding better public services and the ever-watchful bond markets. The fiscal balances haven't improved since Labour gained power; rather, the reverse is true. And the government's fiscal sums are based on what many economists believe, with good reason, are optimistic OBR forecasts. The OBR is not necessarily culpable, given the information and policies it must work with, but a prominent ex-member of the OBR, Andy King, has cast doubt on the most recent OBR forecasts for this parliament. As Paul Johnson, ex-director of the IFS pointed out, 'With spending plans set and ironclad rules being met within a gnat's whisker, any move in the wrong direction would almost certainly spark more tax rises.' With Trump in the White House and trouble in the Middle East, it is more likely than not that there could be yet more major negative shocks.

In such difficult circumstances, it is arguable that governments must remain flexible and refrain from boxing themselves into corners. The economic trends we have seen have, to a significant extent, encouraged discontent and the emergence of polarised factions. This has split the political landscape apart and led to the emergence of single-issue parties like Reform, thus altering the long-established framework of two dominant parties in government. The uncertainty over future outcomes also tends to encourage policies that please those supporting the extremes, inevitably leading to policy mistakes without the luxury of proper cost/benefit calculations or rigorous impact assessments (the policies to watch here include backtracking on competition and consumer protection and easing requirements for listings and bankers' bonuses, as well as intentions to reverse the separation of commercial and investment banking). Of course, we need more investment and innovation, given that the UK has been consistently below other G7 nations in its GDP share of Gross Fixed Capital Formation. We know that business investment remains subdued, so rejuvenating it is a must. But what we are seeing now is the lack of an evidence-based approach of the kind government economists are taught to push for. Instead, we are stuck with fiscal rules that should have been changed more radically than the OBR's attempts in 2024. We and most economists predict that the need to appease bond market fears will result in an increase in the tax take from most of us over the course of this parliament, and possibly beyond. Added to the significant retreat on the winter fuel payments and giving up on health-related benefit reform as we saw in the summer of 2025, it remains clear that more money will have to be found elsewhere. It is true that this would probably just take us closer to the percentage tax take of comparable European countries, but given the current state of the UK economy and the lack of both business and consumer confidence, this is unlikely to be good news for growth.

The rub for Labour is that investment will be subdued and the lag in any expected returns will mostly exceed the length of the electoral cycle, and whatever government comes next will have to grapple with that issue. Given the path the UK has followed since before the Second World War, and on current plans and with such well-embedded trends, we will not soon see the 'economic reset' that Rachel Reeves hopes will happen. Indeed, we will be lucky to do any more than carry on with flatlining real GDP per capita for the rest of this parliament. The government has a declared goal of delivering higher incomes, but the latest forecasts from the OBR and the Bank of England show projected growth up to 2029/30 to be weak, with the outcomes being worst for lower-income households.

Even within the forecasts, then, the 2025 spending review keeps government spending roughly constant as a share of GDP. In July 2025, the OBR warned, in language unusually strong for public bodies, 'Against this more challenging domestic and global back-drop, the scale and array of risks to the UK fiscal outlook remains daunting.' And so, the dilemmas and trade-offs will become ever more pressing as health, defence and other spending rises, with higher interest rates making the already high cost of servicing the national debt even bigger. The notion that this could all be solved by dramatic public sector efficiency gains, as some parties are promising, is ridiculous.

Politicians and most of our media are unwilling to be honest about the implications of all this for public services and tax. Clearly, it will take an enormous degree of political nerve, persuasive leadership and a healthy dose of sheer luck to do what must be done and so stay the political course until a brighter economic landscape appears.

NOTES

CHAPTER 1
1 See https://ifs.org.uk/news/decade-and-half-historically-poor-growth-has-taken-its-toll

CHAPTER 2
1 See https://bankunderground.co.uk/about/

CHAPTER 3
1 See https://www.aston.ac.uk/sites/default/files/2024-09/Full%20Report.pdf

CHAPTER 6
1 Diana Coyle, *The Measure of Progress: Counting What Really Matters,* Princeton University Press, 2025
2 See https://www.ons.gov.uk/peoplepopulationandcommunity/wellbeing/articles/ukmeasures ofnationalwellbeing/dashboard
3 See Coyle, *The Measure of Progress: Counting What Really Matters*

CHAPTER 7
1 See https://www.gov.uk/government/publications/air-pollution-applying-all-our-health/air-pollution-applying-all-our-health
2 See https://www.bloomberg.com/opinion/articles/2025-06-30/ignoring-a-7-trillion-financial-disaster-won-t-make-it-go-away?utm_medium=email&utm_source=newsletter&utm_term=250706&utm_campaign=sharetheview
3 See https://www.cladcodecking.co.uk/blog/post/renewable-energy-percentage-uk
4 See https://dieterhelm.co.uk/energy-climate/climate-realism-time-for-a-re-set/
5 See https://www.bbc.co.uk/news/articles/cq8oygdd3zlo

CHAPTER 8
1 See https://www.ft.com/content/5c905b91-6a21-45d1-8962-14cf2847e084
2 See, for example, https://ifs.org.uk/publications/outlook-public-sector-productivity
3 See https://ec.europa.eu/eurostat/statistics-explained/index php?title=Use_of_artificial_intelligence_in_enterprise

CHAPTER 9
1 See https://www.niesr.ac.uk/wp-content/uploads/2021/10/NIESR-Briefing-Immigration-Attitudes-4.pdf

2　See　https://www.gov.uk/government/statistics/immigration-system-statistics-year-ending-september-2024/summary-of-latest-statistics

3　See https://www.independent.co.uk/news/business/news/impact-of-immigration-on-native-wages-infinitesimally-small-a7545196.html

4　Figures taken from the Oxford Migration Observatory, https://migrationobservatory.ox.ac.uk/

5　See https://www.gov.uk/government/statistics/land-use-in-england-2022/land-use-statistics-england-2022

CHAPTER 10

1　See https://academic.oup.com/ooec/article/3/Supplement_1/i1086/7708125

2　See https://equalitytrust.org.uk/scale-economic-inequality-uk/

3　See John Burn-Murdoch, 'What if the UK isn't actually the sick man of Europe? Britain's illness-related inactivity crisis looks increasingly like a mirage', *Financial Times*, 6 December 2024

4　See https://www.oecd.org/en/data/indicators/benefits-in-unemployment-share-of-previous-income.html

5　See https://ifs.org.uk/inequality/

CHAPTER 11

1　See https://www.resolutionfoundation.org/app/uploads/2025/04/How-to-do-industrial-strategy.pdf

CHAPTER 12

1　See https://www.pcs.org.uk/news-events/news/uk-civil-servants-among-best-world-research

2　See https://inews.co.uk/news/politics/labour-workers-rights-plan-cost-3338087?srsltid=AfmBOooHHVLxnOksWUbqkvZfEF8c6BwHfXIo4KiUko2TrBu1VkLoRApu

3　See https://centreforbrexitstudiesblog.wordpress.com/2024/07/31/how-to-get-growth-more-audits-please-but-this-time-of-the-uks-competition-and-regulatory-regime/

4　See https://www.aeaweb.org/articles?id=10.1257/aer.20231278

5　See https://www.~oxfordeconomics.com/wp-content/uploads/2025/03/Europe-Defence-splurge-will-help-industry.pdf

CHAPTER 13

1　See https://www.economist.com/graphic-detail/2025/06/06/who-is-ahead-in-the-global-tech-race?utm_content=ed-picks-image-link-6&etear=nl_today_6&utm_campaign=r.the-economist-today&utm_medium=email.internal-newsletter.np&utm_source=salesforce-marketing-cloud&utm_term=6/10/2025&utm_id=2087189

ABOUT THE AUTHORS

VICKY PRYCE is an international economist and commentator. She is currently chief economic adviser at the Centre for Economic and Business Research (CEBR) and a visiting professor at King's College. Her books include *How to be a Successful Economist, Women Vs Capitalism, It's the Economy, Stupid: Economics for Voters* and *Greekonomics: The Euro Crisis and Why Politicians Don't Get It*.

ANDY ROSS is a former deputy director in the Government Economic Service (GES) and was the head of professional development for the GES and later for the Society of Professional Economists. He was joint author with Vicky Pryce and Peter Urwin of *It's the Economy, Stupid* and co-wrote *How to Be a Successful Economist* with Vicky Pryce, Alvin Birdi and Ian Harwood.

ACKNOWLEDGEMENTS

We'd like to thank all those economists, statisticians and other researchers, in both the private and public sectors, who diligently produce rigorous analysis and evidence for practical policies, all for the public good. Even when we disagree with them, they are vital for keeping up with the economic state of the country and for informing good policy decisions. The individual researchers are numerous, but we are particularly grateful for all the work done by our ex-colleagues at the Government Economic Service, both while we were there and since we left. Excellent information, data and analysis is contained in Bank of England, IMF, OECD, ECB and Chatham House Working Papers, as well as blogs and research documents and reports. The support from economists at CEBR and ex-colleagues at KPMG, as well as the practical on-the-ground experience from groups such as the British Chambers of Commerce and the London Chamber of Commerce and Industry, has been invaluable. The numerous think tanks of all persuasions – which the UK is fortunate to have – including the IFS, the Resolution Foundation, the Institute for Government, Radix Big Tent and the NIESR, each offered a wealth of brilliant analysis and contacts we were able to pick the brains of. The Centre for Brexit Studies at Birmingham City University kindly allowed us to borrow and reuse the odd idea from the contents of blogs we had authored for them. The data analysis from Better Statistics CIC is fresh and deeply interesting (and they are always ready to challenge the ONS). We are also thankful for other academic work undertaken in universities we are now, or have in the recent past, been attached to, including the LSE, King's College London, Leeds University, Loughborough and Birkbeck. We learned many things about the limitations but also the reach of public policy from our erstwhile political bosses, Patricia Hewitt, Alan Johnson and Vince Cable amongst others, as well as the late Alistair Darling, formerly the boss of both authors, having been at BIS before becoming Chancellor, just as the financial crisis hit. Inspiration has also come from The Leaders Club, Best for Britain and the International Women's Forum. Thanks are due to the Academy of Social Sciences (AcSS), the Royal Economic Society (RES) and the Society of Professional Economists (SPE); we are privileged to be Fellows of all three.

But even more, thanks to the Biteback staff who showed instant enthusiasm when we first proposed the idea and pushed us all along to speed up our deliberations to meet deadlines. There was inevitably, therefore, a limit to how much we could update the text – with so much going on both here and across the pond – while we were drafting the book. But we appreciated the pressure as it encouraged us to cut the waffle, focus and get on with it. Any mistakes and omissions are all our own.

INDEX